ALL-TIME FAVOURITE BOOKS & MOVIES AND THEIR EPIC JOURNEY

VISHWAS PATIL

ALL-TIME FAVOURITE BOOKS & MOVIES AND THEIR EPIC JOURNEY

TRANSLATED FROM MARATHI BESTSELLER
NOT GONE WITH THE WIND
BY NADEEM KHAN

NIYOGI BOOKS

Published by

NIYOGI BOOKS

D-78, Okhla Industrial Area, Phase-I
New Delhi-110 020, India
Tel: 91-11-26816301, 49327000
Fax: 91-11-26810483, 26813830
Email: niyogibooks@gmail.com
Website: www.niyogibooksindia.com

Editor: Jayalakshmi Sengupta
Design: Dsgn Unplugged

ISBN: 978-93-83098-78-1
Year of Publication: 2015

Printed at: Niyogi Offset Pvt. Ltd., New Delhi, India

CONTENTS

PREFACE

The thirst for literature of the highest quality can never be quenched. The works of William Shakespeare, Thomas Hardy, John Steinbeck, Oscar Wilde, Miguel Cervantes and Sharatchandra Chattopadhyaya occupy a permanent place in my heart. I have had the privilege of roaming extensively through these dense forests that contain within them the entire range of human emotions and sentiments. I then began exploring the treasure-trove of movies made on these immortal classics, and partook of their pleasure to my heart's content. *Not Gone with the Wind* was the outcome of my indulgences in the overlap of these two different forms of art.

My obsession with movies is a gift to me from my land of birth—the city of Kolhapur in Western Maharashtra. It was here, in the mid 1920s that the world renowned 'Prabhat Film Company' was established. I grew up in these environs. It was here, while a student in Std V, that I had experienced the thrill of getting the great V. Shantaram to autograph my school notebook. Later, while working as a government officer at Film City in Mumbai, I had the rare good fortune of making the acquaintance of and spending quality time with luminaries like Dilip Kumar, Naushad and Ilaya Raja.

My stay in Film City created the opportunity for me to study the transformation of great literature into great movies. I gorged myself on the exquisite feast laid out for me by the great directors of world cinema like Elia Kazan, John Ford, Oliver Stone, Vittorio De Sica, Roman Polanski, David Lean, Steven Spielberg and Francis Ford Coppola.

Not Gone with the Wind, originally published in Marathi, is a unique exploratory journey through world literature and the extraordinary movies that were made on them. It received the Best Book Award from the Government of Maharashtra. It was also published in a serialised form in the popular literary Hindi magazine *Nayaa Gyaanodaya.* The Bhaaratiya Gyaanpeeth has published a Hindi translation of the Marathi book under the title *Badi Kitaabon par Badi Filmein*, which has been received with great enthusiasm across the country.

My Marathi book provided me with the opportunity of peeping into my readers' minds. A granny from Delhi called me on reading my piece *Not Gone with the Wind*. She talked about how she had melded with the character of Scarlet O'Hara at different levels right from adolescence to grandmotherhood. She related with great excitement how, when she was young, her boyfriend had gifted the novel to her, how the two of them had watched the movie together, and now, at the threshold of old age, how her grandson had gifted her a new edition of the same novel.

My book was particularly appreciated by young students of film institutes. It will certainly help the readers understand the kind of efforts that writers and directors make to plumb the depths of their characters.

Niyogi Books has undertaken to bring out the English avatar of my book. As a writer I happily acknowledge my sense of pride at this development. This work of mine is now equipped to step across the borders of my country into the wider world beyond. My friend Nirmal Bhattacharya has taken particular pains to make this happen. The editor of this book, Jayalakshmi Sengupta, has ensured that every detail is in perfect order for acceptance by a world readership. This English version of my book is presented as one more evidence of her editorial skills.

Transporting the literary wealth of one language into another without loss of flavour and substance is a difficult job. It requires talent and sensitivity to both the languages, as well as to the subject matter. The skill and hard work that Nadeem Khan poured into the English rendition of my book is without parallel. I record my heartfelt gratitude to him.

The great Niagara Falls on the border of the United States of America and Canada continue to push enormous quantities of water over the edge of the cliff unceasingly, day in and day out. It looks so massive, so enigmatic, so magnetically attractive that a number of adventurous spirits get into a barrel and roll over the cliff along with the surge to acknowledge and record their love for the great natural phenomenon. They are known as 'The Dare-devils of Niagara'. Movie-lovers do a similar thing too when they plunge themselves into the limitless waterfall of movies from across Hollywood, France, Britain, and Italy right up to Japan. I consider myself blessed to have got the opportunity to travel through these intoxicating, mesmerising territories in the process of writing these articles.

VISHWAS PATIL

“The ode lives upon the ideal, the epic upon the grandiose, the drama upon the real.”

VICTOR HUGO

I

EPIC JOURNEYS

OTHELLO

AUTHOR William Shakespeare PUBLISHED 1622
DIRECTOR Stuart Burge PREMIERED 1966

'O, beware, my lord,
of jealousy;
It is the green-ey'd monster,
which doth mock
The meat it feeds on.'

Storms of various intensities are quite a regular part of life's experiences. But when the hurricane of suspicion penetrates the bedroom, hovers over the bed, it can raze even mountain-sized human beings in no time. Shakespeare wrote his play *Othello* on this subject around 1604. This tragedy created by the foremost English playwright has mesmerised the world ever since. This play has continued to reverberate through translations and adaptations in many languages across the world. The storm of suspicion that gripped Othello's mind, set ablaze the silver screen too.

Desdemona is the daughter of a rich Venetian senator named Brabantio who loves her dearly and has brought her up like a princess. She is sought after by a large number of suitors, but she remains unimpressed by their looks or wealth. Her attention and respect are for men of courage and calibre. That is the reason why she has fallen in love with the soldier Othello, who is a Moor. Othello is jet black in complexion and older to her by ten to fifteen years. Despite coming from a foreign land, he has risen to occupy the position of a general in the Venetian army. Quite naturally, this inter-racial love affair has created quite a stir in Venice.

One of her suitors, Roderigo, overcome by love for her, seeks the help of his mentor Iago, an unscrupulous man. In the first scene of this tragedy, Roderigo and Iago arrive in front of Brabantio's palatial house in the dead of the night with the intention of harassing him. They start shouting

‘Thou weigh’st thy words before thou givest them breath.’

out that a very dear thing has been stolen from his house. When Brabantio appears at the window, Iago, concealed by the darkness, shouts out his sour message, ‘Even now, now, very now, a black ram is tupping your white ewe. Arise, arise;...or else the devil will make a grandsire out of you.’

When Brabantio learns that his young and beautiful daughter has fallen in love with a black Moor and may have even secretly married him, he goes to the court with a complaint against Othello for beguiling his innocent daughter and besmirching her. Othello explains to the court how the delicate feet of Desdemona walked into the life of one so dark, ugly and elderly as himself. As a casual visitor to Brabantio’s house, he would narrate stirring stories of his adventurous life: his voyages as a soldier across stormy seas; his victories won on the flaming battlefields; his conquests and sieges; his being taken prisoner and sold into slavery; his resourceful escape! Desdemona used to be entranced! Othello talked of his travel across strange lands and stranger encounters—people whose heads grew beneath their shoulders; mountains whose heads touched the heavens; vast, romantic caverns; evil cannibals—and Desdemona listened enraptured. Her eyes would fill with tears of compassion for Othello’s travails. Their frequent meetings, their respect for each other, and the uniqueness of their experience set the strings of love strumming.

When Desdemona arrives at court she publicly accepts Othello. When she is asked who she will render obedience to, she tells her father:

To you I am bound for life and education;
My life and education both do learn me
How to respect you; you are the lord of duty—
I am hitherto your daughter; but here’s my husband,
And so much duty as my mother show’d
To you, preferring you over her father,
So much I challenge that I may profess
Due to the Moor, my lord.

William Shakespeare

On hearing this, Brabantio is quite shattered. He had hoped that as a well-brought-up Venetian girl she would choose someone above the rank of a senator; but by secretly marrying a Moor she had cheated him!

The Duke himself tries to pacify Brabantio by drawing attention to the many virtues of the Moor. But Brabantio is inconsolable. In the presence of all, he pointedly addresses Othello with the fatal lines:

> Look to her, Moor, if thou hast eyes to see:
> She has deceiv'd her father, and may [deceive] thee.

Othello is a simple, straight-forward person, without the gift of the gab of other young people. But he has gravity, dignity and grace. An intrepid soldier, he is dispatched by the Duke to Cyprus to combat the Turks. As he leaves, he assigns Iago the responsibility of escorting his newly wedded bride to Cyprus, in the belief that he and his wife Emilia would take good care of her on the way.

By the time Othello arrives at Cyprus, the war clouds have dispersed, and danger of enemy invasion has abated, almost as if the very thought of confronting Othello on the battlefield has frightened the enemy away. But Othello's troubles are far from over; in fact they are about to seriously gain strength. Othello is a self-made man and soldier who has earned his privileges by dint of character and effort. No surprise then that there are those who hate and envy him, and are scheming to cause him harm. Among such is Iago, handsome of body but ugly of heart. He now unleashes a heart-rending storm in Othello's life that completely destroys him.

Among Othello's trusted soldiers is one Michael Cassio, young, handsome, jovial and eloquent; an object of desire for the young women around. Like Othello, he is also a target of resentment on account of being an outsider—a Florentine. In the eyes of many Venetians, the two are rank outsiders, aliens, risen on the strength of their capabilities, and thus deserving of hate and jealousy. The two are so close that Othello frequently uses him to carry love letters and messages between him and Desdemona.

Othello had lately promoted Cassio to become his lieutenant, a post which Iago has been wanting for himself. Iago believes that Cassio is an upstart, fit merely for dallying with women and children, who knows nothing about the world and its ways; he is incensed at his position being usurped. Determined to avenge himself, the plotting mind of Iago lays out a vicious web of intrigue that would culminate in the annihilation of Othello, Desdemona and Cassio.

Cassio has been given the charge of keeping guard on the island of Cyprus. Iago knows that Cassio has a weakness for the bottle, and exploits this weakness by getting him punch drunk that night. In this drunken state, Cassio is provoked into unsheathing his sword and attacking some people. The scuffle leads to a riot, and Othello wakes up to the clamour. Indignant at such dereliction of duty from a trusted associate, Othello demotes him instantly. Iago tells Cassio:

> ...Reputation is an idle and
> Most false imposition; oft got without merit, and lost
> Without deserving. You have lost no reputation at all,
> Unless you repute yourself such a loser.

He advises that if Cassio wants his position back again, he should plead his case with Desdemona, as the keys of power lie in her hands, and hers is the door that he should knock.

Having played the courier between her and Othello during their courting, Cassio knows Desdemona well. So he instantly meets her. The artless, innocent Desdemona assures him:

> I will do all my abilities in thy behalf....
> Thy solicitor shall rather die than give thy cause away.

Cassio, however, has fallen from Othello's graces. Desdemona's perpetual and persistent entreaties for granting him forgiveness exasperate him.

Meanwhile, Iago keeps on insinuating slanderous ideas through cunningly contrived double-talk. On the one side he advises Othello not to harbour any base suspicions against his wife, and on the other he alerts him:

> Look to your wife, observe her well with Cassio.
> Wear your eyes thus, not jealous, not secure.
> I would not have your free and noble nature
> Out of self-bounty be abused.

Slowly and cautiously, Iago pollutes Othello's mind with poison: Othello is a foreigner to Venice; he has little knowledge of the impetuous Italian swains, ready for amorous adventures, and adept in surreptitiousness. Besides, the same Desdemona had dismissed

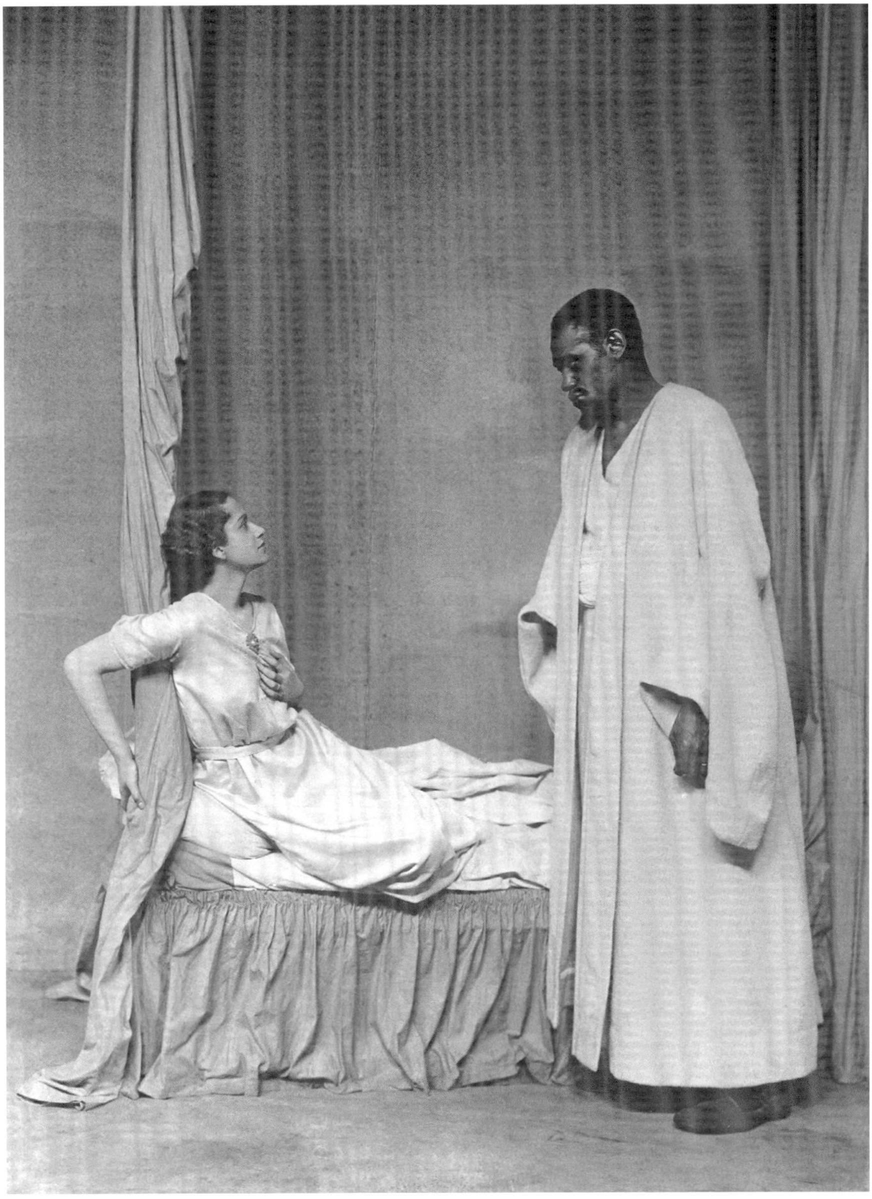

In 1930, Paul Robeson won rave reviews as the first actor of African descent to star in an English performance of Shakespeare's *Othello*.

CREDIT: EXPLOREPAHISTORY.COM/IMAGE DONATED BY CORBIS-BETTMANN

proposals of many fair and handsome aspirants; so why would it be inconceivable one day for her to regret having settled for a dark, ugly, middle-aged person like him? And hadn't she betrayed her own father and brought sorrow down upon his old head? Othello is deeply shaken at hearing all this.

Iago advises Othello to keep Desdemona engaged in conversation, and note the manner in which she pleads for Cassio again and again. And so it happens that the innocent, open-hearted Desdemona continues her campaign for securing justice and restitution for Cassio, and the primed up Othello smoulders inside, ready to explode like a stockpile of sulphur. He possessed neither looks, nor complexion, nor beguiling youth; his race, religion and nationality are different; and he is no strapping youngster either. Othello is now convinced that he has been hoodwinked.

The spark of suspicion sets his every pore on fire, to the point of destroying his reason. He is driven insane at the thought that a trusted friend like Cassio should invade his very bed. It isn't Othello the man alone, Othello the soldier is also shattered. He loses the joy of brandishing his weapons too. His heart, that used to be roused at the sight of troops and banners in battle array, and would stir and leap at the sound of a neighing war-horse, seems to lose all that pride and ambition that are a soldier's virtue; all his military ardour and all his old joys seem to forsake him.

In his unbalanced state of mind, Desdemona would sometimes seem virtuous and at other times a characterless whore, and make him faint with grief. In one such state of uncertainty, he catches Iago by the throat and demands evidence for Desdemona's guilt. At which Iago mentions a special handkerchief—the very first gift of love that Othello had given to Desdemona.

An Egyptian witch had gifted the handkerchief to Othello's mother, which she had handed over to him and whispered that as long as the handkerchief was in the possession of the woman of the house, she would have the good fortune of retaining her husband's good graces. He shakes with rage when he is told that an ordinary soldier like Cassio was seen wiping his beard with it. An extraordinary detestation for Desdemona takes hold of him when he finally sees the handkerchief in the hands of Cassio's mistress, Bianca. Convinced now that he has been cuckolded, he turns to the villain Iago and tells him to fetch poison to kill Desdemona. Iago then advises him:

> Do it not with poison; strangle her
> In her bed, even the bed she hath contaminated.

Before taking this extreme step, he seeks confirmation from Emilia about Desdemona's illicit relationship with Cassio. Emilia is shocked, and she tries with all her might to talk him out of his doubts about the blameless Desdemona. But Othello is in no state to have anyone talk about Desdemona in positive terms. He calls her a 'strumpet' and 'the cunning whore of Venice'.

Iago, meanwhile, manipulates the other characters as well and makes them dance like puppets. He sets Roderigo upon Cassio. When Othello hears Cassio scream in pain, as Roderigo attacks him off-stage, he expresses his satisfaction with Iago and sets off to wreak his revenge upon Desdemona.

The terrible events that bring the play to its conclusion have been delineated by Shakespeare with artistry of the highest order. The tender, innocent Desdemona, who has disdained the comforts of her valiant father's house for love of a dark man from another land; Desdemona, who worships Othello and has surrendered herself body and soul to his service; lies dressed up in her wedding gown, waiting for the arrival of her estranged husband. She lulls herself to sleep with a song she had heard her maid sing, 'The poor soul sat sighing by a sycamore tree,…Sing willow, willow, willow.'

She, of course, does not know that the wicked Iago has set alight a powder keg that is about to blow her domestic bliss into smithereens. Moonlight filters in through the open casements. Enters Othello, completely consumed by suspicion and resolved upon putting an end to her life. He looks first at his wife's face deep in sleep, and then out towards the star-studded firmament, and then breaks out into these immortal lines:

> It is the cause, it is the cause, my soul—
> Let me not name it to you, you chaste stars—
> It is the cause. Yet, I'll not shed her blood,
> Nor scar that whiter skin of hers than snow,
> And smooth as monumental alabaster.
> Yet she must die, else she'll betray more men.
> Put out the light, and then put out the light.

He gives her a last kiss. He keenly wants another, but stops, knowing the next one will break his resolve. His teardrop wakes her up with a start. He tells her to say her prayers and ask for God's forgiveness before he kills her. When she entreats him to disclose the cause of her punishment, he accuses her of illicit affair with Cassio and mentions the handkerchief as evidence. She begs him to call Cassio so that she may clear herself of this accusation, but she is informed that he has already been slain. When she breaks into tears, he shouts her down with, 'Out, strumpet! Weep'st thou him to my face?' Finally, he smothers his blameless wife to death with her own bedclothes.

Meanwhile, Emilia rushes in with news of the stabbings that have happened outside. She is aghast at what meets her eyes inside. Iago arrives after a little while. She begins to realise the role her husband has played in bringing about this disaster. As she starts exposing his black schemings, he stabs her mortally. Before she dies, she tells Othello that she herself had found the fateful handkerchief and handed it over to her husband, and that his wife was completely innocent.

The wounded Cassio comes in now, and further lays bare Iago's wicked machinations. All these revelations, however, have come too late. Othello has so meaninglessly slain his virtuous wife, and he is now in the state of a huge ship that hits the rocks and shatters into pieces and then floats around without the worth of a paper boat.

Distraught with grief, Othello pulls out his sword and stabs himself. 'I kiss'd thee ere I kill'd thee. No way but this—killing myself, to die upon a kiss,' he says, and collapses next to where Desdemona lay on the bed.

Othello's extraordinary tale was not Shakespeare's own creation. It was one among a hundred moral stories written by an Italian named Geraldo Cinthio, set in Italy, with the main characters named Desdemona and Othello. The straight and simple moral lesson that this story preached was that marrying outside one's community brought about unforeseen calamities.

Shakespeare, of course, does not travel down Cinthio's single-line trajectory. By holding Othello firmly responsible for the reprehensible murder of his wife, he improves the dramatic quality of the plot a thousand fold. Shakespeare does not focus upon the act of murder, but studies the motives behind the deed, and the psychological storms that rage inside the characters, relentlessly pushing them towards their crisis. Iago too is no run-of-the-mill villain. In the irredeemably wicked, cunning, destructive Iago, Shakespeare metamorphoses Milton's Satan for the stage. This is the chemistry that has gone into the creation of this masterpiece of a tragedy.

Although Shakespeare himself was a good actor, he had stopped appearing on stage much before writing *Othello*. But the role of the wicked Iago was so powerful that it pulled him back to the boards. Iago is universally considered

‘Brabantio: “You are a villain!” Iago: “You are a senator!”’

the crown jewel among villains. He is himself presented as a consummate actor, with the ability to twirl the other characters round his fingers. A deep understanding of human psychology combined with a natural inclination towards evil makes him the perfect villain.

Iago is the embodiment of a slithering snake with an unquenchable thirst for destruction. Unlike other villains, he does not care to conceal his wickedness. On the contrary, he gets into conversation with the audience, and lets them in to his next nefarious move. Yet, as the other characters fall victim to his malevolence, the audience is left awestruck. He pours his life into these cleverly placed assertions and pretences, and in the process snuffs out the lives of others.

Such is Shakespeare’s virtuosity in the creation of Iago that, unsurprisingly, many reputed writers feel miffed. Even the world renowned George Bernard Shaw has this to say of him, ‘[*Othello*] is pure melodrama. There is not a touch of character in it that goes below the skin; and the fitful attempts to make Iago something better than a melodramatic villain only make a hopeless mess of him and his motives.’

The brave and valiant Othello is simple and artless, incapable of sensing the craftiness of others. It is this little weakness that brings the lofty structure of his imposing personality crashing down. Modern critics like Harold Bloom have this to say of him: ‘The tragedy of Othello is that he did not know his own character as well as Iago did.’ Desdemona, on the other hand, is the personification of virtue and good conduct. Sindhu, from writer Ram Ganesh Gadkari’s *Ekach Pyaala,* carries a deep imprint of Desdemona.

Shakespeare’s plays have always been a subject of inspiration and emulation for stage and screen the world over. A major director like Roman Polanski established his European reputation with the production of a film version of the Shakespearean tragedy *Macbeth*. *Othello* being, of course, one of the most stage friendly of Shakespeare’s plays, Othello and Iago have held the greatest actors in a mesmeric hold.

Paul Robeson, a black actor, created a sensation on Broadway in 1943 in his role as Othello. His performance was of such high quality that it never failed to sweep the audience off their feet. Orson Welles, the maker of *Citizen Kane*, tried his hand at *Othello* too, but without any notable success.

'Watch the greatest actor of our time in the greatest role of his life!' This was the ad-line with which Sir Lawrence Olivier's *Othello* was heralded in 1966, and his performance measured up to all that was promised in the blurb. Othello had seeped into Sir Lawrence's bloodstream as deeply as Hamlet had. He happily abandoned his image of the handsome hero, and sailed through the movie made up as the black, unattractive Othello.

While some of his audience found his rendition a little loud, in my opinion he fitted the bill perfectly, and did full justice to the character of the unfortunate Moor. Particularly, when the seeds of suspicion are first sown in Othello's mind, the change that comes about in his behaviour, his movement, is simply amazing! His stutter, his graceful power-packed walk, the polished performance of Sir Lawrence is a veritable lesson in acting. Then again, when he realises that his wife was innocent, his helpless cries at the unrelenting sky, the storm-waves that lash his visage, the blood-freezing tumult that rocks his heroic frame are unforgettable images. Sir Lawrence Olivier's Othello reverberates in a corner of one's heart in the same manner as the resonance of monster waves keeps echoing long after one has walked away from a tempestuous shore.

Iago is a strongly author-backed character, and has been constructed with great felicity by the playwright. The danger here for Othello is that the slightest slack in its portrayal, and the play or the movie gets swallowed up by the stronger role. Frank Finlay had played the part of Iago against Olivier's Othello. Tall, fair, strikingly handsome, tongue flicking quite like a snake's, Finlay too is an actor's actor.

Directed by Stuart Burge, other than Laurence Olivier and Finlay the film starred Maggy Smith as Desdemona and Joy Redman as Emilia. All four were nominated for the Academy Awards, but none managed to bag it. In 1966, however, at the International Film Festival held in San Diego, although Sir Lawrence missed it out again, Finlay did come away with the Best Actor award. Performers of the stature of Sir Lawrence Olivier, Paul Robeson and Orson Welles have shone in the role of Othello.

On account of being so stage-pliant, *Othello* has left a particularly deep imprint on Marathi theatre. Several illustrious actors have tried its rendition on stage. Its first translation in Marathi was done by Kirtane. But the most celebrated among all, even to this day, is G.B. Dewal's *Zunzaar Rao*. A number of basic English concepts did get left out in the adaptation, but Dewal succeeded in transporting the essence in lucid, pithy Marathi. *Zunzaar Rao* was brought on stage for the first time by the Marathi Gadya Mandal. The role of Zunzaar Rao (Othello) was essayed by Ganpatrao Joshi, and his delicate Kamalja (Desdemona) was Madhavrao Tipnis. Jadhavrao (Iago) was splendidly played by Ganpatrao Bhagwat. The play created another major stir in 1949 when it was staged by the Mumbai Marathi Granth Sangrahalaya to celebrate its 50th anniversary. The great thespian Baburao Pendharkar played the title role, with Snehprabha Pradhan as his Desdemona. K. Narayan Kale came in as Iago, and Pilajirao (Cassio) was none other than Raja Paranjape, while Saaraja (Emilia) was performed by Kusum Deshpande. The play was directed by Chintamanrao Kolhatkar, with P.L. Deshpande doing the background musical score and Godse providing the stage setting. Prabhakarpant Panshikar, who played a guard in this rendition, narrates the episode with great relish. After a number of successful performances, the group fell apart on account of a rift that developed between Pendharkar and Snehprabha.

V.V. Shirwadkar came up with a translation of *Othello* that had some good declamations, but the translation itself wasn't of the highest order. In its few performances at Nashik, Othello, of course, was played by his favourite Baburao Sawant (for whom he had specially written *Nat Samrat*). But the character who really wowed the audience was Iago, played by a powerful actor who was making his debut on stage—Datta Bhat.

The story got itself a modern spin when Prof. Dilip Pardesi readied it for 'Natya Sampada'. The freshly arrived Savita Prabhune did Desdemona. It was Iago again who ran away with the accolades, and this time the character launched the career of the redoubtable Chandu Parkhi. The year 1982 saw another adaptation in the form of *Nishpaap*; and although it ran on for more than a hundred performances, Pant Panshikar still expresses his dissatisfaction with the delineation of the central character of Othello.

The recent arrival of Vishal Bharadwaj's movie *Omkara* has again revived discussion on Shakespeare's play. It created considerable stir even before it was released but it was clearly too far removed from the Shakespearean oeuvre and art to merit a discussion here.

CRIME AND PUNISHMENT

AUTHOR Fyodor Mikhailovich Dostoyevsky PUBLISHED 1866
DIRECTOR Josef von Sternberg PREMIERED 1935

‘Would not one tiny crime be wiped out by thousands of good deeds?’

The year was 1849, and he was 28 years of age. He had got into the company of some European socialists in Russia, and his friends and he had begun plotting against the ruling powers. His group was caught, convicted for treason, and sentenced to be hanged. He stood facing the pitch-black gallows, watching his friends being hanged one after the other. The gallows had turned reddish black with congealing blood. It was now his turn. He gathered the rattling chains that held his arms and legs, and began shuffling towards the gallows. But destiny, they say, is king. The order arrived at the very last moment, commuting the sentence of the survivors to incarceration in the prisons of Siberia. It had to be the good fortune of generations of readers (what else?) that whisked away from under the gallows this master storyteller—Fyodor Dostoyevsky.

Some scholars believe that the very world identity of the Russian people acquired a deeper meaning on account of Dostoyevsky being born among them. At the same time, a writer of the eminence of Maxim Gorky considers him Russia's 'evil genius'. In the manner of Shakespeare, Dostoyevsky too gained immense name and fame across the world. It is no surprise, therefore, that both of them should be the target of envy and hate. An epoch-moulding novelist like D.H. Lawrence has this to say of him, 'I do not like Dostoyevsky. He is like the rat, slithering along in hate, in the shadows, and in order to belong to the light, professing love, all love.'

'It takes something more than intelligence to act intelligently.'

The land of Russia has given to the world of novels two of its greatest works—Count Lev Tolstoy and Fyodor Dostoyevsky. While Tolstoy has given us some of the greatest female characters of fiction, the credit for creating its most compelling male characters clearly belongs to Dostoyevsky. *The Idiot* and *Crime* and *Punishment*—I have read these two Dostoyevsky novels over and over again; and on each revisit, Raskolnikov and Prince Mishkin have given me the deep-felt joy of meeting childhood friends.

Dostoyevsky's protagonist in *Crime and Punishment,* Rodion Raskolnikov, is a poor student, who lives under the sheets of a garret on top of an ancient, dark, dilapidated building in St. Petersburg. Poverty-ridden, distressed, solitary, at odds with society, young Rodya falls under the sway of an outlandish, diabolical notion of cleansing the society. He is driven to realise it and to satisfy his deep-seated desire to avenge himself on life and society. He, therefore, becomes fixated with the idea of killing Alyona Ivanovna, an old crone who runs a pawn shop, from whom Rodya often borrows money.

Pumping himself into a state of high excitement, he hides a short-handled axe in his coat sleeve, and arrives in the ill-lit room of the withered, chicken-livered, tetchy old woman. Keeping a conversation going, Rodya hits her on the head with his axe. The woman collapses on the spot, in a pool of blood. He hadn't realised, however, that her sister, Lizaveta, was in the next room, and was a witness to the murder. She is dumbstruck with terror. To conceal one, Rodya commits a second murder and disappears from the scene.

Committing the crime takes him only a few minutes, but the guilt of its commission follows him like a shadow—everywhere, all the time. He returns to his room in a state of delirium and hits the bed. The next day, he receives a summons from the local police station and that sets him in a panic. He gives himself a scrub, disposes of his blood-soaked clothes and other pieces of incriminating evidence, and presents himself at the

Fyodor Mikhailovich Dostoyevsky

police station. It turns out that he had been defaulting on his rent for many months, and he had been summoned in response to the complaint his landlady had registered.

His conscience incessantly preys upon him. When he hears conversation at the police station regarding the double murder, he faints. To add to his misfortune, his devoted, impecunious mother arrives along with her daughter Dunya. It is love and concern for their dear Rodya that brings the two over to the city. But the Rodya they encounter now is not the boy they knew. The murder has set up such storms of self-loathing as to unhinge his mind, and he resents the company of those he loved; he wants them away!

The self-inculpation that follows the murder forms the core of the novel. That Raskolnikov should have killed two poor, innocent old women so pointlessly sears his innermost being. His state becomes that of a person who is pursued and harried by some vengeful spirit at all hours. Probably in an effort to console himself, in his weakened mental state, he had divided human beings into two classes: the ordinary and the extraordinary. He believed that the most extraordinary among this extraordinary class possessed the nature-given right to shed the blood of ordinary men and move boldly forward over their dead bodies. Napoleon was one such in his list of supremely extraordinary persons. He had even published an article in a local newspaper on this theme some months earlier.

After the murder, though, Rodya is gutted. The storm raging in his mind refuses to be subdued. He realises that he is no Napoleon; he is not the valiant conqueror that he had deluded himself into believing he was. He now sees himself as a particularly pitiable specimen.

Rodya's life moves through another transition when he meets Marmeladov, a public official given heavily to drink. Dostoyevsky has portrayed a heart-rending picture of his destitute family. Although a complete sot, he rails against his own thoughtlessness with every gulp. He is driven to despair by his poverty, yet he cannot snap out of his addiction to the bottle. As a result, there are unending rounds of quarrels, beatings, and a pervading stink of alcohol. The family occupies a niche in hell.

Marmeladov has a young daughter, Sonya, who is quite typical of the young girls we meet in Dostoyevsky's novels. Quiet, serious, soft-spoken, she makes a deep impression on Rodya. She moves about Marmeladov's hell-hole quite like a flickering flame in the midst of a dark storm. She is lacerated by her father's uncontrollable addiction and the resultant disintegration of her family, and makes desperate efforts to keep it together. When all efforts fail, she takes to prostitution. Her modesty and innocence make Raskolnikov fall deeply in love with her. When he declares that she is far more worthy of respect than his mother and sister, he shocks Sonya too.

The Sonya of the novel is an extremely commonplace girl from an ordinary background, a rebuttal of Rodya's concept of ordinary and extraordinary. It appears that Dostoyevsky put a lot of thought into naming his heroine Sonya which is apparently a very popular name among girls in the nomadic families in the Russian frontiers. Deeply riven by natural disposition, Rodya Raskolnikov considers the prostitute Sonya as the embodiment of Christ's compassion and love. Sonya too lavishes her all on him, without asking for anything in return.

Meanwhile, Profiry Petrovich, a detective, is on Rodya's trail. He misses nothing: Rodya's fainting on overhearing the discussion on the murder at the police station; the minute jottings of the pawning activities maintained by the old woman Alyona; the arrival of all her debtors, except Rodya, after her murder to enquire about their pledged goods; none of these incidents escape his observation. Nor does this alert officer miss Rodya's article on ordinary and extraordinary human beings published some months earlier. Profiry keeps close watch, not only on every step that Rodya takes, but also the pace at which Rodya breathes.

Petrovich has no doubt at all about Raskolnikov's culpability. But without any eye-witness or solid evidence to go by, his conclusions are based only upon circumstantial indications. Hence, he gives Raskolnikov the patient advice, 'Confess your crime,' to help him get a lighter sentence.

The volcano of anguish that had been building up in his mind erupts, and in this state Rodya confesses his crime to Sonya. He is crushed by the thought of killing the two innocent women he has. It is as if he has killed himself. Torn to shreds, Rodya goes and sinks into Sonya's embrace and pleads for some remedy for the storm that is raging inside his head. 'You have killed, and you yourself will have to confess.' She puts a cross round his neck and tells him, 'Go to the crossroads; bow to the people, and kiss the earth, because you have sinned to it too, and say aloud to the entire world, "I am a murderer!"'

Raskolnikov acts according to Sonya's advice. When his case goes on trial, he is granted substantial relief by a sympathetic court. The court observes that while Raskolnikov was committing the murders, the doors of the house were wide open. Since he did not have the presence of mind of latching the doors from the inside it indicates that the killings had been done in a state of mental illness. Raskolnikov gets a light sentence and is made to serve his term in Siberia. While he serves his sentence, Sonya settles in a village on the outskirts, and pays him frequent visits.

'What is hell? I maintain that it is the suffering of being unable to love.

Tara Birell as Antonya Raskolnikov with Douglass Dumbrille as Dmitri, in Josef von Sternberg directed *Crime and Punishment* (1935). COURTESY: WWW.DOCTORMACRO.COM

Fyodor Dostoyevsky had become a legend in his lifetime. His novels, originally written in Russian, have been repeatedly translated into many languages. In fact, in the early parts of the 19th century, some Malayali and Bengali men of letters spent time in Russia to ensure that their translations of Dostoyevsky novels came word-perfect. Beginning with Constance Garnett, a large number of English translators have returned to the Dostoyevsky treasure-chest in search of new meanings and fresh understandings.

Dostoyevsky was born on 30 October 1821, in a Moscow hospital. His circumstances were moderate, insecure and typically middle class. The wealth and affluence of Tolstoy and Turgenev's childhood were not a part of his lot. His father Mikhail, a short-tempered, choleric man, was a doctor in the estate of Tulla. It was probably his irascible nature that led a farmhand serf to murder him, leaving a deep mark on Fyodor's young mind.

His mother Maria, in sharp contrast to her husband, was a soft, sentimental soul who loved music and literature. Dostoyevsky was merely fifteen when she died, two years before her husband, depriving the unfortunate boy of maternal shelter. Orphaned thus at a most delicate age, young Dostoyevsky immersed himself in incessant reading, as if he had located the wellsprings of his energy in books.

After finishing his schooling in Petersburg, he took admission in the Academy of Military Engineering there. The move from a stifling, uninspiring home to the open, liberal environs of the academy certainly offered him greater pleasure; but soon he was bored of those dry engineering hours, those practical-sessions and those mind-numbing hours of study. The real feast for him lay in the pleasures of reading. With the dim, dancing flame of a candle for company, he devoured every word composed by the greatest among the greats: Homer, Shakespeare, Goethe, Scott, Balzac, Victor Hugo, and their ilk. In his frenzy he went to the extent of translating a Balzac novel into Russian. He somehow held down his job as an engineer for a year, and then he cut himself loose. From then on, for the rest of his life, he sat as a votary at the feet of the goddess of literature.

He had had to spend four desultory years in Siberian prisons. Remarking on those years he says, 'It was as if I had been nailed in a coffin!' In that terrible school, he got to experience many facets of human life. In prison, as in exile, he moved about in the lives of the common folk—poor peasants, labourers, petty salary earners in the cities—these were his true kith and kin.

His private life was as full of twists and turns as any work of fiction. His first marriage was in 1857, to the widow Maria Dmitrievna. Then began his dalliance with Apollinaria Suslova, a young and stunningly beautiful student. She was a fellow lover of literature, and she satisfied his needs—spiritual and carnal. In these early years some novels were published, and they brought him success, but these happy times did not last very long. Suddenly, in 1864, he lost his wife Maria and his brother Mikhail. Then followed another blow—the flat refusal to marry, by the girl in whose love he stood submerged up to his ears—Apollinaria.

His brother had left behind a mountain of debt. And now, having turned into an extreme loner, he himself took to gambling. To meet his ever-growing need for money, he would routinely take advances from publishers and work as their slave to compensate for these advances. While working on his novel *The Gambler*, he came in contact with a young stenographer named Anna Snitkina. The writing wound up in a month's time, but Anna's entanglement with his life became more permanent. With a fearful heart he proposed marriage, and happily she accepted.

He, however, continued to be tormented by financial anxieties. His stepson, Pavel, begging money from all and sundry, almost all the while, his own addiction to gambling, his occasional epileptic fits and other such annoyances became his ever-present companions. In 1868, while he was living in Geneva, a daughter named Sophia was born to him, but within three months she died. A second daughter too died in infancy. His third one became mentally unbalanced. Thus had this great writer to witness the destruction of his children's lives.

The last few years of his life saw him reach great artistic heights and acquire considerable wealth. In 1879 his major novel *The Brothers Karamazov* was published in a serialised form in the periodical the *Russian Messenger*. It is regarded as one of the greatest novels in world literature. Dostoyevsky had planned to write a sequel to this work, but this was not to happen. His health steadily worsened, and he passed away on 27 June 1881.

On the issue of identifying his best novel, critics are still divided. While some consider *Crime and Punishment* as his greatest work, others give this place of honour to *The Brothers Karamazov*.

What is the kind of magic that lies at the core of *Crime and Punishment*? Dostoyevsky once noticed a small item in a newspaper that reported the murder of an old woman who was a pawnbroker in Moscow. The killer was an adolescent student. This great writer looked at the event with a slightly different perspective, and created a new chapter in the art of novel writing. It was as if a tiny acorn had found fertile ground and metamorphosed into a mighty oak. Another great novelist had been similarly moved to artistic creation on reading a small news item. A young girl's carthorse had died in an accident, thus depriving her family of their only source of livelihood. Thomas Hardy had transformed this little incident into *Tess of the d'Urbervilles*.

When Dostoyevsky had first prepared the outline of *Crime and Punishment*, he had planned to position Marmeladov as the central character of his novel. But Raskolnikov came along, and without Dostoyevsky realising when, his crime and its guilt-ridden punishment, unobtrusively, took over the entire work.

Seen at a superficial level, as a murder story, it should have moved straight along the line of a regular mystery narrative. But with the magic touch of Dostoyevsky, what emerges is an imposing work of art that examines the very depths of the human mind. *Crime and Punishment* is amazingly saturated with infinite love and compassion for human kind. Dostoyevsky appears to have poured his soul into every word with which he delineates the families of Raskolnikov and Marmeladov. A pen that can explore human relationships and interactions at such profound levels can only be described as phenomenal. In my opinion, Dostoyevsky's Marmeladov belongs to the same set as Charles Dickens' Micawber and the Spanish Miguel Cervantes' Don Quixote.

The letter to Raskolnikov from his mother describing their state of abject poverty is so full of tender emotions that it reminds the Marathi reader of Sane Guruji's *Shyamchi Aai*. Then there is the heart-rending episode of Marmeladov's deranged wife, lamenting the fate of her children as she stands with a begging bowl in the street.

Plays and mystery novels have created their template of the typical investigation officer. In Profiry Petrovich, however, Dostoyevsky has created a secret police officer far removed from this stereotype. He is fat and stodgy. With great skill he weaves his web around Raskolnikov's crime. In a session with Rodya, prior to his confession of his crime, Petrovich tells him, 'Have you ever seen a moth fluttering about a candle flame? Well, he (the killer) will be just like that; he'll circle round me as if I were that flame.' He tells

Rodya that he has planted his agents all around the killer. Where could he go? Even the wilderness will rise up to gobble him! At that point, the completely bewildered Rodya cannot help but ask, 'Then—who—was the murderer?' Petrovich almost recoils at this question, startled by its unexpectedness, and replies, 'Why, it was *you*, Rodion Romanovich! You murdered them!'

Sonya reminds one of Ophelia in Shakespeare's *Hamlet*. The two women belong to the same tribe; two innocent lives crushed by circumstances for no fault of their own! As different from Sonya's lot, Ophelia at least had the benefit of being born in a happy, responsible household. Hamlet and Raskolnikov keep returning to mind for the fascination of their pathos.

Many scholars credit *Crime and Punishment* for laying the foundation for the modern novel. Its off-shoot, the stream-of-consciousness novel, takes one's breath away! For all this, it is probably the world's first great work of art that has refused to be framed into a high-quality play or film. There have been over 25 film adaptations of *Crime and Punishment*. They hardly created any stir. *Crime et Châtiment*, made by French film-maker Pierre Chenal in 1935, is widely regarded as the one single effort that does justice to its subject. The same year, Columbia Pictures had made an 88 minute movie on the novel, directed by Josef von Sternberg. Francis Coppola, the director of *The Godfather*, made two movies in 1983 called *The Outsiders* and *Rumble Fish*. These movies carry deep imprints of the characters portrayed in the novel. In 1998 *Crime and Punishment* was produced for television, directed by Joseph Sargent in which the role of Profiry Petrovich, played by Ben Kingsley of Gandhi fame, received good reviews. Another recent film *Crime and Punishment in Suburbia* directed by Rob Schmidt in 2000, loosely adapted from the novel, is so laden with violence, sex and abusive language that the final product bears no resemblance at all to the original masterpiece.

It is said that the poet can reach where the sun's rays cannot. By the same token, it may be said that neither the eyes of the camera nor the brightest flashlights have the ability to penetrate the dark depths of the human mind that have been accessed by great writers like Dostoyevsky. This is where the language of cinema finds itself inadequate. However, in the firmament of novels, *Crime and Punishment* established itself as the pole star, long ago.

ANNA KARENINA

AUTHOR Leo Tolstoy PUBLISHED 1876
DIRECTOR Clarence Brown PREMIERED 1935

'She brought herself to ruin and two good men...'

Anna Karenina is regarded as a trailblazer in the world of literature. Its span is expansive as that of a mighty river. Family, love, infatuation, deception, all these elements have been explored by Leo Tolstoy in this magnum opus. Anna herself is the unparalleled empress of the world of novels who has left her readers captivated for the last 150 years. The high standard that this remarkably beautiful novel has gone and set has created, in a sense, a problem for all the writers who followed. It has held directors, actors and playwrights in a state of perpetual hypnosis.

Anna Karenina is a tale of love and ruin set at a time when Russia itself is in throes of great change. Anna, her husband Alexei Karenin and her lover Vronsky have been braided together to form the central substance of the novel. Running parallel is the story of Konstantin Levin, a country landowner. While narrating their saga, Tolstoy uncovers a wide range of issues of the contemporary Russian society. From the existing feudal system to politics, family, religion, gender, morality—everything finds detailed exposition and discussion in this novel. The novel is at once a picture of the collapsing social order of Russia and also the collapsing institution of marriage with all its fault lines.

They've got no idea what happiness is, they don't know that without this love there is no happiness or unhappiness for us—there is no life.'

Tolstoy's Russia is divided into three main divisions: the first is the virtuous, god-fearing world of the poor, the second is the world of entrepreneurs, and the third is the glittering world of rich aristocrats. To this world belongs Prince Stepan 'Stiva' Arkadyevich Oblonsky, a high-ranked noble of the Russian aristocracy. He gets amorously entangled with his children's French governess, which causes great distress to his wife Darya Alexandrovna, nicknamed Dolly, and their happy household is transformed into a battlefield.

Oblonsky's sister Anna arrives from St. Petersburg to her brother's house in Moscow with the hope of sorting matters out between the warring couple. Anna is the wife of Alexei Alexandrovich Karenin—a senior statesman in Tsarist Russia and twenty years her senior. Alexei is a gentleman, kind and considerate. They own a palatial house, and are blessed with a lovable eight-year-old son Sergei, or Seryozha.

While travelling to her brother's house, in the railway carriage Anna meets Countess Vronskaya, the mother of Count Alexei Kirillovich Vronsky, a cavalry officer with the rank of Captain. He arrives at the station to pick up his mother, and is instantly infatuated by Anna's beauty and deportment. Their first meet is marked by a rather tragic event—a railway worker accidentally falls in front of a train and is killed. It portends the melancholic trajectory that their own affair will take, and anticipates Anna's own sad end. Up to this point Vronsky had been courting Princess Katerina Alexandrovna Shcherbatskaya, or Kitty, but one look at Anna, and he tosses Kitty away like a crumpled piece of paper. It is of no concern to him that Anna is married, has a young child and that others have a claim upon her.

Anna is conscious of the excessive fascination she holds for Vronsky, and knows that this is queering the pitch for poor Kitty, and is not at all inclined to complicate matters and provoke discord.

Once, while she is travelling by train to St. Petersburg to meet her husband, very early in the morning the train halts at a tiny station in the midst of heavy snowfall. There, in the freezing cold, Anna finds a person whose presence startles her. 'I didn't know you were going, Captain. What are you coming for?' she breaks out.

'What am I coming for?' Vronsky repeats, looking straight into her eyes. 'You know that I have come to be where you are,' he says; 'I can't help it.'

'It's wrong, what you say, and I beg you, if you're a good man, to forget what you've said, as I forget it,' she replies.

'Not one word, not one gesture of yours shall I, could I, ever forget…'

Anna begins by repulsing the advances of Vronsky; then, in spite of being a married woman, she starts enjoying the vain pleasure of being the object of desire for a lusty, young, unmarried army officer; and finally she gives in to his lures; how, she herself does not understand.

It is at the ball where Vronsky seeks her out for a number of dances that the physical contact with him intoxicates her. After ten years of domesticity with Alexei, love and passion had quite disappeared from her life. The bodily contact with Vronsky, and his ardour for her excites her and rekindles her passion. She makes a few attempts at turning down his advances, but cannot—does not—resist them for too long. This warmth that develops slowly between Anna and Vronsky, the delectable pull of this love amidst restraint, their whisperings, their mutual attraction, are realistically portrayed to paint a beautiful picture.

The affair of the wife of an important aristocrat falling in love with a young, unmarried army officer is bound to set tongues wagging. It creates a storm in the St. Petersburg society. While Anna becomes the object of contempt among the upper-class women, Count Vronsky too becomes the target of anxiety for his family. They are worried that by succumbing to the charms of a married woman, their young man is ruining the prospects of a wonderful career in the army. However, the goodness of heart and the richness of character that Anna possesses, Vronsky does not. Critics have also accused Anna's husband, Alexei, of being a very cold and dry character. A rich aristocrat, he has the reputation of being an excellent administrator, who gets to the depth of any matter he has to deal with. After years of government service—with all the qualities required for being successful in it, such as punctuality, hard work, commitment to duty—he has turned into a dry person. He attends parties only for recording his presence, not for having a nice time, and has no time for his young wife.

One important reason for *Anna Karenina* occupying the highest rungs of world literature is the beautiful episodes that Tolstoy has crafted. The episode of the annual

Clarence Brown

steeplechase race in which Vronsky is due to participate takes an interesting start. After checking out his mare he goes over to meet Anna, and finds her on the garden terrace waiting for her son's return. 'What's the matter?' he asks her, 'You are ill?' At which, after considerable cajoling, she informs him, 'I'm with child.' His child. The news does not disconcert him. For a while he paces up and down the terrace, then goes up to her resolutely, and tells her, 'Leave your husband and make our life one.' She, however, cannot accept this line of action.

Anna goes to the races to see Vronsky in action. This time her husband Alexei observes her from close—her excitement, her agitation, her extreme concern over Vronsky's fall. Feeling upset at her blatant exhibition of consternation for Vronsky, he politely escorts her out. In the carriage he mildly upbraids her for her unbecoming behaviour, at which she spits out, 'I love him, I am his mistress; I can't bear you; I'm afraid of you, and I hate you....You can do what you like to me.'

Alexei, of course, does not care to have a wife who has been seeing another man so freely and even flaunted her love for him so openly. On the other hand, by contemporary Russian laws, filing for divorce would require evidence to prove infidelity. Besides, prolonged litigation would also hurt his social prestige. That leaves him with only one alternative—to have Anna break her relationship with Vronsky. Anna, however, refuses to oblige and continues with her illicit affair.

Contemporary social circumstances obstruct easy resolution of such triangulation. Seeking or obtaining divorce is a difficult exercise. Only the offended party can apply for divorce. In the event of divorce being granted, the offending person is not granted permission for remarriage. It will also lead to Anna's beloved son being separated from her. She can hope for nothing better than spending her life as Vronsky's mistress. And in that case not only she, but her child from Vronsky will also be denied all rights of inheritance.

So, one day, she simply abandons everything—her ten years of domesticity, her dear son and everything else, and presents herself at Vronsky's door. She tells him that she has left her earlier life behind, and all she has now to call her own is he. That night she dreams a terrible, terrifying dream. She dreams that she is married to both Alexei and Vronsky, and that she is sleeping with both of them at the same time.

Another important episode is of her illness. One day, out of the blue, Alexei gets a telegram from his wife that reads, 'I am dying; I beg, I implore you to come. I shall die easier with your forgiveness.' With little hesitation he sets off for St. Petersburg. In the hall he notices on the hatstand a military overcoat. He is informed that she has just

'I think...if it is true that there are as many minds as there are heads, then there are as many kinds of love as there are hearts.'

Greta Garbo as Anna Karenina with Fredric March as Count Vronsky, in Clarence Brown directed *Anna Karenina* (1935).
COURTESY: WWW.DOCTORMACRO.COM

delivered Vronsky's baby girl. He finds Vronsky sitting desolately in her boudoir. He goes to her bedside and finds her babbling in a semi-delirious state. Such is the enigmatic charm she exercises over both her men that she reduces them to uncontrollable tears. In her feverish state she begs her husband to forgive Vronsky, and gets them to hold each other's hands. For three days, she is ridden with fever, delirium and unconsciousness. On the third day, the doctor sees some signs of hope. Alexei breaks into tears and sobs out to Vronsky, 'This is my position: you can trample me in the mud, make me the laughing-stock of the world, I will not abandon her, and I will never utter a word of reproach to you.' He also willingly accepts Vronsky's child from Anna as his own.

The largeness of Alexei's heart staggers a self-centred person like Vronsky. He considers himself as completely annihilated by the magnanimity of the man's character. In this state of mortification he reaches home and shoots himself in the chest with his pistol. He misses aim, however, and only manages to wound himself rather badly. Anna reverts to her relationship with Vronsky.

The resumption of Anna's liaison with Vronsky convinces Alexei that there is no way to hold her back, and he agrees to grant her divorce. Thrilled at this turn of events, Anna and Vronsky begin dreaming colourful dreams of their future, and set off on a pleasure trip to Italy. But Anna has another change of heart. She wants Vronsky, of course, but she does not want a divorce either. She loves her son dearly, and cannot accept the idea of separation or dissolution of ties with her beloved Seryozha. She cannot settle down to the pleasures of the flesh either. She is forever vacillating between pleasurable immersion in her love for Vronsky, and bouts of extreme tetchiness, insecurity and irritability, to the point that she becomes an enigma for Vronsky.

After returning to St. Petersburg from Italy, Anna gets desperate to see her son. Although she does care for her daughter from Vronsky, her deepest attachments are still with her Seryozha. On the morning of the boy's ninth birthday she gathers courage, barges into her husband's house and gets into the boy's bedroom, where Seryozha is just getting into wakefulness. She gathers him in his arms and smothers him with kisses. 'It's my birthday today,' mumbles the smiling boy. 'I knew you'd come.' As she fondles him, she cannot hold back her flood of tears. Confused, the boy asks her why she should be crying, to which she answers, 'I won't cry.... I'm crying for joy. It's so long since I've seen you. I won't, I won't.' Exactly at the fixed hour of 9 o'clock, Alexei enters the room. She casts a rapid glance of repulsion and hatred towards him, and almost runs out of the room. In her agitation she forgets to give him the parcel of toys she had chosen with such love and sorrow the day before in a toy shop.

The latter half of the novel is full of gloomy, dark clouds. Ugly, frightening shadows of insecurity forever loom over Anna. Even small periods of separation from Vronsky whip up a frenzy of questions: Where would he have gone? Which beautiful young woman would he be spending his time with? Vronsky tries hard to set her mind at rest, and lavishes his love upon her. Anna, however, remains unconvinced. Tolstoy makes a very telling comparison between Anna and her brother's wife Dolly. Dolly is less attractive, less affluent, and also less blessed with her husband's attention. Yet, she comes to terms with her circumstances as also with the profligate tendencies of her husband. She does not desire to be another 'Anna'.

Subjected to unrelenting insecurities and suspicion, Anna's relationship with Vronsky goes from bad to worse. Anna had fallen for a rich, handsome, graceful and, most importantly, romantic hero of a cavalry officer. But the poor man is as much circumscribed by practical circumstances, traditions and the rules and regulations of society as any other man. He cannot leap into the sky to suit Anna's romantic fancies. Her jealousy and mistrust increase with each passing day. She tortures herself with visions of pretty young damsels prancing around her Vronsky. She develops a tendency for self-destruction and a morbid fascination with death.

The city, she believes, is too full of temptations, and she would be safer with her handsome Vronsky settled in the country. A vicious cycle emerges—Vronsky begins to tire of her irrational, blow-hot-blow-cold whimsical behaviour, and withdraws from her, which sets off more severe bouts of jealousy and rage, which makes him withdraw further. She gets to hear that Vronsky's mother, Countess Vronskaya, is negotiating her son's marriage with a Princess. As a result of all this, the chasm between Anna and Vronsky widens and deepens, and they have frequent clashes. Consumed by insecurity, Anna loses all contact with reality. The world, for her, has turned wicked, horrible and loathsome.

Vronsky thinks back to the time when he had first met her. As Tolstoy writes, 'And he tried to think of her as she was when he met her the first time…mysterious, exquisite, loving, seeking and giving happiness, and not cruelly revengeful as he remembered her on that last moment.'

In the last part of the novel, Tolstoy very skilfully creates the turbulence into which the family is sucked, and the devastation it causes to the lives of so many characters. Reminiscent of Shakespeare's play, once the seeds of doubt find space in Othello's head, he rises like a man possessed. Beyond the temptation scene, the play takes off on its upward course, destroying everything that comes its way. The novel too takes total charge of the reader's mind as it hurtles towards its climax. '…[D]espair poisoned the wounds of her tortured, fearfully throbbing heart,' writes Tolstoy.

'There,' she says to herself, looking into the shadow of the railway carriage, at the sand and coal dust which cover the sleepers—'there, in the very middle, and I will punish him and escape from everyone and from myself.' With this, out of a false sense of vanity she flings herself under the wheels, and thus ends a beautiful life just to teach Vronsky a lesson.

This is what she gets as a comment from Vronsky's mother Countess Vronskaya, 'Yes, hers was the fitting end for such a woman. Even the death she chose was low and vulgar...[S]he was a bad woman. ...She brought herself to ruin and two good men—her husband and my unhappy son.'

After the runaway success of *War and Peace*, Tolstoy was planning to write a major historical novel on Peter the Great, and got its outline ready too. But an important event occurred in Tolstoy's life that made him change his mind. The mistress of his friend and neighbour Bibikov, named Anna Pirogova, a tall, full-blown woman with a broad face and an easy-going nature, threw herself under a freight train at the Yasenki station. Before doing so, she had written a stinging suicide note to the man, 'You are my murderer. Be happy, if an assassin can be happy. If you like, you can see my corpse on the rails at Yasenki.'

Tolstoy was present at the autopsy of Anna conducted at the railway station next day. He observed that although her appearance was bloody and mutilated, there was a mysterious, desirable trace of a smile on her red lips. The event left Tolstoy profoundly overwhelmed, and the ghost of Anna refused to settle down. The issues of chastity, treachery, and turbulent, violent death haunted him.

His wife Sonia has made interesting entries in her diary regarding her husband's agitated state of mind. She writes that Tolstoy first visualised her as the agent of evil in the world. One whole chapter in one of the early drafts of the book, devoted to a description of Anna, is entitled 'The Devil.' But as he began brooding over the character, as its nuances began to emerge, he turned more and more sympathetic, till at last she held him in sway. It was through this process of deep cogitation that an altogether transformed personality finally emerged.

It is quite true that Tolstoy goes into descriptions of hundreds of dead bodies in *War and Peace*. But the encounter of one single dead body of Anna

‘If you look for perfection, you’ll never be content.’

Vivien Leigh as Anna Karenina, in *Anna Karenina* (1948), directed by Julien Duvivier.

COURTESY: WWW.DOCTORMACRO.COM

on a railway station had shaken him up to the core. Out of this singular experience was born Anna Karenina, who has straddled world literature across the ages as one of its greatest heroines; a one-of-a-kind character whose heart, while pulling her inexorably towards her lover, melts for her husband as well. On the one hand she stakes her life for her young son, on the other she worries about loss of beauty by going into confinement. The number of facets to her personality! She wants to possess two men at the same time: her husband Alexei for depth of character and Vronsky for his passionate ways. She doesn't realise, however, that life does not offer such two-in-one deals; it is her fickleness of mind that lies at the root of her tragedy.

The world of cinema has had some actors whose presence has imparted a golden sheen to the silver screen. To this charmed circle belongs Greta Garbo, who first essayed the role of Anna in M-G-M's silent movie *Love* in 1927. Eight years later M-G-M came out with a talkie version, this time named *Anna Karenina*, where again they chose Greta Garbo to play Anna. Indeed, the persona of Greta carried some of the enigmatic qualities of Anna. She discharged the role of a woman torn by the conflicting pulls of two lovers and a son with considerable panache. She had the benefit of highly experienced people in cameraman William Daniel and director Clarence Brown. Interestingly, for their silent movie M-G-M had made the story end on a happy note; fortunately, they did not commit the same sin for their talkie version, and allowed the movie to end as a tragedy.

In 1948 came the second version of the novel, this time a British movie with Vivien Leigh playing the title role. It was nine years after Ms Leigh had made her sensational debut on the silver screen with *Gone with the Wind*. However, neither the M-G-M movie nor the British version can be considered classics. Both the movies show Anna's brother Stepan Oblonsky, Princess Kitty and Konstantin Levin as losing their lives. Vivien Leigh has put in a creditable performance as the neurotic, unbalanced Anna.

The latest *Anna Karenina* was presented in 1997 with a lot of fanfare by the director Bernard Rose. The movie is noted for its beautiful depiction of nature at its Russian best. The sound effects are also amazing. His Anna, played by Sophie Marceau, does not measure up to the standards set by Greta Garbo and Vivien Leigh. The first two movies finish off with spellbinding scenes. The gust of wind blowing across the railway station, with Greta Garbo/

Vivien Leigh walking into it with tragedy etched all over her countenance, they make for soul-stirring cinema. But this said, none of the movies captures the word picture Tolstoy sketches to describe the heart-wrenching events leading up to the suicide.

No moviemaker has succeeded in capturing the mental, emotional and spiritual journey of the three main characters with which Tolstoy captivates the reader's mind—the helpless lover Vronsky, the bewildered husband Alexei, and the fickle, enigmatic Anna who slips away from the normality of decent human existence, loses all contact with reality, and gets relentlessly pushed towards the dark abyss of death. Despite having performers of the calibre of Greta Garbo and Vivien Leigh, the movies fall short of interpreting the mental agonies and human interactions as effectively as they are found in the book.

One important fact gets highlighted on watching the three Anna movies: independently, the cinema seems inadequate in imparting the joy that a novel does; the viewer needs familiarity with the original novel to truly enjoy the movie. The need for this crutch of the original writing, however, was not felt at all for *Gone with the Wind*, *The Bridge on the River Kwai* or *Schindler's List*.

As it happens, looking at the scope and the various themes that it straddles, *Anna Karenina* is ideal material for presentation in great cinematic form. But great novels require not only deep study, but also absorption through every pore; they need makers like David Lean, Ingmar Bergman or John Huston who absorb the characters into their bloodstream to create their own epics in celluloid. Two of the *Anna Karenina* movies did have their divas in Greta Garbo and Vivien Leigh, but they missed out on inspired enough architects to conceptualise a cinematic temple commensurate with their divine talent. On the whole, while the novel has reigned supreme as a piece of literature, in the sphere of cinema though it has caused many a film-maker to miss his bus.

TESS

AUTHOR Thomas Hardy PUBLISHED 1892
DIRECTOR Roman Polanski PREMIERED 1979

‘...our impulses are too strong for our judgement sometimes.’

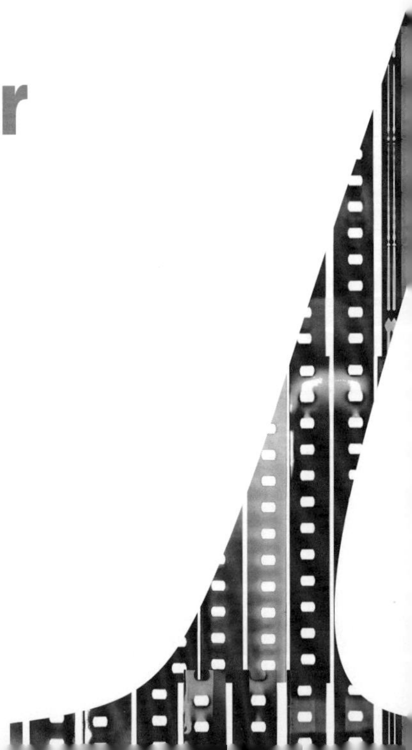

A high-quality novel possessing sizzling drama, extraordinary characters and the strange chemicals of vast life experiences does not necessarily find its destiny in a high-quality movie. Sure, the novel *Gone with the Wind* was followed within a few years by a movie that projected its magic on the screen. Despite the presence of talents of the calibre of Greta Garbo and Vivien Leigh, the film version of Tolstoy's Anna Karenina did not achieve any noticeable artistic height.

The world renowned Thomas Hardy wrote his *Tess of the d'Urbervilles* in 1891. The novel arrived carrying a storm on its tail. Both *Tess of the d'Urbervilles* and *Jude the Obscure* were greeted with such venom by the critics, and Hardy had to face such opposition at every step that he stopped writing novels and turned to writing poetry for a while. *Tess of the d'Urbervilles* eventually brought him handsome financial returns but it had to wait a full ninety years to be presented with full honours on the screen.

Tess of the d'Urbervilles is Hardy's twelfth novel where Tess represents the dark fate of a vulnerable woman who gets mired in tragic circumstances and is persecuted for no intentional fault of hers; a poor, young, innocent peasant girl, in this case, who is neither sophisticated nor worldly—the very character traits that leave her totally unprepared for the travails that beset her when she is thrown to fend for herself.

The story opens in a small village in Dorset. Farmer John Durbeyfield is seen on his way home, when Parson Tringham calls out to him as 'Sir John'. The priest, who is a local historian, tells him that he had been going through their family history, and as per records his family name has been found to be d'Urberville and not Durbeyfield. The d'Urbervilles were an ancient noble family, and in days of yore owned lands, palaces and vast wealth.

The thought that he has noble blood coursing through his veins makes John mad with joy. Pleased as punch, he turns towards the village pub. By the time he returns home dead drunk, it is well past midnight. He is due to leave at daybreak next morning to carry beehives to the Casterbridge market. He has four children, the eldest being Tess, and his wife's worry is that one missed trip to the market would mean hunger for the entire family.

Next morning Tess, who is barely 16, is persuaded to make the trip on behalf of her father. After a fair distance has been covered, young Tess falls asleep with the reins in her hand, and she does not notice the speeding wagon coming from the opposite direction. The sharp shaft of the wagon penetrates her horse, Prince, and kills it on the spot. Tess is overpowered by sorrow and guilt. The horse was their source of earning. Through her carelessness she had compromised the lifeline of her family. How would they now make ends meet?

They learn that a few miles from their village, in Trantridge, lives an old woman by the of name Mrs d'Urberville, who has her own mansion. Going by the name, John's family believes that the old woman belongs to a branch of the same family as theirs. It is decided that some investigation would be in order; it may land them some employment or financial help. Tess is dispatched to the manor house on this enterprise; her mother hopes in her simple way that if there is a male heir around at Trantridge, Tess might well finish off being the new baroness.

When Tess reaches the mansion, she does not get the occasion to meet the old baroness, but runs into her 25-year-old son Alec. On seeing her, the libertine's desire is

Thomas Hardy

‘Beauty lay not in the thing, but in what the thing symbolised.’

immediately roused and he welcomes her with pretended warmth. When Tess returns home empty-handed it greatly disappoints the family. But within a little while arrives a letter from the old baroness, promising her plenty of job opportunities at the manor. She could well become the manager of their poultry farm. The parents' hopes rise, but Tess harbours a slight suspicion as the handwriting of the note seems rather masculine.

When the carriage arrives to pick her up on the appointed day, Tess bids her parents goodbye with a heavy heart. Soon, on way they come across another carriage in which Alec d'Urberville is seated. He gets her to come into his carriage and sets the horse on a gallop. Alec suggests that she holds him tight. Tess senses his lecherous intentions and lets her hat fly off her head, and gets off the carriage with the excuse of retrieving it. She refuses to get back into the carriage, declaring that however long the distance, she would prefer to walk it. As a close relative, she expects some sympathy and consideration from him. ‘Artful hussy!’ is how he responds, and moves on.

Alec has no sympathy for Tess. For him she is only a maid, a poultry-keeper; to be exploited at will. Tess has no desire to stay on in the mansion, but with grinding poverty at home she is left with little choice. She would only add to her old parents' miseries by returning. Alec who wants to use her for his pleasure is surprised at the spirit and vanity of the worthless working woman who could have easily considered it an honour to be the mistress of the heir of a noble house!

Alec's lecherous intention reaches a point when, frustrated at not being able to make Tess succumb willingly to his desires, he forces himself on her and rapes her. Tess is devastated and curses and berates Alec for being a heartless wretch. She decides to flee her oppressor and finding an opportunity slips out one morning to return to her family at Marlott.

It was her mother who had pushed her towards Trantridge in the naïve hope of landing a good son-in-law, and her father had seconded this enterprise with great joy. Now, when she tells them about the stain she has brought back home, her father holds her alone to be blamed.

Marlott is rife with rumour. At church, people look at her with such suspicion that she stops visiting it during the daytime and returns only after dark. Time deals her a further blow when she finds that she is with child. Taunts follow her everywhere she goes.

In the 14th chapter of the book Tess baptises her illegitimate, severely sick and dying infant herself, worried for its soul. It is an episode sketched with great persuasion and delicacy of language. In the middle of the night she calls her young brothers, sprinkling a little water on their faces to awaken them and then lifts the infant off the bedsheet. Hardy writes here, 'She took the baby from her bed—child's child.' She christens it 'Sorrow'. The next day the infant dies.

The vicar grants that even though the baptism had been performed with due doctrinal process, out of fear of public outrage he wouldn't be able to bury the infant in the churchyard. Losing control, Tess snarls at him, 'Then I don't like you! And I'll never come to your church no more!' Tess returns at night, and with the help of an old woman she inters her child in an unconsecrated corner outside the churchyard, amidst notorious drunkards, suicide victims, thieves and vagabonds.

Deeply disillusioned, she leaves her village and decides to travel to another village, Kingsbere, where her ancestors had been laid to rest. The second important phase of her life begins here.

She joins a dairy farm run by Richard Crick and meets Angel Clare here. Hardy has created the character of Angel as a foil for Alec d'Urberville. Angel's father and his two brothers are all priests but Angel is more inclined towards agriculture and dairy farming. Angel has in fact seen Tess before and been struck by her innocence, at a village fair they had both attended, some years ago. He immediately recognises Tess who appears to him as a sober, happy, energetic, virtuous child of nature. He too has a generous heart and a flawless character, and does not care either for wealth or titles. While the other dairymaids yearn for a look from him, he seems to have eyes only for Tess.

On the advice of his parents, Angel had more or less decided to tie the wedding knot with a young girl named Mercy Chant. But having met Tess, he now decides that she should be his wife. He confesses his love to her and proposes marriage. 'I would rather be yours than anybody's in the world,' returns the sweet and honest voice of the distressed girl. 'But I CANNOT marry you!' Tess pleads. She is consumed by the thought that she would be quite unacceptable when Angel gets to know about her past: the brutality committed upon her by Alec d'Urberville and her dead child. When she consults her mother on the subject, she is however told that such incidents often happen with young girls and is advised not to reveal any of it to Angel.

Tess is quite determined that Angel should know everything of her past life, but cannot bring herself to tell it to him face to face. So she puts it all in a letter and slips it under the door of his room. When Angel continues to show the same interest in her,

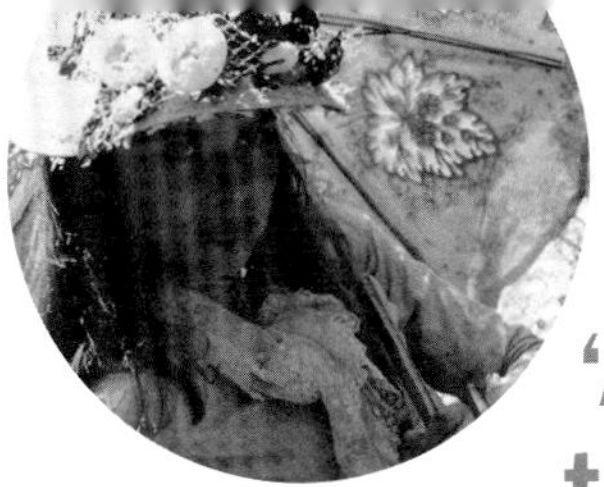

'A strong woman who recklessly throws away her strength, she is worse than a weak woman who has never had any strength to throw away.'

she believes that Angel has accepted her past, and accepts his proposal for marriage. It is only on the eve of her marriage that she notices the letter under the matting; it had slipped in there and Angel was still unaware of her ugly history. She tries to find him alone and begs that he should hear her out, but he brushes away her entreaty by saying that they would have enough time for conversations after marriage.

The night after the wedding turns out to be a truly dark one for the simple girl. When Angel tells her of the physical relationship he had with an older woman in London, Tess is encouraged to confess the atrocity committed upon her by Alec. While she happily forgives him his trespasses, he is utterly shaken by her confession. 'Am I to believe this?' he screams. She begs for forgiveness but he is in no state of mind to relent. Deeply resentful, he tells her, 'You were one person; now you are another...the woman I have been loving is not you...another woman in your shape.'

She begs him to keep her as a maid, a slave. 'Angel!' she tells him, 'Angel! I was a child—a child when it happened! I knew nothing of men.' When he absolutely refuses to give in to her pleas, she offers him the option of divorce. She brings to his notice that she was not the one keen on marriage. But Angel is impervious to her pleas. His love, it appears was only a mask, unconcerned, spurious. Tess is helpless against this indifference. His walking out of the room a defeated man, his directionless meandering, Tess catching up with him, the two of them moving with slow, purposeless steps, their faces registering disillusionment and despair, the background darkness of the night slowly giving way to the early light of dawn— some of these scenes have been beautifully captured on film.

When Tess returns to her native Marlott, her old village is no longer hers. Disowned by her father for bringing shame upon him, abandoned by husband, poor, innocent, virtuous Tess is misfortune's child. In search of life and livelihood, Tess travels to the impoverished village of Flintcomb-Ash to eke out a living. There she once again runs into Alec d'Urberville, who is now a half-baked priest. At seeing her, all his old passion is revived. In an effort to somehow win her heart, he tells her, 'I have enough and more than enough to put you out of anxiety, both for yourself and your parents and sisters. I can make them all comfortable if you will only show confidence in me.'

Tess, however, cannot get her husband Angel out of her mind. She writes letters to him, 'Angel, I live entirely for you...I would be content, ay, glad, to live with you as your servant, if I may not as your wife; so that I could only be near you, and get glimpses of you, and think of you as mine.'

As she sits at home one evening, her sister Liza-Lu suddenly arrives with the news that both her parents are seriously ill, and that her father is on his deathbed. The father soon passes away. Tess learns from various sources that her ancient family of d'Urbervilles is under a curse, because of the many sins committed by her ancestors. One such ancestor had tried to abduct a young girl in his coach, and the girl had died in an attempt to escape. Tess considers herself doomed to suffer for the misdemeanours of her ancestors.

After abandoning Tess, Angel goes away to Brazil. He brushes away the entreaties of the other dairy maids, Marian and Izz, friends of Tess, who remind him, 'Look to your wife if you do love her as much as she do love you.' Meanwhile, poor Tess's troubles are nowhere near over. After the father's death, the family has to relinquish their house. With no roof over their head they are reduced to pitching a tent by the wayside. With no solution in sight and despite her abhorrence Tess finally bows to the pressure of circumstances and becomes Alec's mistress. In return, Alec rents a house for her at a coastal resort called Sandbourne, and the rest of the family is housed elsewhere.

Alec never stops dinning into her head that her husband would never come back, and exploits her circumstances to the full. But one day, Angel arrives at the doorstep of Mrs Brooks' house at Sandbourne, where Tess lives. Angel learns of Tess's tragic tale and is full of remorse for having abandoned Tess because of her past misfortunes. Tess appears on the threshold but she does not walk into his open arms. 'I waited and waited for you,' she says from the doorway. 'But you did not come! And I wrote to you, and you did not come!...He has won me back to him.'

A shattered Angel leaves for the Sandbourne railway station. From the landing, Mrs Brooks overhears Tess's heartbreaking sobs as she tells Alec, 'Now he is gone. Gone a second time, and I have lost him now for ever...and he will not love me the littlest bit ever—only hate me!...O yes, I have lost him now—again because of—you!' She is so overcome with despair that she picks up a carving knife and plunges it into Alec and kills him. She then heads towards the station, and runs after him as she espies him on the highway. Pale, breathless, quivering in every muscle, she overtakes him and says, 'Angel, do you know what I have been running after you for? To tell you that I have killed him!'

The two are on the run thereafter. Sensing time is running out on her, Tess holds her husband's hands and asks, 'Angel, if anything happens to me, will you watch over Liza-Lu for my sake?' After some rest, they are back on the wilderness of the heath. Suddenly, they find themselves confronting colossal stone pillars, thick and tall as tree trunks. They are in Stonehenge. Dog tired, Tess stretches herself out on an oblong slab, and holding Angel by the hand, she slips into deep slumber. When she regains consciousness, she realises that they have been surrounded. 'What is it, Angel?' she says, starting up. 'Have they come for me?'

Towards the end of the novel, Angel and Liza-Lu are seen walking together. Convicted of murder, Tess is hanged. A black flag flutters over the prison tower. Angel and Liza-Lu stand still and lower their heads, as if in prayer. The drama that black destiny had begun with Tess's life finally comes to a close.

Thomas Hardy was born in Dorset in 1840, and died in 1928, thus living through 88 years of eventful life. Fifty of these years were spent as a famous writer and a successful poet. *The Mayor of Casterbridge, The Woodlanders, The Return of the Native*, *Under the Greenwood Tree*—are some of the great novels he has written. His father was a master mason, and his mother would usually be engrossed in reading Latin and French romances. At the age 22, young Thomas went to London as an Architecture intern. He could find no publisher for his *The Poor Man and the Lady* written in 1867. Later, of course, his novels were such runaway successes that they made the fortune of many a publisher.

As a novelist Hardy achieved lofty heights. The magic woven by Hardy's novels continues to mesmerise readers across the world for 150 years. Hardy was a truly fortunate writer who became a fairy-tale hero in his lifetime. His novels would be sent by boat to Japan, where eager readers would crowd the docks in their hundreds, waiting for the boat to arrive, and welcome the book with traditional fanfare. During the last years of his life he had reached the pinnacle of popularity. Tourists from all over the world would visit Hardy, making his house a tourist spot. Reminiscent of the Moghul emperors giving their subjects a glimpse of themselves by appearing on the palace casement, Hardy too would meet his admirers in the lobby of his house. Since the assemblage would become too big to manage, lots would be drawn for getting the privilege of shaking hands with the master.

Tess came out in 1891, and it challenged the values and religious traditions of the Victorian era. Before coming out as a book, it was published in a serialised form in the newspaper *The Graphic*, and it attracted immediate attention. Its heroine, and the events visited upon her, delivered a shock to contemporary social and aesthetic norms and customs. The Bishop of Wakefield publicly burnt a copy of the book to record his protest. The rape committed upon a village girl and her giving birth to an illegitimate child were shocking ideas for the society of those times. That is why well-known publishing houses like Macmillan had advised Hardy to remove those episodes from the book. But any change in his manuscript was completely unacceptable to the author.

Hardy's strength lay in the creation of excellent characters and the description of the geographical backdrop of his region, Wessex. He has portrayed with great skill life as it existed in rural England of the Victorian era. Shepherds, farmers, village fairs, weekly markets, dense forests, grasslands, heaths and hillocks, all come alive through his words. One can hear the shrieks and groans of the prehistoric aborigines buried under the mounds.

Hardy's Wessex is a mix of reality and imagination. His characters Eustacia Vye, Jude, Michael Henchard, Bathsheba Everdene, and many others have found a permanent place in the hearts of countless readers. He was particularly good at sketching women characters; in the process Hardy removed many layers off a woman's heart: the fun-loving Bathsheba Everdene of *Far from the Madding Crowd*, the lively Eustacia Vye of *The Return of the Native*; Tess was a close relative. Initially he had wanted to name the novel *A Pure Woman Faithfully Presented*. The other title he had decided for the novel was *Too Late Beloved*. Scholars and critics now regard *Tess of the d'Urbervilles* as Hardy's best novel.

It had been already made into a film in 1913 by J. Searle Dawley and again 1924 by Marshall Neilan when Polanski noticed it in late nineties. Why, among the great film directors of the world, should Roman Polanski have fallen in love with the novel? Why should Tess have so charmed and mesmerised its readers and audiences? The answers are hidden in Polanski's life, his brilliant screenplay and his shared affinity with Hardy, in understanding a woman's heart.

Roman Polanski was born in Poland on 18 August 1933. As a young boy he was witness to the worst atrocities of the Second World War. When he was eight, his mother died in the Auschwitz concentration camp. He

'What is hell? I maintain that it is the suffering of being unable to love.'

Nastassja Kinski as Tess in Roman Polanski directed *Tess* (1979). COURTESY: AUTHOR

himself somehow managed to escape with his life from the infamous Kraków concentration camp. He wore out many a doorstep to keep himself alive. It happened once that some Nazi soldiers were practising target shooting when young Polanski passed by. For fun they decided to use his head as target. It was by the sheerest luck that he managed to escape.

Singed in childhood by the Second World War, accused in middle age for raping a minor, exiled, doomed to see his beloved wife murdered, honoured with an Oscar for Best Director for *The Pianist*, Polanski has journeyed through all the by-lanes of life. Polanski learnt his first lessons in direction in Lodz, Poland. The atmosphere in Poland was not quite conducive to film-making then. In a cultural exchange programme Polanski went over to Paris where his studies acquired depth and breadth, and here he made his first feature film *Knife in the Water*.

The movie did not at first appeal to Polish audiences but when it was nominated for the Best Foreign Film Oscar, the attention of the world turned towards this 30-year-old director. He was hailed as the creator of movies that projected extraordinary psycho-sexual tension.

Polanski did not let the disappointment of missing the Oscar pull him down. He collaborated with Gérard Brach, and within 17 days wrote the screenplay for *Repulsion*, the story of a young Belgian girl named Carol, a split personality who loves and detests sex at the same time. He picked Catherine Deneuve to play the uninhibited character of Carol. The movie was so dense and terrifying that the Censor Board had to invite a psychologist before certifying it for exhibition. *Repulsion* brought Polanski rave notices.

Polanski had experienced the vicissitudes of life; as a result, he carried the conviction that family life always ends in tragedy. He later went on to make *Rosemary's Baby* which dealt with the black magic that found adherents in Manhattan.

During the making of *The Fearless Vampire Killers*, he came in contact with American actress Sharon Tate. They stayed as a live-in couple for two years. Despite the emotional bonding that tied them together, Sharon did not raise the issue of marriage, knowing Polanski's declared position on the subject. However, on 20 January 1968 they did formalise their partnership into marriage. Sharon and Polanski split their time between London and Los Angeles.

When Polanski was busy in London writing the script of *The Day of the Dolphin,* Sharon left for the US without him. Polanski was pacing around, discussing the subject with his colleagues, when a call came from his agent at Los Angeles: 'There's been an earthquake at home! Sharon is dead!' All he said was, 'Oh, no! No!' and collapsed. In fact, Sharon and her friends had been brutally done to death in her Los Angeles home by the notorious Manson gang. Sharon was in her ninth month of pregnancy at that time. A mountain had collapsed on Polanski's head. It was with great difficulty that the doctors brought him under control with tranquilisers.

It was months before Polanski could come to terms with Sharon's death. His wife's passing away had crushed him. But what hurt him more was the kind of kite-flying and rumours that began circulating about him: Sharon and Polanski were drug addicts; they were closely associated with an African who practised black magic; Polanski indulged in all kinds of voodoo rituals at home. What hurt him particularly was that a respected magazine like *Time* should get into the smirch campaign.

Tess has very delicate associations for Polanski. He has dedicated this film to Sharon Tate. After the death of his wife he found a copy of this book on the shelf in his London house. She had read it during her pregnancy, and in the copy left a note for her husband, suggesting that it could be turned into a top-class film. Hardy's heroine Tess had withered before she could reach full bloom. A wicked society had snuffed out Sharon Tate, too, before she could live to maturity. Perhaps it was this parallel between their two lives that inspired Polanski to make the movie; perhaps it was Sharon's undeclared desire to play the character of Tess on screen.

It is not as if Hardy alone looked upon the character of Tess with love and compassion. Polanski too overflowed with compassion for her. In the Roman Polanski movie, the camera pans beautifully as Tess moves towards the manor, making her way through the tangle of bushes and bramble, presaging the difficulties she is getting sucked into. Alec's evil is also beautifully captured through his shenanigans with his horse.

Tess and Alec's journey through one of the most ancient groves called 'The Chase' has been very effectively portrayed by Hardy. Roman Polanski and his cameraman too have worked wonders while filming this episode—thick dark jungle, branches reaching down like shadows, sudden shafts of light appearing and disappearing from the canopy, thick curls of mist enveloping the horse and its riders. In this dark, misty atmosphere, the passion-besotted Alec asks Tess for a kiss. Tess instantly responds that she does not care for him. After a sleepless night, Tess is ready to drop dead. Alec keeps taking his horse deeper and deeper into the forest. He can feel Tess's head lying limp against his back. He quietly brings his horse to a halt and tries to gather her in his embrace. As she tries to push him away, he slips down from the horse and gets scratched in the process. The sight of blood frightens her, and in her simplicity she tries to pacify him. The scratch is really nothing, but he senses that the time has arrived for him to indulge his lust for Tess which had been burning inside him for so many days. He makes full use of the opportunity and rapes her. Hardy has dealt with this episode with minimum words and some ambiguity, but Polanski captures it with great sensitivity.

Polanski has presented the episode where Tess goes to the priest requesting for a burial ground for her son a little differently, but very effectively. In the movie the priest is shown as shooing the bees away from the hive in front of the church. Tess's back is towards the camera. She keeps the sobs firmly out of her voice and tells him of the passing away of her child and the baptising that preceded it. The expressive manner in which the actress Nastassja Kinski puts it across leaves one stunned. Her purple-tinged face in a tight close-up is worth studying.

Roman Ploanski deserves hundred per cent marks for his choice of Tess. Selecting the right person for the right role is a mark of a great director. When the entire burden of the story happens to rest upon the main character, the choice becomes critical. The slightest error, and not all the technical legerdemain can save the movie from crashing. Tess is seen as the victim of a callous society. The novel identifies her family background as primarily responsible for her misfortunes. But Polanski has been criticised for holding the men in her life responsible for her travails. Nastassja was chosen as a deliberate effort at whipping up sympathy for Tess, the criticism goes. I believe that Nastassja as Tess is one of the major strengths of the movie. Her beautiful tear-brimmed eyes remind one of dark clouds; they are so unspeakably expressive and meaning-laden.

As the movie progresses, as one scene gives way to the other, the virtuosity of Nastassja Kinski gathers strength. With her lustrous complexion, jet black eyes, thin lips, tall and graceful Nastassja playing the 16-year-old Tess is everybody's dream-girl—a darling daughter, a perfect life partner for the young men, a great sister-material for the young. It is not through her beauty alone that Nastassja enchants; when the situation demands, her expressive face reflects the agonies that she as Tess has suffered in life.

The Tess portrayed by Hardy was not merely a statuesque beauty with big innocent eyes and expressive mien. The film-maker was required to re-create for his audience not just the ethereal beauty of Tess, but the throbbing anguish of her star-crossed life. On repeated viewing of Polanski's *Tess,* I felt that Nastassja was tapping into her personal sorrows to give her role such authenticity. What showed through her portrayal was what she had undergone as an individual.

It was this curiosity that set me on the trail of her past life. She was the daughter of German actor Klaus Kinski, and was born on 24 January 1961. She has more than 60 movies to her credit. During the decades of 70s and 80s she was identified as a sex symbol. Her nude photograph with a python, taken by world renowned photographer Richard Avedon, became famous.

Nastassja, who would later gain fame, faced extreme penury and humiliation as a child. Her parents were divorced when she was eight, and mother and daughter had to face grinding poverty. Often they would collect their free food from the church and eat it by the wayside. Arranging for the next meal was a major issue. At the age 16 when she played Tess, she would have remembered the distress of those days. The abysmal dearth, the afflictions of those days have been immortalised by her through her acting prowess. Besides her imperishable portrayal of Tess, her other movies like *Texas* and *Paris* also gained popularity. Her role of Tess won for her an Oscar nomination for Best Actress, and brought her the prestigious Golden Globe Award.

As director, Roman Polanski left no stones unturned. He sent Nastassja Kinski over to England, where she took special training to remove all traces of her German accent. He also had to recreate for his audience the greenery, the greyness, the other natural aspects of Hardy's Wessex. He chose the legendary cameraman Geoffrey Unsworth to take charge. Geoffrey wasn't keeping good health. But his college-going daughter was doing *Tess of the d'Urbervilles* as a part of her curriculum, which gave him an affinity for the novel. The movie was to be filmed in German, French and English simultaneously.

Polanski had to face many problems for shooting this period film. Victorian England had long vanished, so he had to search out suitable sites in Normandy and Brittany. All traces of modern times—including TV antennae—had to be wiped out from the chosen villages, and he had to pay heavy compensation to the villagers.

One cannot fail to register the amount of work put in by both Polanski and Unsworth. Tess is hard at work on the threshing machine along with other workers. An old oil engine is chugging away by her side. Alec arrives there to conciliate her. The scene has been captured flawlessly. A disappointed Tess has set off towards her village from the dairy farm. As she takes a break in the dense bracken in the forest, a deer, as soft-hearted as she, comes to her; when she sets off at daybreak the next day, the fifty to sixty deer hunters ride by with their loud calls! Shot in the early morning mist and dew, it makes an enchanting scene. Unsworth threw himself so totally and so uncaringly into his work that his frail health could not take the strain, and he died in harness. The rest of the filming had to be completed by Ghislain Cloquet. Art director Pierre Guffroy used all his skills to erect churches, dairies and houses of Victorian times. Anthony Powell created the costumes to match the times.

Tess wasn't received with any noticeable enthusiasm in France. Many ran it down as merely a documentary on dairies. After frequent deletions, the length of the movie has now been reduced to 170 minutes. While excellent in other technical areas, in the matter of editing the film is quite loose, for which of course, Polanski himself is responsible. Much against his wishes, an edited version of the movie was later shown in many countries, and except for France, it was well received everywhere.

There was the case of sexually abusing a minor, still pending in the US courts, against Polanski. So he had to stay away. But his movie was received with great enthusiasm. The movie received nine nominations for the Oscar, but could convert only three: Best Cinematography (Geoffrey Unsworth–Ghislian Cloquet), Best Art Direction (Pierre Guffroy) and Best Costume Design (Anthony Powell). Against expectations, the Best Director award did not go to Polanski. He did get the Critics' Award for Best Direction, though. He had to wait till 2002 to land the Best Director Oscar for *The Pianist*.

There is an old proverb in England which holds that if a man goes bad, he is considered bad; but a woman gone bad is evil. The proverb fits our modern, progressive times rather well. It was with this scale that people had measured Tess during Hardy's times. An accusation laid at Hardy's door was that he brought women's emancipation to a halt by placing a knife in Tess's hand. Many believe that she should not have allowed her passion to overpower her self-control. However, the manner in which the drama of black destiny finally comes to a close does not appear inappropriate.

The manner in which both Thomas Hardy and Roman Polanski look at Tess's tragic journey shows that they share the same soul, the same values and the same sympathies. Watching Polanski's *Tess* reproduces for us the same pleasure as re-reading the novel.

MUGHAL-E-AZAM

ADAPTED FROM Syed Imtiaz Ali Taj's *Anarkali* (1922)
PUBLISHED 1922 DIRECTOR K. Asif PREMIERED 1960

'*Mohabbat joh darti ho woh mohabbat nahin... ayyashi hai, gunaah hai*'
(Love that is scared is not love... it is debauchery, it is crime)

An artist often holds a concept close to his heart and works upon it for several years, before he finally manages to create an immortal piece. The subject of Gandhi stayed with Sir Richard Attenborough for twenty years. Similarly, K. Asif started working on Mughal-e-Azam in 1944, but by the time his dream was realised August 1960 had dawned. Nursing such dreams is not different from sharing the bed with a snake. A living mission, a writhing, wriggling dream which bites, stings and pinches, and keeps one restless for as long as it stays.

Mughal-e-Azam is a beautiful product of the fertile imagination of some of the most talented minds. In the late 1800, writer Abdul Halim Sharar had written a work of fiction built around *Anarkali* (pomegranate blossom), supposedly one of Akbar's favourite dancing girls. This story gained popularity and was adapted into literature, art and cinema. Syed Imtiaz Ali Taj, an Urdu dramatist, is remembered above all for his 1922 play *Anarkali*, with the purpose of creating a love story that would enchant all. It was staged hundreds of times before being adapted for feature films in India and Pakistan, and finally reproduced as the famous film *Mughal-e-Azam*, in 1960.

According to history, it was after many prayers, and with the blessings of saint Sheikh Saleem Chishti of Fatehpur Sikri, that prince Saleem had been born to Akbar. The very son would, however, grow up to rebel against the beloved father, and break his heart in a struggle for power. The movie *Mughal-e-Azam* is about this epic struggle between a father and a son but built around the fiction of Anarkali. Here it is about the conflict between an Emperor who is determined to crush his son's love affair in the interest of the future of the country, and a son who too is determined enough to wage war on his father for the sake of his beloved. Historically, however, Saleem had rebelled against his father purely for thirst of power and not for love of any Anarkali. The Saleem of history was also a philanderer who had several liasons with many a femme fatale. The story, then, which is imaginary, may thus be termed semi-historical.

Director Kamruddin Asif, or popularly K. Asif, formally purchased the film rights of the play from Imtiaz. Like Shakespeare who tapped the *Lives* of the historian Plutarch and used the historical characters to his convenience to create great masterpieces, K. Asif's team of writers performed the same magic. Asif joined hands with Aman (Zeenat Aman's father, also known as Amanullah Khan) to create a beautiful script. For the dialogues he put to work great writers of Urdu and Hindi like Ehsan Rizvi, Kamaal Amrohi, Dr Sabdar, Amanullah Khan and Wajahat Mirza for a few years. A situation was allotted to each for writing a scene, and a joint reading was held after that. This churning got the script and dialogues into shape.

The stupendous character of Akbar is the priceless gift of the affection that existed between a visionary director like K. Asif and a phenomenal actor like Prithviraj Kapoor. When one thinks of Tukaram, one can only think of Vishnupant Pagnis; in the same manner, when one thinks of Akbar, it can only be Prithviraj Kapoor, and nobody else.

A product of the stage, Prithviraj was forever breathing down director K. Asif's neck: 'How do I essay Akbar?' During the shooting, Asif had given Prithviraj a few tips: let alone the set, even at home he was to behave like a king; he was never to pick up anything; he was to address the servants in a regal manner; issue diktats; he was to keep a regal bass-note to his voice. Prithviraj took these tips so much to heart that, according to old timers, his voice changed during the course of the movie.

In the movie, when Akbar goes to pay his homage to Sheikh Chishti, he walks barefoot on the hot sand. For rehearsing this, Prithviraj practised walking on the sands of Juhu, it is said. Once, at the Film City, Dilip Kumar, who was directing Sudhakar Bokade's *Kalinga* at that time, reminisced, 'Asif took repeated re-takes of Akbar's barefoot visit to Sheikh Chishti, to the point that even Prithviraj was a little disturbed. What, after all, was so special about that scene? We often used to make fun of the director in our private conversations. But when the movie came on to the screen, pulling on his cigarette, Asif would ask his friends, "Now say, which of the two walks shows greater delicacy, an elephant with wax on its back or my Akbar walking over the sand?"'

Initially, the producer of *Mughal-e-Azam* was Shiraz Ali Hakeem. He had Chandramohan to play Emperor Akbar and Sapru for Saleem. Nargis had been given the role of Anarkali. A bit of shooting had been also been done. Music director Anil Biswas had composed a few pieces too. Dilip Kumar was a new arrival then, and he still had to get star airs. Once Naushad related this incident to me: 'A few people suggested Dilip Kumar's name to Asif, to which Asif responded, "I have no intention of gambling on a trainee horse and getting my Mughal-e-Azam Airavat (divine elephant) stuck in the bogs."'

The movie surmounted innumerable obstacles during its production journey of nine years. There were many mountains to cross. The country was torn into two. Many Muslim artists left for Lahore. Producer Hakeem, a close friend of Barrister Mohammad Ali Jinnah felt it unsafe to live in India. He sold off his 'Famous Studio', packed the negatives of *Mughal-e-Azam* to rust in boxes, and left for Pakistan. Later senior actors like Chandramohan and Sapru passed away. Asif, however, marched on relentlessly.

Despite all the political changes, young Asif refused to be diverted from his mission. The desire to present the majestic image of Emperor Akbar on the silver screen was an obsession with him. Born in the small town of Ittawa in Uttar Pradesh, Asif had come to Mumbai to test his fortunes. His uncle Nazeer was a successful name in the film industry. Instead of standing in a beggar's line for a feast, it was better, he thought, that his nephew earned a decent living. He opened up a tailoring shop for him. But the nephew continued to do the rounds of film studios. 'I'll make such films that I'll leave everyone gasping for breath!' he would brag in the vicinity of Ranjit Studios.

In 1945 he directed a movie called *Phool*, and then he came up with the Dilip Kumar-Nargis starrer *Hulchul*, neither of which brought him much success. Hakeem's abandonment of the *Mughal-e-Azam* project caused him further disappointment. But he never let the fire in his heart die. Then came to Mumbai a moneybag who was equally fixated with Akbar—the construction magnate, Seth Shapoorji Pallonji. Akbar was the favourite topic of Shapoorji's wife too. Asif went and met him instantly. 'Azam' meant 'the greatest of the Mughals', explained Asif to Shapoorji, and went on to tell him the tale he wanted to film. Shapoorji bought the idea, and brought in his firm, Sterling Investments Pvt. Ltd., to finance the project.

A lot of water, meanwhile, had flown under the bridge. When superstar Chandramohan passed away, Dilip Kumar, who was on the ascendant, landed the role of Saleem. The original Anarkali changed too. During the making of *Hulchul* Dilip Kumar and Nargis had had a spat, and she had decided not to work with him. The search for a new Anarkali began. For some time attention rested on Nutan, the girl from Maharashtra. Soon, the search got tiring, and shooting began without her. Along with Durga Khote of the original list, Asif assembled a brand new cast and began to shoot. In the early days Dilip Kumar was not particularly happy doing Saleem. From the screenplay, and even during the shooting it appeared that the story belonged to Akbar alone. It was with great difficulty that Asif brought him round. A special wig was flown in for him from London. But Dilip Kumar's grouses did not stop. When Asif got irritated, Dilip would tell him, 'You are pressurising me!' And Asif would reply, 'I am making Mughal-e-Azam, not Saleem-e-Azam.'

K. Asif made the movie in the manner of a sculptor, sitting with his chisel and hammer and creating an immortal masterpiece. Keeping the original play *Anarkali* as its spine, the screenplay was made more elaborate.

There is this emotionally charged scene when the Prince Saleem comes to bid the Empress Jodhabai goodbye: on the one side we see the mother's soft heart, on the other her steely imperial determination; the sword slips from the mother's trembling hands and clatters to the floor! Another unforgettable episode is when Prince Saleem challenges the authority of his father for the sake of his beloved in the presence of the full Mughal court!

It was also for the first time that Indian audiences witnessed such an enormous battlefield on screen. The advance of the armies, the combat between the forces of Saleem and Akbar required money and it flowed like water. The Indian Army had lent its cavalry for the battle scenes filmed on the deserts of Rajasthan.

On the eve of battle, Akbar goes to meet his son in his camp. The thought of plunging his sword in his own progeny had made his heart go heavy. Saleem greets him with a sarcastic: 'The Emperor has come in the disguise of a father!' Just as father and son begin closing distance, Saleem's friend Durjan Singh arrives after having freed Anarkali from the Emperor's prison. He has lived by a Rajput's word given to a friend. Anarkali can be seen right behind Durjan, as terrified as a hunted doe. Having got Anarkali back, Saleem declares, 'There is no reason left for battle.' The enraged father throws off his mantle and retorts, 'Battle shall take place! It most certainly shall!' As he is leaving the tent, he lets loose a barb at the girl, 'Anarkali, your life is an invitation of misfortune for Saleem.' The entire scene is worthy of finding a place in the works of the best dramatists.

K. Asif put as much money into the movie as others would have spent for twelve. In this context, I remember a story, which was often told to me by the cinematographer of *Ganga Jamuna*,

Dilip Kumar as Prince Saleem and Madhubala as Anarkali, in the K. Asif directed *Mughal-e-Azam* (1960).
COURTESY: AUTHOR

S.V. Babasaheb. Asif had arranged for a pair of pearl-studded footwear for Akbar that cost Rs 4000. During those days, when a primary school teacher earned Rs 20 a month, it was a huge amount. When Mathur saw these expensive shoes, he was furious. 'Kamruddin,' he shouted, 'why are you getting into such exorbitant expenses in the name of grandeur? You think these shoes are going to be visible to the camera?' Asif lit a cigarette in his typical manner, and laughed, 'My dear boy, when the Akbar who is going to put on these shoes gets to know their price, his walk and his delivery will acquire a special swagger. It is not his shoes, but the expression of his face that I want you to capture on film.'

Money was also blown in massive quantities to build the *sheesh mahal* (glass-palace) set, erected after months of hard work. It became the subject of much comment. Not surprising then, there were enough people who wanted to flay him.

Two movies by the name of *Anarkali* were announced, one of them to be produced by Kamaal Amrohi for M & T Studio. Amrohi had a major contribution in *Mughal-e-Azam* as screenplay and dialogue writer. But the two were good friends, and it was by calling upon this friendship that Asif dissuaded Amrohi from his project.

During those times there was this factory by the name of Filmistan Studio which ran day and night, churning out movies. Nandlal Jaswantlal readied *Anarkali* for Filmistan and screened it in the span of one year. With Pradeep Kumar as Saleem and Bina Rai as Anarkali, the movie became a superhit on the strength of its beautiful songs composed by C. Ramchandra. The Anarkalis of both these movies reached great heights because of the soulful, melodious voice of the nightingale Lata Mangeshkar.

Filmistan's *Anarkali*, the story of a dancing girl who challenges the might of the mighty Mughal, had become a runaway hit on the strength of its songs. It was imperative for the lyricist Shakeel Badaayuni and the composer Naushad to come up with something equally lilting.

They settled upon *Pyaar kiya toh darna kya* out of the many that Naushad had readied for the sheesh-mahal song. About 15 years ago I had the occasion to visit Naushad at his bungalow in the company of composer Ram Kadam, and had the rare fortune to listen to some other pieces composed for the movie.

After all these years, I distinctly remember the piece prepared for *Anarkali* dancing at the Durbar, which Naushad played for us on the harmonium:

Nigaahein neechey kiye sar jhukaaye baithey hain
Wahi to hain jo mera dil churaaye baithey hain
(Sitting there with head bent, eyes lowered,
He's the one who has stolen my heart)

The envious dancing girl, Bahaar, sings a song to welcome Saleem home after a victorious campaign. It is sung against the background of a boat race. The song that got in was '*Teri mehfil mein kismet aazmaa kar hum bhi dekhenge*', leaving out the one that has Madhubala and Nigar Sultana playing in the water on the banks of the Yamuna.

K. Asif lived a very simple life near Gowalia Tank. *Mughal-e-Azam* was being shot at Mohan Studios in Andheri East, where he would go by taxi. He was known for his helpful, compassionate, prodigal nature. There were enough envious people who created a din during the sheesh-mahal controversy. The expenses had been so stupendous that even a millionaire like Shapoorji was nervous. He began complaining, 'Asif is pauperising me. No director can shoot in sheesh mahal!' He decided to take the baton away from Asif. A similar uproar had been created by those envious regarding the novice Coppola during the making of *The Godfather*. Poor Coppola would get nightmares of the film being handed over to Roman Polanski.

At the request of Shapoorji, the film-maker Sohrab Modi promised to complete the film for him. When he arrived to see the sheesh-mahal set, K. Asif was quietly having a smoke in a corner. As Sohrab Modi was leaving the set, his car developed a snag, and the company car went to drop him home. On way, the driver could not hold himself back. 'Sir,' he said, 'Mr Asif is a strange person. Here he insists on fetching diamonds and pearls for Anarkali, plays with rubies and emeralds during the day, and himself lives in a ramshackle house. Just has a couple of pairs of vests and pajamas, and sleeps on a mat. Spends his salary away on friends. Good man, he is.' When he reached home Sohrab Modi telephoned Shapoorji, 'Your director Asif is an artist to the bone. If you mean well by the movie, don't think of turning it over to me or to anyone else. Let him finish it.'

Dilip Kumar and Madhubala were playing out the immortal story of Saleem and Anarkali. The duo were deeply in love with each other in real life. The two had reached the pinnacle of professional success, both were unmarried, and of the same faith too. The spanner in the works was Madhubala's father Ayaatullah Khan. For him, the successful actress was the goose that laid the golden eggs. Born in poverty, he crowed that he belonged to a higher denomination than Dilip Kumar.

During the nine-year period of the making of the film, the love affair of the two went through its ups and downs. In a case related with the making of *Naya Daur*, Dilip Kumar declared in full court at Girgaum that he loved Madhubala deeply, and would continue doing so till his last breath. But Ayaatullah would forever be present on the sets like a Pathan with his whip. Around this time the Shammi Kapoor starrer *Naqaab* was being shot in Pune. With the excuse of meeting his friend, this king of the silver screen would often visit Pune, as the story goes, and meet his beloved occupying the next suite on the sly. The passion of their private life is reflected in their on-screen performance. The jealous Bahaar brings the surreptitious rendezvous of the prince to the notice of the Emperor. The Emperor arrives there red with rage, intent upon chewing the girl up alive. The helpless Anarkali backs off from the advancing king, and scampers into the arms of Saleem, and collapses in his embrace. The terror on the face, the concentration and the extreme agony expressed here have never reappeared in any of her other films.

Madhubala's ethereal beauty, her innocent childlike laughter, and her endearing frivolity are inimitable. When the song *Mohey panghat pey Nandlaal chhed gayo rey* was being filmed, the barrister scion of a rich family would come to watch the shooting. He exploited his passing acquaintance with Asif, and under cover of being in love with the song, he sat for hours together, absorbing the celestial beauty of the performer from the corner of his eye. He marked his attendance at the studio for eight continuous days. Later this man would become the President of Pakistan—Zulfiqar Ali Bhutto.

Shooting the intimate love scenes of Saleem-Anarkali under the very nose of the ever-suspicious father tested the director's problem-solving skills. In particularl it became a challenge to film the passion-laden scene in the royal garden, with Tansen's (Ustad Badey Ghulam Ali Khan's) romance-soaked song floating in as voice-over, before Ayaatullah's eagle eyes. K. Asif, however, knew of the old man's weakness for gambling. He called over Taranath Gandhi, handed him Rs 25,000, and told him to lure the old man away, and keep him away. Gandhi took the Pathan away to a far corner of the studio, and steadily went on losing right through the day. Meanwhile, K. Asif canned the now famous love scene.

Suddenly one day, the doctors announced that the 21-year-old beauty was suffering from an enlarged, perforated heart. When Ayatullah learnt of his daughter's affliction, he was heartbroken. On the one hand, the Saleem-Anarkali film was nearing completion; on the other, her illness was gaining strength. Tensions began to appear in the personal lives of Dilip and Madhubala. Dilip went to the extent of staying aloof. When Dilip was on the set, an energy would enter the disease-racked body of the woman; when he was missing, she would droop like a dead flower. Which was why, perhaps, when she sang the following lines, the pathos of the poem becomes evident on her face:

Muhabbat ki jhooti kahaani pey roye;
Badi chot khaayi jawaani pey roye
(At the fakeness of the love story, I cry;
At the injury suffered by youth, I cry)

Studios then were not the air-conditioned ones we see now. Characters wearing the heavy costumes of imperial courts would sweat under the tin roofs. They didn't have the make-up vans of today that can put a king to shame. But under the hot tin roof, through years of hard work, the story of Saleem-Anarkali continued being filmed. Their on- and off-screen love, their skirmishes and their distances, these were all like dancing on the razor edge of the sword.

If *Mughal-e-Azam* is examined today frame by frame, Saleem at places looks confused, even cruel. But Anarkali is a completely devoted, committed lovebird. Looking at the shadow of death on the horizon, it was as if she was telling Dilip Kumar and his world:

Dhadaktey dil ka payaam le lo
Tumhaari duniya se jaa rahey hain,
Utho, hamaara salaam le lo
(Take this message of the throbbing heart:
I am departing from your world;
Rise, and accept my goodbye)

Mughal-e-Azam was released on 5 August1960, at the Maratha Mandir cinema hall. It came decked up as a newly-married bride. It was released simultaneously at 150 theatres across the country. It is said that there was not enough coloured ink left in the market to make the posters. Excitement was at its peak among the filmgoers. People had come from Pakistan, Myanmar and Sri Lanka to watch the film. People stood in line for three continuous days and night to get their tickets.

The arrival of the movie confirmed the obsession-driven K. Asif as a genius. Shapoorji recovered his 15 million rupees many times over. Asif then began the production of his next movie *Love and God*, with Guru Dutt in the lead, and Simi Grewal as the female lead. But Guru Dutt passed away within a very short time.

K. Asif had intended to spend on the same scale on this movie as the earlier film, and create another magnificent dream. But at the relatively young age of 48, this mission-maniac passed away in 1971, causing the Indian film industry an irreparable loss.

Seeing *Mughal-e-Azam* forty-five years after its first release, it is clear that if anyone deserves a tribute, after K. Asif it is its cameraman R.D. Mathur. If it hadn't been for the technical skill that Mathur brought into this movie, the magnificence of the Mughal period would not have been recreated with such authenticity on the screen. It was the first Indian movie to have achieved the standards of a Hollywood movie. On close examination it appears that all the lenses, filters and other equipment available in Hollywood were put to full use here.

Mathur's camera was far ahead of the Hindi films of those times. For *Citizen Kane*, Director Orson Welles and cameraman Gregg Toland had adopted the style of scenes jumping from one frame to another like the blooming of flowers. The shot division of *Mughal-e-Azam*, likewise, astounds us with the magic wrought by the director and the cameraman. The lighting, too, was as impressive as Josef von Sternberg's works.

When colour arrived in filmdom, *Muglal-e-Azam* was in the final stages of completion, and K. Asif got a two-reel piece filmed in colour. The result was so satisfying that he went with his latest demand to Shapoorji: 'Let's re-shoot the entire movie in colour.' But the budget-limit had long been exceeded. Shapoorji had arrived at the end of his patience, and he would have none of it.

Later, in 2004, the entire movie was given its hues. The close-up scenes look well done;, Madhubala particularly looks beautiful in the song '*Mohey panghat pey Nandlal chhed gayo re*'. But the long panning shots cause the grains to split. In short, it's quite like our grandparents' portraits, taken at the village fair, filled in with colour by the drawing master-cum-artist of the sub-divisional school.

The release of the fully coloured version of *Mughal-e-Azam* was organised in 2004 at Eros, the premium cinema hall in Mumbai. I cannot forget the face of the emotion-choked Dilip Kumar on that occasion. Reminiscing on those old times, Dilip Kumar said, 'O Lord, I pray to you from the bottom of my heart. Please get all the actors, the technicians and the seniors associated with *Mughal-e-Azam* together once again.'

There was no Anarkali in history, but mixing up fact and fiction, history and legend, K. Asif created an unbelievable mix called *Mughal-e-Azam* and gifted a priceless piece of art to the world.

Films were made yesterday, they continue to be made today, and will be made tomorrow too. But the history of the Indian film industry will have to tarry a bit at this milestone of a movie before it proceeds further.

Lord, truly, where have those times gone? Where have those people vanished?

ALL QUIET ON THE WESTERN FRONT

AUTHOR Erich Maria Remarque **PUBLISHED** 1929
DIRECTOR Lewis Milestone **PREMIERED** 1930

‘We were all at once terribly alone; and alone we must see it through.’

The novel was burned.
The film on the book was banned.
The writer was exiled from his homeland.
But the truth?
Nobody can slay the truth or stark reality.

Three quarters of a century later *All Quiet on the Western Front* has brought the novelist Erich Maria Remarque and the director of the movie Lewis Milestone true immortality.

The anti-war note struck by this novel contributed a few stones towards the construction of the future United Nations Organisation. The director of this immortal film in his old age believed that directing this movie earned him great merit. He had been able to alert people to the war-mongering manufacturers of armaments who had emerged in the interim; people who made their living out of setting countries at war with each other.

The notable quality of this piece of art is that it does not focus on any particular war or any particular country. It speaks against all wars that have ever been fought, and all belligerent tendencies the world over that cause such wars to happen.

All Quiet on the Western Front has Paul Bäumer, Albert Kropp, Müller and Leer, none beyond twenty, as some of its main characters. They are the so-called proud 'iron youth' of Germany, as hammered into them by their teachers, enlisted to fight for the proud traditions of their German fatherland.

The central focus of the book is the trench war, with its slush and its hand-to-hand combats. The 'front' of the trenches of Remarque's novel—a more apt term would be the 'rear-side' view of civility and basic humanity—a naked display of brutal, obscene, demonic warfare! Under the guise of patriotism and love for fatherland, these youngsters are plundered, and their flesh torn off them by the merchants of war. They are not even married, with only their old parents at home. An occasional boy has had a girl, with whom he had a clandestine affair like a half-burnt cigarette.

Bäumer's class is 21 strong, late adolescent, bursting with romantic notions on life. They are hurried through a ten-week programme where polishing boots is chosen over polishing the intellect. Intelligence does not count; what counts is the system, the deadening drill. In the manner of circus animals, they are trained to jump at the crack of a whip to get ready for the never-ending war with rockets exploding in the sky, the deafening noise of canons interspersed with the rat-tat-tat of gunfire and blindfold bombings!

They lie in chest-deep trenches dug into the earth, the rims of the trenches laced with sandbags for additional protection. They sneak out, crawl forward, run into a machine-gun spray, and dodge their way back into the safety of their trenches. The bombs land closer and ever closer, like fuses hissing and crackling towards their load of dynamite, and finally hit the trenches. Young lives are blown into smithereens, and dismembered limbs land back in the trenches. Some nurse their comrades, some others roast horseflesh to put into their bellies. In the theatre of war, men are just so much wax, so much dung. The earth from the trenches settles under their nails like black and blue poison.

Pitiable beyond words, tender young recruits keep streaming in to be roasted on the embers of war. Communal latrines with no doors, where twenty men sit answering the call of nature side-by-side as if on a train, another drill conducted under the watchful eye of their seniors.

They are not even grown-up enough to be ready for martyrdom! Müller carries course books in his backpack and does mental sums under heavy bombarding. The narrator Bäumer loves sketching the pictures of birds. Some are hit by stomach ailments, some others with memory of their dear ones back home!

On the front we meet chest-high fog and the smoke of the lethal weapons. Hiding behind the smoke and fire we also meet the moon. A few heads and the barrels of the guns peep out above the fog. There are the searchlights that go mopping the darkness

Erich Maria Remarque

out of the sky. The smaller cannons sound like the barking of wounded deer. The rockets in the sky vomit out green smoke from the edge of the clouds. The cannon balls kick up slush from the earth. Suddenly there's the murderous loud scream of a roasting mare. The words in the book present mind-numbing pictures; the eye of the camera has limitations, and can't reach so deep.

As with the soldiers, one day the earth too is engulfed in flames, and the next day it is squelching wet. They want to burrow themselves deep into the pit to gain protection from the ear-shattering noise; they hold the earth in a tight hug to escape the blaze of the explosives, to save their limbs from being sawn off by its serrated tongue. During such moments there is no friend closer, no parent more loving than earth.

In the early part of the novel we meet Kemmerich, whose leg has to be amputated. He looks terrible, yellow and pallid. Death peeps out from the edges round the pupils of his eyes. The friends visiting him really have an eye on his boots. Once he moves on, they hope to gain ownership of those soft yellow leather boots. Their own legs have rotted in the slush in the trenches, the rats have nibbled at them. Kemmerich dies, but even before his body loses its warmth, the orderly wants the corpse moved out. There is a line of live bodies waiting outside for the bed to become available.

Under the name of military discipline, there is a corrupt, ignorant, artificial system at the front that roasts the skins of the youngsters. Corporal Himmelstoss, the commander of their squad, a former postman, is 'reckoned to be the stickiest bastard in the whole barracks'. He makes the men run. Full pack on back, rifle in hand, the trainees are made to do their drills on wet, freshly ploughed earth. 'On your feet! Advance! Get down!' he roars, and after some time of rolling in the mud, the recruits are turned into masses of mud themselves.

The fundamental issue that Remarque has raised here is this: who incites such ruinous war? Why? For whose benefit? The protagonist and narrator of the story, Paul Bäumer, expresses the opinion of his pal Albert Kropp:

> He reckons that all declarations of war ought to be made into a kind of festival, with entrance tickets and music, like they have at bullfights. Then the ministers and generals of the two countries would have to come into the ring, wearing boxing shorts, and armed with rubber truncheons, and have a go at each other. Whoever is left on his feet, his country is declared the winner. That would be simpler and fairer than things are out here, where the wrong people are fighting each other.

Erich Maria Remarque was tall, fair and handsome, with a head of platinum blonde hair and a strong, well-groomed physique. Although at first appearance he was the quintessential Aryan of Nazi conception, he was a sworn enemy of Nazism and its desire for world dominance through force of arms. He was born on 22 June 1898 in Osnabruck, to a lower middle-class Catholic family that was ever on the move, looking for affordable rents. From early childhood Remarque was exceedingly interested in literature and possessed precocious writing skills. His school essays often made his teachers suspect him of plagiarising.

As a matter of fact, Remarque had wanted to become a composer of music, but very early in life he ran into dehumanising war. At the age of eighteen he was on the war front. Five times he was wounded, the fifth time grievously. For fifteen months he lay in a critical state in a hospital, thus bringing his life as a soldier to a premature end.

While his physical wounds were deep, his emotional wounds went deeper. The violence, the bloodshed, the naked dance of death, the slaughter that shattered one's faith in mankind—for the first time ever, Remarque's young generation experienced the terrible reality of war, first-hand. The experience unhinged them. It took Remarque a good ten years to sort out the causes of his terrible disillusionment.

He sold tombstones, drove a van for a tyre manufacturing firm, taught for a short while, worked as deputy editor for a periodical, and went through many more sundry jobs, but the ghost of war couldn't be shaken away. Catharsis finally arrived only when he sat down and poured all his angst into a conscience-stirring book. For two full weeks he sat up till late in the night organising his thoughts, and that was when the novel began taking shape.

His wife loved the concept so much that she advised him to give up his job if need be, so that he could devote himself to it. Friends, however, advised caution, and thought chucking a comfortable job with a fashion magazine would be suicidal. 'Whoever wants to dig up the ten-year-old graves of a long forgotten war?' said one publisher. 'Throw this manuscript away and sit peacefully at home.' Another big publisher gave it to him on his face, 'There is no demand for war books at all, gentleman!'

When *All Quiet on the Western Front* was first published in German in 1929, it exploded like dynamite. It was the time when the Nazi party was strengthening its hold on Germany. After many major German publishers had turned down the book, it was finally published by a Jewish firm called Ullstein. Within three months it sold 300,000 copies. Within a short period of 15 months a total of 2,500,000 copies were sold in different languages of the world. Along with European languages it was also brought out in Urdu, Tamil and Marathi.

It went on to become an immortal piece of art, a stinging indictment on the meaninglessness of war and its brutality; the armaments manufacturers and traders, and the ambitious politicians who built their careers by instigating hostilities.

The war poets of English literature had already done a powerful portrayal of the horrors of First World War and its warping effects on humanity, but their efforts did not have the continuity, and therefore the explosive quality that this novel brought with it. It was for the first time that a prose rendition of those nightmarish days hit society with stunning force. It was as if it knocked the top off the bubbling, smouldering, subterranean disaffection of the past ten years, and caused it to finally boil over. Remarque had himself undergone branding by the conflagration of First World War, and that is why the hot breath of soldiers on the war-front, and the wringing out of their lifeblood come out so authentic page after page.

All Quiet on the Western Front created quite a convulsion, acquiring the form of a hurricane in Remarque's own Germany. It, of course, miraculously transformed his life: from being only a casual presence in the world of letters, at age 33 he became its world renowned voice; quite as if a backstage boy had suddenly been propelled into stardom! The book became a bestseller from the moment of its arrival.

The Literary Academy of Germany declared *All Quiet on the Western Front* as the last will of the dead to their living brethren; its message reached even those houses that remained unscathed by the war. The stark realism and the massive shock the novel administered were not easy to withstand. This could be a reason why, as happens with movies, the English version was subjected to 'cuts'. But there were always enough connoisseurs of literature who insisted that the novel brought to light the reality that lay behind the biggest, the most searing, the most repugnant event they had experienced, and it expressed their despair in a formidable manner.

The success of this novel by purely literary standards found enemies along the way, but Remarque and his publisher used smart publicity strategies. One accusation was that the novel's structure was flawed. Novels should have complications and sub-complications, and should finish off with resolutions of those complications. Critics who looked for such straight and simple structures were bound to find several faults in *All Quiet on the Western Front*. But it has been proved, over and over again, that real experiences are bound to break these artificial moulds and create new standards.

Great scholars have sung praises of Remarque who passed through the literary firmament like a comet. H.G. Wells considered him incomparable. Many others showered *All Quiet on the Western Front* with fulsome praises.

The speciality of Remarque's writing is that even while talking of grim realities, his words are laced with compassion. In the manner of Victor Hugo and Premchand, he too jolts his readers with his boundless sympathy for humankind.

It would be impossible for such a stormy novel to escape the notice of Hollywood. The founder President of Universal Pictures, Carl Laemmle, and his son Carl Laemmle Jr., instantly bought the filming rights. As a gift on his 21st birthday, Senior gave the responsibility of its production to his son.

It is true that the father-son duo had bought the filming rights with great enthusiasm, but making a movie on *All Quiet on the Western Front* that the audience would find interesting and digestible was a difficult task. Unlike all other movies of the genre, this one, instead of glorifying war, focuses on its violent and destructive nature. The romantic element was worth only one scene. In the opinion of cinema professionals, it was a losing proposition.

The Board of Directors of the Universal Company set itself against it. The novel was a success, yes, but they advised father and son to abandon the illusion that the movie would succeed too. The book, however, had taken such a firm grip on Laemmle's heart and mind that he stood up in open opposition to the Board. He told them to forget about the profit-loss arithmetic, and promised to produce a film the coming generation would be proud of. He assured them that the movie would touch every moviegoer's conscience. If they hadn't read the novel yet, he advised them to do so immediately and suspend professional calculations for a little while.

The renowned director of silent films, Lewis Milestone, was given the responsibility for the movie. Milestone was independent thinking, and known to

'Forgive me, comrade; how could you be my enemy? If we threw away these rifles and this uniform you could be my brother just like Kat and Albert.

Lewis Ayres as Paul in Lewis Milestone directed *All Quiet on the Western Front* (1930).
COURTESY: AUTHOR

be a rather unreliable director. The other movies done by him until then were *Rain*, *The Front Page*, *Of Mice and Men* and *A Walk in the Sun*. *All Quiet on the Western Front* would be his first talkie. He combined with Del Andrews, Maxwell Anderson and George Abbott to evolve the flashback technique of narration.

Hollywood was also curious to know who would be selected to do Paul Bäumer. The director invited Remarque himself to come over to Hollywood and do the role himself. Though the writer agreed that he was young enough, he preferred to be left alone to do his writing. Milestone wanted a new face for the role.

Lew Ayres was a young composer of music who had earned limited success, and was very keen to do movies. For two consecutive days he is believed to have woken up Milestone from his sleep at seven in the morning appealing for a chance. The irritated director told him to stay away from the movie and to stop pestering him. Even Laemmle father and son didn't want him. The thought of an unknown hero for a big budget movie did not attract them. But when Lew Ayres came through the tests Milestone exercised his director's prerogative and won the argument. Ayres turned the opportunity into gold. Without getting into melodrama Ayres gave a controlled performance, and recorded his protest against war on the strength of his passion. The officer who guides the boys on the front, Stanislaus Katczinsky, was played by Louis Wolheim, while John Wray did a great job as the sadistic instructor Himmelstoss.

Just as Remarque portrayed the terrible reality of war in words, Lewis Milestone did it on screen. As the narrator Paul Bäumer says, 'If they had sent us out into the trenches without this kind of training, then probably most of us would have gone mad. But this way we were prepared for what was waiting for us.'

There is a scene where Bäumer is hiding in a pit when a French soldier comes rolling into the same pit. With a reflex reaction Bäumer stabs him in the chest. The soldier does not die instantly. As he groans in fevered pain, Bäumer is consumed with remorse. He tries all that he can to help him ease his pain. Both the book and the movie have sketched this scene with great sensitivity and Ayres has essayed Bäumer with great authenticity.

Milestone had to create the blazing battlefield, the demoniacal trench front, and the flaming German villages. Army officers like Captain Charles, who had experienced war first-hand, were incorporated into the unit. This 40-acre front was erected in the backyard of Universal Studios. The set remains intact as a tourist spot even today—the original set got burnt down in 1960. What we see today is its reconstructed version. The shooting took place for 23 consecutive weeks.

Milestone was in search of some real-life trenches too—trenches created by the explosion of cannon shots; trenches that could take in a horse; where logs, twisted iron bars and the skulls and ribs and thigh bones of animals lay buried; trenches where the dream-world of adolescent youngsters lay castrated; where these dumb birds were murdered in the name of ambition and patriotism; Milestone had checked out these graveyards that went by the name of trenches.

Another 930-acre location called Irvine Ranch was used for the trenches. A river runs through it, and it was used for the scene where the war-weary boys meet the French girls. They don’t understand one another’s language, but the signals of youth are good enough. In the dead of the night the three German soldiers swim across the river and emerge naked on the other side. They do not forget to carry eatables and wild fruit for their girlfriends. Other than this small interlude, there is nothing romantic, either in the book or in the movie, but this scene alone, which hurt French national pride to have German soldiers flirting with their women, prevented the movie from being exhibited in France

Milestone exploited fully this nearly 1000 acres of war zone for his movie. Twenty tons of black powder and ten tons of dynamite were used for these war scenes. Arthur Edeson, the cinematographer, says that except for live bullets, they used actual weapons deployed in a war. The total cast for the movie was 5000 strong, including 2000 war veterans. The sheer presence of such an enormous crowd, their manoeuvring on the screen, the quick battlefield mobilisations; the entire atmosphere left the audience stunned.

An explosion scene was once being shot from quite close, with the cameraman and the director sitting on a crane. The mud kicked up by the explosion was so huge that its impact injured Milestone. From that day onwards the two started using, unfailingly, large German helmets during shooting schedules.

During the course of the production Milestone began experimenting with new ideas. He used a special crane for filming the marching soldiers and for shooting them advancing through the rolling smoke and fire. The concept of the ‘storyboard’ began from this film. The book ends on a rather flat note relative to its earlier parts, but Milestone wanted a proper, impactful finish for the movie. His office was strung out with individual pages of the novel hung up on the wall with clothes-clips, like clothes hung out for drying

Milestone did not have a single worry regarding the screening of his movie; he knew he had created a masterpiece. Other executives were not so relaxed. They had poured a lot of money into it, and only a superhit could balance their account.

When *All Quiet on the Western Front* was released in 1930 audiences fell as much in love with the movie as the readers had with the novel. The critics loved it too. Some commentators suggested that the movie should be exhibited till the term 'World War' got excised from the dictionary. Some praised it for its excellent reproduction of the squelching wet corpses of the innocent youngsters lying near the doorsteps of the selfish, ambitious merchants of war. Yet others came up with the naïve hope that none would now dare to wipe out mankind in the name of war.

Today, Milestone is chiefly remembered for *All Quiet on the Western Front*. He always resented that his other films were ignored in comparison. When the movie was released in Germany, Dr Joseph Goebbels came into limelight because of his trenchant opposition to it. Remarque shifted to Switzerland to avoid risk to his life, and then settled in the US. Lew Ayres was universally appreciated for his portrayal of Paul Bäumer. After watching the premier, a novitiate actress Ginger Rogers fell in love with him and in due course became his wife.

Some social thinkers and politicians have always held that after watching the movie, society would lose faith in the power of the army. That was why the liberal America welcomed the movie with open arms to begin with, but banned it in 1939, at the threshold of the Second World War. The German Nazis condemned it as the bluff of the corrupt Jewish mind, and banned it too. Along with the Australian Parliament, a number of belligerent countries blocked its screening. The film was subjected either to the scissors or to the hatchet.

Lewis Milestone won the Oscar for the Best Director. The movie itself won the Best Film Oscar, which was given to producer Carl Laemmle by the head of M-G-M, Mr Louis Mayer himself. Mayer remarked that along with the Oscar, Carl deserved the Nobel Peace Prize too.

Finding an appropriate closing for the movie had become a problem for Milestone. In the book, all the young soldiers of the company in the trench get knocked off one after another. Milestone resolved the problem with great imagination. The book mentions Bäumer's particular fascination for butterflies. In the movie, he espies a butterfly at a distance from his trench hide-out. With the mouth-organ playing in the background, Bäumer climbs out and goes after the butterfly. The movie ends showing a hand advancing to catch the butterfly, and then there is sound of the gunfire. The director does not show Bäumer's face, it shows the hand shrinking and sinking ever so slowly, like the wings of a dying butterfly. The last frame shows the graveyard plains in a long shot, pocked with hundreds of crosses. Superimposed upon these images come these adolescent boys, their faces carrying raw emotions as they turn back towards the camera while entering the bootcamp—the enthusiasm of getting into the army!

Delbert Mann's remake of *All Quiet on the Western Front* in 1979, as a TV movie with feature film quality, ended differently. Lying injured in the trench amidst the burning plains, the expressive-eyed Paul Bäumer hears a bird. He senses it sitting on the bare, stunted tree in front. With great excitement he begins sketching the bird. The shot of a gun is suddenly heard from a corner, and he crumples, dead. The sketch of the wet bird on the paper, as well as Paul's young corpse are seen stretched out in the slime inside the trench. The invisible bird has died. The corpses of the demons stand hanging at the gates of the world.

True connoisseurs feel that there should never be remakes of outstanding movies like *Gone with the Wind, Casablanca, Citizen Kane* and *Pyaasa*. Director Delbert Mann's remake was a valiant effort to stay honest to the novel; but it was only an effort. In terms of imagination, the inspiration behind it, the emotional turmoil of life in the burning trenches, and the strength derived from all these factors gave the Milestone movie an artistic merit that was much higher than Mann's.

Portraying horror, at its most abject, could not be the sole motive behind Remarque's effort. I believe the novel is a lamentation raised by a sensitive artist in the interest of peace. In the manner of the war poets of the Second as well as the First World War, the Japanese poet Toge Sankichi had also struck a similar note of lament to protest against the carnage wrought by the obliteration of Hiroshima. His poems were a denunciation of those war-mongering forces that brought the world to the threshold of annihilation to serve their own selfish ends. Emasculated by diseases resulting from exposure to radioactivity, the poet cried out in anguish that those who were trying to stifle him were committing a crime against humanity.

GONE WITH THE WIND

AUTHOR Margaret Mitchell PUBLISHED 1936
DIRECTOR David Selznick PREMIERED 1940

'After all tomorrow is another day.'

The victorious steed of Harry Potter is at full gallop these days, moving full tilt in all directions across the globe. Along with fame, its author J.K. Rowling has gathered royalty in fairy-tale proportions, and is now richer than the Queen of England. A similar heart-warming phenomenon had occurred in June 1936 that had turned book trade upside down when Margaret Mitchell, an unknown novitiate in the world of letters, had descended on the literary horizon with her tome *Gone with the Wind*. A thousand copies sold would have made the young writer happy enough, but Macmillan let loose a raging storm with the publication of this novel. The ordinary reader was, of course, blown off his feet, but the scholars too had to hold their hats from blowing away.

Shakespeare's plays, Cervantes's *Don Quixote* and such other medieval classics took a few centuries to leave their native shores; *Gone with the Wind*, however, has gone on to sell 350,000,000 copies. From America to Japan it is difficult to find a bookstall or a railway-station kiosk where this book is not prominently displayed. Sixty-five years down the line, this great work of art is still settling down with the readers, and the potency of its magic is nowhere near fading.

A well-made movie on a good quality book often muddies the waters a little bit. Instead of doing the book justice, the movie often robs it of its sheen. David Selznick converted *Gone with the Wind* into a major movie which brought in many Academy Awards. Clark Gable and Vivien Leigh who played the lead roles became the toast of the land. The Metro-Goldwin-Mayer (M-G-M) production of *Gone with the Wind* is one of the world's all-time great creations, and it would be downright silly to expect any artistic endeavour to overhaul the lofty standards it had set. However, eight months ago I took up the novel and it left me truly dumbstruck. I have read it three times in succession, yet I cannot break the spell it casts over me. This intensive reading has convinced me that however well made a movie, however mind-boggling its scale, it can never hope to capture much of a book's chemistry. Limitations of the medium and the three-hour barrier may be just two among many other valid reasons, but a movie can never hope to replicate the multiple strands that get woven into a novel, nor deliver the long-term impact, awe and wonder that a novel can.

What are the exotic chemicals that reside in the innards of this incomparable 500,000 word novel? What strange world is it on whose canvas its contours have been painted? In 1860 Abraham Lincoln took over the reins of the United States of America, as its 16th president, with a firm hand. While technically slavery had been outlawed in 1804, some southern states had never cared for the abolition; seven of them had declared their secession from the Union to form the Confederate States of America (Confederacy). Flaunting their stock of slaves was for them a measure of social prestige. As Rhett Butler mentions in the novel about the true capital of the southerner, 'Why, all we have is cotton and slaves and arrogance'.

Southerners were chivalrous, adventurous people, for whom life and education carried no meaning if they could not handle a pistol or a gun, or tame a runaway horse. As soon as he assumed office, Lincoln sent a huge army to bring the rebellious southern states to heel. The Confederates responded to this assault with great ferocity. This internecine conflict, which is known in history as the American Civil War, had its epicentre in Atlanta. It is in its state of Georgia that this story unfolds.

The novel opens with a description of the natural attractions of the Georgian landscape—thousands of acres of its red earth brought under the plough, its blades upturning the sod in blood-red furrows, crisscrossed to prevent the rains from carrying away the topsoil; its slow, sleepy meandering rivers. On this heart-warming landscape, however, the terrifying shadow of impending war soon rolls in. At the very outset we are introduced to its protagonist Scarlett O'Hara—mischievous, wilful, of 16 or 17 with a leonine waist; an attractive young fortune's child, for sheer spirit she has no match in the three neighbouring counties. Scarlett is extremely conscious of her slim figure and good looks, and never more than pecks at her food. She is ambitious, and never allows anything to stand in the way of fulfilling her desires. How she comes to fall in love with the gentle and dignified Ashley Wilkes she herself does not know, but love him she does, despite a complete lack of enthusiasm from his end, and loves him with all the intensity of her passionate nature.

It is dusk, and she is seen waiting for the arrival of her father Gerald, whose routine is to ride in leaping over the fences. Gerald is an Irish immigrant to Georgia, and through dint of hard work has worked himself into the position of an affluent landlord. He is upset with Scarlett for falling in love with Ashley, and advises her to snap out of it. Of his three daughters, she alone possesses the courage and character to take charge of his substantial wealth, and run his immensely successful cotton plantation 'Tara'. He has been grooming her to take over this responsibility after him. Love for the land, he teaches her—love for the earth, the black mother—is the greatest of all love.

A grand barbecue and ball has been arranged that evening at the big Wilkes' mansion at their plantation 'Twelve Oaks'. Scarlett has heard about Ashley's formal engagement to his cousin Melanie Hamilton, but she is not one to let circumstances defeat her. She sets off for Twelve Oaks with the intention of abducting him for a walk under the stars, and working her magic upon Ashley. She finds Melanie and Ashley moving around hand in hand, mingling among their guests. It isn't on a whim that Ashley has chosen Melanie for his wife. Innocent as a child, she seems to possess just three faculties: simplicity, affection and artlessness.

Set afire with irrepressible passion, Scarlet gives the slip to her youthful admirers, and pulls Ashley into the library, throws herself upon him and reiterates her love for him. Ashley tries to laugh it off by saying that there are all those young swains whose heart she has already stolen, and she can make an exception of him. But Scarlett is in such a frenzy of arousal that she clings to him and mumbles apologies for being so helplessly in love with him. When Ashley gently extricates himself from her grasp and walks away she is wild with rage, and throws whatever she can lay hands on at the receding figure.

Margaret Mitchell

This is when Rhett Butler, who has been lying concealed behind a coach listening to the exchange, rises up and gives her a villainous, scornful laugh. He applauds Scarlett for the unladylike spirit she displayed with Ashley. Infuriated and humiliated, Scarlett spits out, 'You aren't fit to wipe Ashley's boots!'

Rich and foppish, Rhett Butler is characterised as a scoundrel and an irredeemable reprobate. A raised eyebrow and a scornful laugh are his trademark habit. He rules over the borders of the southern states and their shady trade, and is notorious for baking his bread on the embers of war. He also has the looks and reputation of an irresistible ladykiller, and no woman anywhere in his vicinity is considered safe. As a 'romantic blockader', he proudly proclaims that he and his kind flourish on the crumbling ruins of nations at war.

Scarlett, marries Melanie's brother Charles on the rebound. Barely two months into the war, Charles dies of measles, and Scarlett is bound by tradition to wear black, and not allowed to speak to young men. Till only a short while earlier, Scarlett was the acknowledged belle of the balls. The dance halls; the mincing steps locking into heady, irresistible music; the riotous, fawning, applauding crowds—these were the stuff that Scarlett rejoiced in.

Widowed at 17, when she has barely arrived at the threshold of youth, Scarlett goes into a depression over all the restrictions placed upon her. She feels resentful and restless. At a dance organised for raising funds for the Confederacy, she runs into Rhett, who shocks the assemblage by bidding 'one hundred fifty dollars—in gold' for a dance with Scarlett, who is still dressed in black.

Scarlett's heart and soul are still sold on Ashley and as he is about to leave for the front, she once again gathers him in a passionate embrace, and promises to become his servant for life at just one 'Yes' from him. Ashley expresses his admiration for Scarlett as a person, and declares she is as beautiful of soul as she is of body. He respects her for her noble mind, but refuses to succumb to her passionate pleas.

As Atlanta is besieged, as it chokes in the smoke and thunder of war, Melanie is in the throes of labour pains. Scarlett is on pins and needles worrying about the safety of her Ashley's unborn child. The burning city, the heart-rending cries of wounded soldiers, groaning hospitals, severe shortage of medicines—the pictures that the novel paints of the horrors of war are traumatising. In its power and descriptive skill of the miseries of warfare, the novel is the equal of *All Quiet on the Western Front, War and Peace* and *Les Miserables*.

The scenes of the prodigious fire that engulfed Atlanta have been raised in various media. It is said that even the great Broadway versions of *Gone with the Wind* carried very competent presentations of the fire episode. But even before the fires begin to rage, the

'Why, land is the only thing in the world worth workin' for, worth fightin' for, worth dyin' for, because it's the only thing that lasts.'

Vivien Leigh as Scarlett and Clark Gable as Rhett Butler in *Gone with the Wind* by the Selznick International Pictures, 1940; directed by Victor Fleming. COURTESY: WWW.DOCTORMACRO.COM

nightmarish agonies of Melanie, the non-availability of a doctor to help her deliver, the desperate search launched by Scarlett, her frantic screams and cries for help—these are descriptions that find their best presentation only in the novel. Crazed with anxiety, Scarlett rushes towards the hospital. On the way she locates a doctor engulfed by the wounded. Overworked, exhausted with caring for hundreds of wounded soldiers, his apron splashed all over with blood, fresh and stale—is he really a doctor? Could he be a butcher? The novel is so suffused with such episodes and characters that expecting them to be shoehorned into a three-hour display for the cinema screen is expecting the impossible.

After her son is born, Melanie and Scarlett make a difficult, dangerous journey to Scarlett's home Tara. When in an effort to entice him, Scarlett had clung to Ashley and cried her heart out, Ashley had very insightfully told her that if there was one thing she loved over everything else it was her ancestral plantation—Tara. Tara was her obsession, and there was nothing she would not do to retain and revive her war-ravaged estate. When she returns to Tara, she finds it deserted. Her mother has died of typhoid, and her lionhearted father has been broken and unhinged by the buffetings of time. But nothing, nothing can break Scarlett's spirit. She locates a hoe and sets off to repair the devastated land.

Groaning under the burden of hiked taxes, the land was under threat of being confiscated. When the former Yankee overseer of Tara, Jonas Wilkinson, presents himself with the offer of buying off the property, she sends him packing with curses, but that does not resolve her problem. The one person who can help her out with the money is Rhett Butler; and however repulsive the thought, she stiffens herself to marry him, or even be his mistress if he can provide the money for bailing out Tara. To make herself attractive, she sews a presentable dress for herself out of her fine green velvet curtains. Rhett, however, merely mocks at her and turns her away. This is when she runs into the rich Frank Kennedy, and seduces him into marrying her. Tara is saved. Along with the impoverished Chinese farmer Wang Lung in *The Good Earth* and the matriarchal Ma Joad in *The Grapes of Wrath*, Scarlett is peerless and profound in her total devotion to the soil.

Scarlett's second husband Frank dies too, killed while out on a Ku Klux Klan meet. While she is still in mourning, feeling personally responsible for having brought about Frank's death, Rhett arrives. He gives her a pep talk, and comes straight to the reason for his sudden visit. 'I'm going away tomorrow for a long time and I fear that if I wait till I return, you'll have married someone else with a little money. So I thought, why not me and my money? Really, Scarlett, I can't go all my life, waiting to catch you between husbands.'

Though Rhett has got Scarlett to marry him, the thought agitates him that although she has taken him as her third husband her true affections are still reserved for Ashley.

Rhett has been no stranger to the pretty women available in the market. It is not as if he thirsts after pretty women any more, but the thought that he has no place in Scarlett's affection leaves him gutted. Two marriages contracted and run through, Ashley still sits there in the sanctum of her heart, refusing to vacate. Rhett, a practical man of the world, hardened and shrewd, knows this all along. But he too loves the irrepressible wildcat beauty that Scarlett is, and loves her passionately. Now into her third marriage with Rhett when she continues with her reckless obsession with Ashley it seriously wounds Rhett's manly pride. Once, heavily under the influence of liquor, he holds her head tight between his palms and barks, 'I'll remove him from your mind forever this way. I'll put my hands so—one on each side of your head—and I'll smash your skull between them like a walnut, and that'll blot him out.' He is jealous of Ashley, she tells him, and he accepts it unhesitatingly.

Disgusted with his wife, Rhett sets off to London with their little daughter, Bonnie. He takes her on a shopping spree and buys her everything she wants. But what she wants most of all is her mother. For the girl's sake he returns home. Scarlett is pregnant. Rhett asks her sarcastically whether the father is Ashley. A quarrel ensues, she loses her balance and goes tumbling down the long staircase. For the first time in her life, she is seriously ill, having lost her child and broken her ribs. Rhett is remorseful, and nurses her with great affection and care. The extroverted, unscrupulous degenerate inside him collapses; he crawls up to Melanie, and cries like a child in her lap.

The world of both Scarlett and Rhett revolves around little Bonnie. The irrepressible child is forever riding her pony, leaping over bars in the company of her father. The premonition of the impending tragedy has been very well developed, both in the novel as well as the movie. Bonnie's fear of the dark, her hallucinations about the teddy bear in the darkness of the night, with the bear sitting on her chest and suffocating her, are presages for what follows. One day, she tries to make her pony leap over a too high bar, slips off the pony, and is crushed to death. The one link between Rhett and Scarlett is snapped, signifying the death of their effort to bridge the gap.

The death of Melanie also affects Rhett deeply. It was Melanie who had showered tenderness on his outlandish life, and the passing away of this sister-figure plunges him in sorrow. He walks out on Scarlett.

It's only after his withdrawal that Scarlett comes to her senses. But tenacious as she is, she expects him to come back to her someday, and once again returns to her land—Tara, and with typical resilience, she raises herself again to grapple with its soil.

A novel that conquered the world and brought it to its knees! But who was this Margaret Mitchell who created this extraordinary piece of literature?

An extraordinary individual who was fated to live the strife-ridden, stormy life of her heroine Scarlett, Margaret was born on 8 November, 1900 in the city of Atlanta, Georgia. She belonged to a wealthy, progressive, politically prominent family. Her mother Mary Isabel was the firebrand president of a suffragette organisation who flew into a passion at any whiff of injustice; her father Eugene Muse Mitchell was an attorney and historian. The history of Atlanta would come trippingly off his tongue. A brisk 5' 8" person, he is clearly the model on which Margaret has created the character of Scarlett's father Gerald.

History and revolution were the two subjects into which Margaret was immersed from head to toe from early childhood. Her maternal grandmother Annie Stephens would tell young Margaret colourful tales of her own experiences of the war—her husband Russell Crawford Mitchell, enlisted in the Confederate States Army, had been severely wounded at the Battle of Sharpsburg, and reputedly walked fifty miles with a couple of bullets in his head.

At home, she was called Peggy. She was bold, playful, robust and vivacious. When she was five, her father had bought her a hairy pony; she loved riding the animal a whole lot more than doing mathematics, to which she was particularly hostile. The Bonnie of the novel is quite clearly a portrayal of her own young self. When she was 19, she fell off the pony, while trying to make it leap over a wall. A passer-by spotted her and probably saved her life. For all her wilfulness and impetuosity during these hell-may-care days, she never missed out on her dancing lessons.

The winds of women's liberation were blowing strong then. Women had just about gained their voting rights. But with her smoking and drinking and gallivanting with friends at all times of day and night, Margaret was way beyond the limitations that bound other women. During these days of self-indulgence she met the rowdy Berrien 'Red' Upshaw. Broad shoulders, all of six feet and two inches, rusty red hair, dark green eyes, such was our prince charming. He had been thrown out of college for rowdyism; he drank hard, he womanised hard. The company of such a renegade was an invitation to disaster, and her family was sick with apprehension. But Margaret bothered more about her green-eyed, scorn-spewing Red than she did about family feelings.

Around this time also came John Marsh. Red's schoolmate and roommate. John too was smitten by Margaret. Overruling all objections from family, Margaret finally had her way and married Red on 2 September 1922, with John standing as the best man. Instead of changing for the better, Red only worsened after marriage. He drank heavily and frequently beat her; welts would stand out on her uncovered back where the cane connected. His gambling and womanising went on too without let or hindrance. After a heavier than usual beating, when she could not take his violence any more, she called in John to knock some sense into him. When all of John's pleadings failed to bring Red round, she finally divorced him and walked the altars with John. Once when they crossed each other on the street, Red very lovingly invited her home. Soon, however, his basic nature erupted and he punched her in the eye.

There were many such tornados that whirled in and out of Margaret's life. While Red Upshaw lacerated her innermost self for life, John Marsh burst upon her like a cloud of love and compassion. In the novel, even after securing the profligate, intractable, bothersome high-society crook Rhett Butler for herself, Scarlett gravitates over and over towards Ashley, quite like a young calf towards a juicy truss of fresh grass.

Even before the romance with John and Red, there was another storm that had visited Margaret's life. Right at the threshold of youth, on the point of graduating in 1918, she had fallen in love with another Harvard student, a young army lieutenant, Clifford West Henry. The personality of Ashley in the novel has been created as a composite of the two persons who left such a permanent imprint on Margaret's mind and heart—Clifford Henry and John Marsh.

Clifford and Margaret had committed themselves for marriage, but as the War began, the Atlanta Government decided to dispatch him to France. Dreading that this seemingly temporary separation may well turn out to be a permanent deprivation, they had got secretly engaged. When Margaret received news, one day, of his martyrdom on the battlefront, she was devastated. She later created the images of soldiers returning from the front as she remembered—emaciated, terror-stricken, ghoulish, crawling apparitions. These strangers dawdle for a while in front of Tara, slake their thirsts, and crawl on. It is in this backwash of broken humanity that Ashley also returns—hunger-crazed, wizened, skeletal.

Margaret Mitchell was first noticed as a successful newspaper features writer. During the four years she worked for the *Atlanta Journal*, she studied the history of Atlanta, as also the sequence of events leading up to her times. But she had to quit her newspaper job due to an ankle injury that refused to heal properly. After always having blown hither and thither like a wild wind, here now was young Margaret, confined to the four walls of home—and domesticity. The world, around this time, was sinking into the abyss of the Great Depression. In her personal life too Margaret was trying to come to terms with physical pain. Her ankles and joints caused her great misery. What does one do in an empty house all through the day? She landed an answer to this all-consuming question—read, of course. Her poor husband ploughed her with crates upon crates of books, and she sat consuming them like a person possessed.

The urge for expression tugged at her heartstrings, sent her into swoons and agitated her. Her fingers were itching to unlock the floodgates to the sea that was raging inside her. John gifted her a second-hand Remington, and in 1926, *Gone with the Wind* began finding words. Margaret's submergence was so complete that her closest friends often ragged her, 'Poor girl, busy writing the greatest American novel!'

She didn't need to go anywhere looking for characters and backdrop. A rare stockpile of tempestuous experiences had accumulated right inside her. When she began, she wasn't quite sure of either the structure or the direction her novel should take. She was like a motorist who just grips the steering tight and moves on. From the very start, she had identified the presence of two very strong, compelling women characters, one of them to be the rebellious, wilful kind. The Scarlett of her imagination was patterned on the combined personality of her grandmother and her own self. Wild, flighty and pungent, Scarlett hankers after another woman's husband and pursues him relentlessly.

The initial intention was to have her shape out as a vamp; but her visceral energy, her undaunted spirit, her fierce commitment towards the well-being of her paternal estate, Tara—as the novel evolved, Scarlett went on hoodwinking her creator out of her originally assigned role. The vamp finally revealed herself to the world donning the heroine's crown. Melanie, who had started off as the lead woman, had to settle for the second place.

It was after a good three years had gone by that the structure of the novel emerged. Just two people really knew that Margaret was busy writing a novel—her husband John and a friend named Lois Cole. Cole worked in the publication department of Macmillan Company. He would be handy when the time came for publication.

Around 1932, Margaret moved out of her Peachtree Street house. The house has now been converted into a Museum in memory of its most famous occupant. It had been a lucky house for her because this was where her writing had caught pace and she managed to complete the bulk of her novel. She had also lived out some hardships there. Sunk up to her neck in her writing, she would be racked by arthritis. Her tonsils had to be removed, her teeth went bad. The irony was the amount of unsavouriness she lived through while lading page after page with delectation.

Try as she might, she could not get Red Upshaw out of her system. Even after the divorce, the worthless, iniquitous, brass-necked rogue had settled deep into her subconscious self. Scene after scene, he kept popping up as Rhett Butler with his raucous, derisive snigger. Unprincipled, adulterous and villainous, at the same time generous, pleasant and desirable, he virtually rode her very breath.

In her personal life, she was haunted by adversities. In early 1934, as she was crossing the street, a drunken driver blew her off the road like a balloon. She survived but her spine was seriously damaged, which left her with a permanently painful back. She had to wear an elastic-and-mesh corselet under her blouse to hold her back up. Nothing, however, kept her from writing for hours together. The road mishap had also aggravated the agony in her legs. Converting this agony into a masterpiece like *Gone with the Wind* is a miracle by itself. In her creative trance, Margaret had hammered out around 1100 pages. A few episodes she had written over and over again. When sometimes the imagination flagged, when there was a lull in the play of fancy, she would lovingly go over the completed chapters again and again. Her husband occasionally felt that they should publish the novel themselves, but the sight of milady's massive, mountainous manuscript would scotch such fancies.

Harold Latham of Macmillan was on a tour of the South, scouting for some powerful new talent. At Atlanta, Cole put in a strong recommendation for Margaret's novel. He added that the only person who really knew how the work had shaped out would be her husband. But judging by the passion with which she had occasionally narrated the subject to him, if she had managed to trap that passion into her writing, then very likely a literary miracle was at hand.

When Latham made enquiries of Margaret regarding her novel, she was quite thrilled. But the next second she remembered the sheer size of her script, and she baulked. Ten years had gone by since she had begun; so many pages had curled up and turned yellow, and were dotted with pencil scribbles. Unnerved, she turned Latham away. 'Not now, another time, maybe.' But then some close friends got after her, pumped her up.

A few days flew away in her 'Should I? Shouldn't I?' The last day of Latham's stay at Atlanta dawned. Margaret hurried home, and quickly gathered up the chapters. At the other end Latham was getting restive; he had a train to catch. His suitcase was inadequate for the bundle he was delivered and so he went for another bag. The happy writer returned home exhausted, and hit the bed. Latham had, however, lost his sleep. He was reading through a brand new writer's maiden presentation, and her lofty flights of fancy had rendered him speechless.

The manuscript was raw, and needed some editing, and 18 months rolled by in this exercise. At a point Margaret got her husband to dispatch a telegram to Latham, 'Return manuscript if not keen'. The wait was getting more and more painful to bear. And then another accident. While they were entertaining at home, a heavy whiskey bottle slipped from a guest's fingers and splintered on Margaret's head. The pain was excruciating. Her arthritis never left company either. Good news just refused to arrive. What did arrive were conciliatory letters from Latham. He assured her that he was completely submerged in her manuscript. He was having his consultants go over it too. Till then, would she kindly bear with him?

Finally, a telegram arrived, informing the writer that Macmillan were very happy with the script, and were dispatching the agreement alongside. Margaret burst into tears. She hadn't dreamt of such a finale, she told close friends; all she had wanted out of her labour was joy for her husband and some relief from her arthritis.

Pre-publication activities speeded up nicely. It was clear to everyone that the novel was a classic. Latham advised her to just sit and fill in the blank spaces and tighten up the end, and the world would be at her feet. It seemed like a dream. Even after the novel was finished, in her innocence Margaret continued to believe that Melanie was the heroine. But Scarlett had been counted out on all ten fingers, and there was lot of her left still!

She was originally named Pansy, and got changed to Scarlett just before the book went for print. In a computerless world, she had to sit substituting one name for another every single page. Much discussion happened over the titles *Another Day* and *Tomorrow is Another Day*, till the author came up with *Gone with the Wind*. It sounded nice and racy, and had been used in passing in the preface too.

At long last, on 10 June 1936, the book was released. There is no success bigger than success, they say. The novel hit the market and all of America was stricken by the Scarlett O'Hara--Rhett Butler fever. Margaret was in a state of panic. Her phone rang incessantly; every five minutes the telegram boy banged at her door; and letters—it was a downpour. Admirers gathered at her front gate and at her backdoor to meet her, or at least catch a glimpse of her; autograph-seekers sprinted towards her. With the husband out at work, there was no one to answer the phone or the doorbell except her.

Moving out became difficult, with her readers chasing her everywhere. One day, she was visiting a departmental store to buy herself a dress. As she was changing in the trial room, she noticed that a few women were staring at her through a crack in the door! It gave them a kick to know how their favourite author looked half-dressed!

'Come for our programme!' 'Come for dinner!' Whoever wanted such fans? Fame and popularity gave her such a scare that she fled into the hills for some rest. Scarlett herself had not fled with such alacrity when Atlanta was besieged. She told friends that if she had known how difficult life would become with the writing of her novel, she would not have handed it over to Latham.

Never had Margaret expected this over-vaulting fame or fawning. She had merely set out to write a novel relating the tragic memories of the war years. In her own words, what she had expected to churn out would be rotten, worthless, ordinary stuff. But during the actual moments of composition, she seemed to have been taken over by a genie! The conflicts endured by her ancestors in Ireland, her father's ceaseless struggle, how her family stood up to the Civil War and the Yankees, all of these she had poured out on paper with great passion.

The memories of the grindings they had suffered in the Civil War were still fresh among the ordinary Americans. To these were added the biting winds of the Great Depression that penetrated their bones. They felt anew its sharp stings and scalds as they read her work. Devastated by the prolonged slump, they loved the devotion Scarlett exhibited for her land and country. She had withstood the lashes of extreme adversity, but never let circumstances bend her or break her. Her words of hope became their mantra as she lifted a fistful of earth and declared, 'As God is my witness, as God is my witness they're not going to lick me. I'm going to live through this; and when it's all over, I'll never be hungry again. No, nor any of my fold. If I have to lie, steal, cheat or kill. As God is my witness, I'll never be hungry again.'

During this period, on 7 July, bang came a call from her first husband, the irrepressible Red Upshaw. 'Read your book. The one thing that stands out of every line is that you still love me.'

'Pshaw! Why should you think that?'

'Your Rhett Butler, he's been lifted straight out of me.'

She, of course, denied it strongly. A little apprehensive, she asked, 'What exactly do you want?' He gave her the quintessential Rhett Butler snigger and replied, 'Tell you all when it's time, OK?' Margaret would insist again and again that Rhett was not patterned on either Red or any other living person. She feared that Red would slap a defamation suit against her.

The delirious, excited readers were convinced that a movie had to be made on the story. In fact, it had begun creating waves in the silver world of Hollywood even before the book was published. Movie agents and producers had landed galley proofs of the novel and were bending their backs to procure filming rights. The readers too had visualised a magnificent silver-screen presentation of the tale, and they were also the first to see in their mind's eye Clark Gable playing Rhett Butler.

Lots of them believed that the author had in mind the handsome, elegant personality of Gable as she wrote Rhett's character. Gable, initially, was not too keen on playing the part, his worry being that he doubted his ability to carry the sheer weight of the expectations the audience had built around him. He was the last member of the film unit to read the novel. Once he understood the nuances of the character, he happily accepted the challenge.

'With enough courage, you can do without a reputation.'

Vivien Leigh and Clark Gable in *Gone with the Wind*. COURTESY: AUTHOR

The famous producer David Selznick dropped a bombshell when he announced in a newspaper the price he was willing to pay for the cinema rights for the novel—$50,000, a figure nobody could have dreamt of during those times. Margaret was swamped with doubts, one being whether Selznick would care for the accent that marked South Georgian language. Selznick, of course, was an established wizard at presenting masterpieces on the silver screen. 'If he has produced such supreme classics like *David Copperfield*, *Anna Karenina* and *A Tale of Two Cities*, why do you think he won't consult you?' her friends reasoned with her.

The preparations leading to the production of *Gone with the Wind*, the production itself, and the spectacular success it met with are all now part of American folklore. Under Selznick's stewardship, it took two full years of preparations before shooting began for this magnum opus. They could as well have been equipping themselves for a major invasion—the property items required for the sets totalled 1,250,000. The screenplay writer Sidney Howard slogged night and day with his colleagues and prepared as many as six complete drafts. The six incomplete ones were put into wraps and shelved. The final draft was finished in February 1939. It contained 685 scenes and used up 20,017 words for dialogues.

Alongside the screenplay, George Cukor, the earlier director, and cameraman Ernest Haller conceptualised each scene in details. In the style of Walt Disney, a storyboard would be put up where notes would be entered for each scene with regard to camera angles, close ups, long shots, medium shots, colour schemes, etc.

The art director had sketched out as many as 200 sets, out of which ninety were actually erected. There is this episode where Atlanta City is in flames, and from out of this fire and frenzy, Rhett Butler drives Scarlett and Melanie out in a buggy to safety—an important scene in the novel, and filming it required immense preparations. As many as 53 structures were erected and a 7,000 foot long road was made for the purpose.

The irony, though: here was the Atlanta conflagration being filmed, and still no sign of Scarlett O'Hara! The guests had arrived, the musicians had lined up, but where the dickens was the bride? Who would fit the bill? All of America was agog with excitement. Scarlett O'Hara was one of her kind, acknowledged as one of the greatest heroines of world literature. Nobody, just nobody measured up to Selznick's image. There would be 'Breaking News' then too in the newspapers. One day it would be Jean Arthur; on another, Loretta Young, or Shirley Temple, or the famed beauty Betty Davis; then it would be Norma Shearer, Katherine Hepburn or Lana Turner. The Scarlett role had literally stolen sleep from the eyes of the Hollywood dream girls. A number of them turned into gym regulars to get that waist to measure sixteen. David dispatched director Cukor and others to the four corners of the world to scout around for the perfect girl.

Vivien Leigh was doing a play in London. She had been reading *Gone with the Wind*, and she announced to her friends that she would be in Hollywood soon; she it was who would do the Scarlett role. Her friends, of course, found her clairvoyance thoroughly amusing.

The shooting began on 26 January1939. Just three weeks before that Selznick had taken an amazing and tough decision of replacing the director—who had been sweating over the movie for the past two years—George Cukor. Victor Fleming was brought in as replacement. A last minute change of director was an awfully risky step to take, but Selznick took the gamble, and what followed was history. The incident also reveals the complete sway Selznick held over the pre-production and the production of the movie. Fleming brought a major advantage to the movie—before he turned director, he had been a very successful cameraman. The regular cinematographer of the movie, Ernest Haller, was, of course, a superb technician himself, and was the acknowledged czar of location shooting. This is probably the reason for the beautiful visuals in the movie—the coming together of two outstanding imaginations!

January 13, 1939—the figure 13 did indeed turn out to be inauspicious for 1399 conceited aspirants of America. On this day David's brother brought Vivien Leigh to the sets at Atlanta, pulled him out of his work, and announced, 'I've brought you your Scarlett.' David looked the girl up and responded, 'It just may be that you're right.' Quick screen tests were taken the very day, and the opportunity of a lifetime landed in Vivien's lap.

It is quite true that the characters of Ashley, Rhett, Melanie and Scarlett as they appear in the movie do not have the depth and density the author had given to them in the novel. It is also true that the anti-war sentiments of Rhett and Scarlett, so evident in the book, are clearly lacking on screen. The poetry that is so palpable in the delineation of Ashley and Melanie also seems to have got lost in the film, say some critics.

I believe the characters of Rhett Butler and Scarlett O'Hara are the author's greatest achievement. The interplay of tension between them, their concord and discord, their clashing personalities and their intemperate lifestyle have been beautifully crafted. Scarlett says at one place, 'We both are rascals.' In the high drama of the novel, when the two are together on the stage for a sufficiently long time, the reader cannot help but get the sensation of speeding in a Japanese train.

The heroines of world literature that are generally placed on the top rungs are Flaubert's Madame Bovary, Tolstoy's Anna Karenina and Hardy's Tess. Measured by contemporary values, what crimes had Scarlett not committed? Whisking away for herself a person who was due to marry her sister; getting prisoners of war to labour on her saw mill; dishonest, thieving, her list of offences is endless. Once, when Rhett berates her on this issue, she expresses helplessness. What choice did she have if the good lord had stuffed the boat with so many lives and handed her the helm? To keep it from sinking, she had no alternative but to fight to the extent to which she was capable of fighting.

For the purpose of sustaining interest in a novel, play or movie, it is considered convenient to place the most overpowering events towards the later end of a story. The first half of *Gone with the Wind* is replete with such poignant events like the devastating Civil War, people and places caught and crushed in its sweep, the calamitous famine, all of Atlanta consumed by raging flames. What, then, would be left for author and director to hold audience interest in the second half? Plenty! The inherent conflict in Rhett and Scarlett's temperament and the taut interplay of their thrust and parry; the gentle, pedigreed, saintly presence of people like Melanie and Ashley; the frolicsome, spirited Bonnie; all of these elements have been so skilfully manipulated—by both author and director—that the story retains its edge-of-the-seat tension up to the very end.

In the end, the image of Scarlett one is left with is not that of a scheming, murderous, dissolute vixen. In the face of insurgencies, rebellions, loot and rapine, she stands out as a hardy, spunky, forceful woman of spine. In the world of Hindi books and cinema, the woman protagonist is always depicted as a sweet, self-effacing, goody-goody bundle of virtues. It is important for Indian readers to closely examine the persona of Scarlett, which runs so completely counter to their own stereotyped, hollow concept of womanhood. Flaubert's Madame Bovary puts her house up for sale to support her extravagant lifestyle; Scarlett doesn't. Hardy's Tess crumples under the onslaught of merciless fate and unrelenting sorrows; Scarlett doesn't. Tolstoy's Anna responds to defeat by annihilating herself under a running train; Scarlett doesn't. Scarlett stands straight, looks misfortune in the eye, and dares it to break her. This is the secret of her success.

Margaret Mitchell was awarded the prestigious Pulitzer Prize for the writing of this novel. With just this one single novel, she collected enough glory for all time, an achievement that hasn't been surpassed these last sixty years. Some literary critics classify the work as a historical love story. For me, this matchless creation offers much more. The horrifying manifestations of war; contemporary Southern society; the insurrection; the grinding, gutting suffering it lived through during the Civil War; its love for the soil! I truly envy the subliminal energy that drove this supreme writer to such creative frenzy. The torrent beyond the words, the surge, the vividness of style, a deep awareness of history, dialogues that would put a playwright to shame; I fancy, if Shakespeare and Tolstoy could ever read this novel, they would toss their hats in glee.

It's now 150 years since the Civil War, and 75 years since the Great Depression. The allegation that the author traded with the emotions of the readers of contemporary times cannot hold now. History has been left behind; the novel, however, marches on.

The last days of this great writer were spent in considerable agony. Her unprecedented success did not fill her with conceit. On the contrary, from 1940 onwards, she threw herself into social work. She ploughed the money she had made into activities like building hospitals and clinics for blacks as well as whites, and the rehabilitation of villages ravaged by the Second World War. On 19 August 1949, as she was crossing a neighbourhood street, she was brought down by a speeding taxi. After five days of coma, she passed away.

A STREETCAR NAMED DESIRE

AUTHOR Tennessee Williams **PUBLISHED** 1947
DIRECTOR Elia Kazan **PREMIERED** 1952

‘I don’t want realism. I want magic!’

gallery of novelists, or the high altitudes of drama, or the perennial flow of poetry—there is always a small section marked out for the greatest masters. For a novice to break into these hallowed areas is well-nigh impossible. The venerable have achieved these elevated, sacrosanct grounds after years of hard labour and relentless meditation—after dedicating their entire lives to the service of their muse. Across the span of the 20th century, two Americans have earned the privilege of sitting shoulder to shoulder with all-time greats like Kalidasa, Shakespeare and Ibsen—Arthur Miller and Tennessee Williams. With *A Streetcar Named Desire*, Williams may well have reached the pinnacle of his art.

The subject of pretence, the wearing of a mask, would appear to be trivial to many, but it was enough for Tennessee Williams to delve deep into its psychology, and construct a mighty work of art that succeeds in stunning theatre and movie-lovers alike. The script of *A Streetcar Named Desire* took total possession of the writer during the process of creation. It rode on the shoulders of an accomplished director like Elia Kazan. It first shook the stage at Broadway, and later sent tremors across

'I have always depended on the kindness of strangers.'

the glittering world of the cinema. It traipsed into the region of immortality and ensconced itself there. It compelled a few generations to re-examine the values that shaped their lives.

The story is about a young couple Stanley and Stella who have their little apartment in a workers' quarters in New Orleans. Stella cares for nothing more than disappearing into the arms of her rough-hewn husband. Into this happy love nest arrives a guest—Stella's elder sister Blanche DuBois—and begins rocking the nest with some vigour

Stella and Blanche were born in a family of landed gentry; but their father's profligacy had completely decimated their once substantial wealth. Stella, sensible and balanced, had torn away the mask of false family honour and vanished wealth, and squared up to take on the world of reality. She had married a strong-built, short-tempered, virile young worker, Stanley, and settled into happy domesticity in a tacky workers' colony in New Orleans.

Stella is four years younger to her sister Blanche. Home-loving, affectionate, with a heart full of sympathy for all, she welcomes her elder sister with genuine warmth and affection, when she arrives to stay with her.

Blanche herself is not so generous. In Blanche, Williams has created an extraordinarily complex character—helpless, insecure, deceitful, frivolous, libidinous, self-indulgent, yet with a twisted kind of innocence that evokes sympathy. She had caught her very young husband in bed with an older man. When she had revealed to him what she knew, he had blown his brains out with a pistol.

Blanche is, however, no angel either. The blood of her philandering father runs through her veins. At the school where she taught, she had lured a 17-year-old boy into a relationship. The father kicked up a rumpus when he got to know, and she was dismissed. On the other hand, she has dissipated whatever resources had been spared by her father. Hounded from all places for licentiousness, down to her last cent, she finally arrives for shelter to her sister's house. Fearful of her past chasing her here, she takes to spinning endless yarns about herself.

Tennessee Williams

Stanley Kowalski, not loquacious, but outspoken, doesn't mix much, has his own pride, works during the day and sits with select friends in the evening for poker sessions. His pokey, two-room flat is a palace to him and he is the undisputed king of his world.

Blanche comes into this set-up with her valise and wardrobe trunk stuffed with her expensive clothes and furs and pearls. She loves to brag about her ancestral wealth and culture, and of course, her millionaire friends. While Blanche detests Stanley's brusque manners and looks for every opportunity to put him down, he on the other hand is deeply suspicious of the classy front she presents and does the same to her. For Stella, though, Blanche is a parent figure, and her heart bleeds for her.

Harold Mitchell is one of Stanley's intimate evening poker buddies who hasn't married because he considers looking after his bedridden mother as his first responsibility. Blanche finds in him an attractive opportunity to settle down, and lays out her web to snare him. She blithely lies to him that she is younger to Stella and that she still holds her teaching job.

Blanche's arrival in the tiny apartment sets it wobbling, and the happy Kowalski household takes a few punches. In one instance when the men are absorbed in their game of cards, Blanche switches on the radio and begins to waltz romantically to the music. Mitch is distracted but Stanley is furious. Stella stands up for her sister and tries to shout him down. In a violent rage, Stanley hits her. Eventually, Stella is hustled out to neighbour Eunice's apartment above. Stanley, recovering, lets himself be doused under a cold shower.

When he fully recovers his senses, he is racked with shame and repentance at having turned violent on his wife. Dripping water, still in his clinging wet drawers, he steps out into the pavement. He throws his head back like a baying hound and bellows, 'Stella! Stella, sweetheart! Stell-lahhhhh!' After a little while the upstairs door opens and Stella begins her slow descent down the winding staircase. Eyes glistening, hair in a mess, she reaches him. Then they fall hungrily into each other's arms.

The next day, when the storm has completely subsided, Blanche wants to know how Stella could be 'insane enough to come back in here after what happened'. When Stella defends him, 'There are things that happen between a man and a woman in the dark—that sort of make everything else seem—unimportant!' Blanche snaps back, 'What you are talking about is brutal desire—just—Desire!—the name of that rattle-trap streetcar that bangs through the Quarter, up one old narrow street and down another.'

Stanley happens to overhear this conversation, and gets into investigating Blanche's dreary past with some more vigour, and presents his findings to Stella. The supply-man at his plant, Ford, is a frequent visitor at Laurel, where Blanche lived and worked. He brings stories of her wanton activities, conducted from a seedy hotel called Flamingo, to which she had shifted after Belle Reve had slipped away. The management of Flamingo soon sent her packing. She shifted base, but soon gained such notoriety that she was chased out from there too.

Noticing his friend Mitch's leanings towards his sister-in-law, he reveals all to him. He wouldn't want Mitch 'to jump into a tank with a school of sharks'.

When Stella organises a small birthday party for Blanche, Mitch does not come. Blanche is convinced Stanley would have poisoned his ears. After another spat over Blanche, Stanley comes back to Stella, takes her clumsily in his arms and says, 'Stella, it's gonna be all right after she goes and after you've had the baby. It's gonna be all right again between you and me the way that it was…the way we used to get the coloured lights going with nobody's sister behind the curtains to hear us!' Stanley has also brought a birthday gift for his sister-in-law, and he hands it to her in a small envelope. 'Ticket! Back to Laurel! On the Greyhound! Tuesday!'

After Stanley tells him about Blanche, Mitch uses his own sources to confirm the stories. He feels terribly betrayed by all the lies Blanche had been dishing out to him. When he accosts her and wants to know the truth, Blanch gasps: 'I don't want realism.' 'I want magic! Yes, yes, magic! I try to give that to people…I don't tell truth, I tell what ought to be truth.'

She uses the ruse of confession to explain her story:

'I stayed at a hotel called the Tarantula Arms!' she tells him. 'That's where I brought my victims. Yes, I had many intimacies with strangers. After the death of Allan—intimacies with strangers was all I seemed able to fill my empty heart with…I think it was panic, just panic, that drove me from one to another, hunting for some protection—'

And then she was driven out of Laurel. 'So I came here. There was nowhere else I could go, I was played out…and—I met you. You said you needed somebody. Well, I needed somebody too. I thanked God for you, because you seemed to be gentle—a cleft in the rock of the world that I could hide in!'

The pathos of the scene gets sharply heightened by the arrival at the door of an old Mexican flower vendor woman. She carries bunches of gaudy tin flowers that lower-class Mexicans display at funerals. '*Flores*. *Flores*,' she wails. '*Flores para los muertos* (flowers for the dead)!'

The woman's wail continues through the scene, as Blanche begins to crumple in front of Mitch. What did she want? Death? Bodily desire? She opted for desire. Any man

'Physical beauty is passing—a transitory possession—but beauty of the mind, richness of the spirit, tenderness of the heart—I have all these things—aren't taken away but grow! Increase with the years!'

COURTESY: WWW.DOCTORMACRO.COM

would do for her—known, unknown, traveller, bookseller, young boy— who would take her and prevent her from slipping into the void.

She fought against the parade of death at Belle Reve, and slipped into desire. 'Not far from Belle Reve,' she rambles on, 'was a camp where they trained young soldiers. On Saturday nights they would go in town to get drunk—'

'*Flores par los muertos, flores—flores…*'

'—and on the way back they would stagger onto my lawn and call—'Blanche! Blanche!…Sometimes I slipped outside to answer their calls…later the paddy-wagon would gather them up like daisies…the long way home…'

When Mitchell clumsily gathers her in his arms and kisses her, returning his embrace, she says, 'Marry me, Mitch!' His hands drop off her waist. 'You're not clean enough to bring in the house with my mother,' he tells her.

'Go away, then!' she screams, incensed, and as he hesitates, she runs out of doors and lets out a loud yell that has people gather around her, and startles Mitch enough to send him clattering awkwardly out of the house. Blanche staggers back and collapses, and is soon sucked into her dream of her millionaire admirer who has promised to take her out on an expensive cruise of the Caribbean.

When Stanley enters, excited over the arrival of his child, Blanche informs him of the invitation telegram she has just received from her millionaire admirer. Stanley offers to patch up with her. 'Well, it's a red letter night for us both. You having an oil millionaire and me having a baby.' He offers her a drink, which she turns down. As Mitch had done a while before, Stanley begins to rip through her fables and pretences. But Blanche burrows deeper and deeper into her make-believe mist. 'A cultivated woman, a woman of intelligence and breeding, can enrich a man's life immeasurably! I have those things to offer…Physical beauty is passing. A transitory possession. But beauty of the mind and richness of the spirit and tenderness of the heart—and I have all of those things—aren't taken away, but grow! How strange that I should be called a destitute woman? When I have all these treasures locked in my heart, I think of myself as a very, very rich woman!'

Then darting a scornful glance at Stanley, she says, 'But I have been foolish—casting my pearls before swine!'

More than the drink inside him, it is her superior attitude that scalds him. 'Swine, huh?'

'Yes, swine! Swine! And I'm thinking not only of you but of your friend, Mr Mitchell. He came to see me tonight…I gave him his walking papers.'

Her constant humiliation and her relentless lies provoke Stanley beyond all limits and there is no one to stop him. He begins by getting her down. 'There isn't no millionaire.

And Mitch didn't come back with roses 'cause I know where he is...There isn't a goddam thing but imagination!...And lies and conceit and tricks!...And look at yourself! Take a look at yourself in that worn out Mardi Gras outfit, rented for fifty cents from some rag-picker! And with the crazy crown on! What queen do you think you are?' As Blanche moves backward through the door into the bedroom, Stanley lunges after her. She smashes a bottle to attack him with, but he overpowers her and carries her to the bed, where he rapes her.

The last scene opens on the poker players on the kitchen table. Stanley swears to Stella that he has not touched Blanche. In any case, the practical person that she is, she has no choice except to take her husband on his word.

Stella cleverly exploits Blanche's delusion about her millionaire friend who is arranging to pick her up for the Caribbean cruise. Along with her neighbour and friend Eunice she helps her pack for the journey. A doctor from the State Mental Health Institution and a matron, a sinister figure in her severe dress, arrive at the porch. Blanche puts up a struggle, but soon resigns herself. She is ready to leave the real world of men and join the others who live in their worlds of imagination too. 'Whoever you are—I have always depended on the kindness of strangers,' she tells the doctor, and walks out holding him tight by his arm.

The poetic sensitivity with which he portrays stormy passions puts Williams among the foremost dramatists of post-war America. He was born on 26 March 1911 in Columbus, Mississippi, and was christened Thomas. The sobriquet 'Tennessee' was gifted to him in his college days, and he took it on as his nom de plume.

When the stock market crashed in 1929, Tennessee was still in college. His younger days were spent in penury. By the time he was 15, the family had shifted in and out of 16 rented apartments. He hadn't shown any great pace in school academics. In fact he was quite disinclined towards studies. That, combined with straitened circumstances, led to abandoning college midway. His father found him a place in the factory of the International Shoe Company, the firm for which the old man worked. But his heart was never in it. He preferred matching words to matching shoes. He began scribbling out short stories. He also squeezed out time to finish his graduation in 1938 from the Iowa State University. When the Second World War began, he did a stint as a writer with Metro-Goldwyn-Mayer.

Williams' first important play was *Cairo, Shanghai. Bombay,* followed immediately by *The Fugitive Kind*. In 1945 came *The Glass Menagerie* where he exposed a few skeletons from his family cupboard. When he came out with *A Streetcar Named Desire* in 1947, the play catapulted him to the pinnacle of his career. Right across his career Williams examined the pretences, the sexual impulses and chicanery that beset humankind in their interaction with society, their thirst for spirituality, and the passion that raged within them at the same time.

His *Cat on a Hot Tin Roof* fetched him his second Pulitzer Prize in 1955. In early youth he developed strong homosexual tendencies. Personal indulgence in this area and close observation caused his experiences to percolate through his pen into his writings. The characters of Blanche, Stanley and Maggie (Margaret) in *Cat on a Hot Tin Roof* are the product of this process.

April 1947, Arthur Miller's *All My Sons* was creating major waves on Broadway. Directed by Elia Kazan, it left a deep impression on Williams. He instantly wrote to Kazan, confessing that he had no memory of seeing a more beautifully directed play at Broadway. The stage props were revolutionary too. He believed that the country was in desperate need of such a wake-up call, even if through the stage. He informed Kazan that he was writing a similar note to Miller. He wrote that he had just come out with a new play whose production rights he had handed over to Irene Selznick, and did not forget to add that Irene would have a copy of the manuscript delivered to him. He was not sure whether the play would hold enough interest for the director.

A Streetcar Named Desire was originally titled *The Poker Night*. When word got around Broadway that Williams had handed over production rights to a novitiate like Irene Mayer Selznick, there were murmurs. All that people knew was that she was the wife of the celebrated producer David Selznick and the daughter of Mayer of the Metro-Goldwyn-Mayer trio. When Kazan heard that someone had been hired as director, he was rather disappointed. Facts, however, were otherwise. Williams was insistent upon Kazan, declaring that he alone could do justice to his work.

As it happened, when the manuscript arrived, it was Kazan's wife who read it first, and then really got after her husband to read it. When he read it first, Kazan expressed some doubts and suggested a few changes. But the first face-to-face with the playwright was an event of epiphany for him. All doubts were resolved, and the foundation of a great friendship was instantly laid. From the very first meet, Kazan found Williams enigmatic and incomprehensible. He fitted the image of a sailor back from mysterious lands, or a prisoner just out after a long time in captivity.

Kazan immediately recognised the life experiences behind the theme as genuine. The writer had, of course, coloured them with his imagination. There were any number of off-shoots resulting from a creative vision but the theme was firmly rooted in reality—this Kazan sensed rather strongly.

In his autobiography *The Life*, Kazan writes that he often reflected on the grand large-heartedness of Williams' character on the one side, and the violent passions that he was prone to on the other, and the interaction between these two aspects of his personality. He could then understand the welts he could see.

To confirm this impression Kazan undertook research in Williams' personal life, and found that large portions of the play sprang out of the author's family experiences. His parents' images are very easily noticed in his characters. The mother Edwina was a status-conscious woman locked up in unhappy matrimony with a violent, abusive man in Cornelius Williams. Cornelius was a rover and philanderer, rather prone to using his fists. Williams grew up in a dysfunctional family where violence and passion held sway, and this left a deep impression on his personality. He went deep into the dark corners of his past to ferret out nuggets for use as art. Once at the shooting, when he saw Brando as Stanley tossing plates off the dining table in anger, he started laughing. He had seen it all happening at home.

In a letter to Kazan, Williams admitted that there was much of Blanche in his character. Lusting for companionship, Blanche needed a cleft in the rock in which she could hide. Williams was searching for his own cleft in the rock. From earliest childhood he had grown up in an emotional desert. He picked up considerable notoriety for his homosexual relationships. In the fall of 1948 a teen-aged boy of Sicilian descent named Frank Phillip Merlo walked into his life. This relationship lasted many long years, until infidelities and drug abuse on both sides ended it. Their years together were Williams' happiest and most productive. Shortly after their break-up, Merlo was diagnosed with inoperable lung cancer and Williams returned to take care of him until his death. In the years following Merlo's death, Williams was plunged into a period of severe depression and increasing drug use, resulting in several hospitalisations until he died at the age of 71.

There are some works of art that not only attract glory unto themselves from the moment of their birth, but also bring with them a golden seam of good fortune for many others. *A Streetcar Named Desire* was first performed on Broadway on 3 December 1947, and its film version arrived four years later. This play-movie combine bestowed upon the world of entertainment a number of unprecedented, priceless gifts—a dramatist of the highest quality in Tennessee Williams, an amazing directorial talent in Elia Kazan, and a sizzling, explosive, world-straddling actor in Marlon Brando!

Even after the resounding success of the play, Kazan was unwilling to direct the movie. He had just finished *Panic in the Streets*, and was busy preparing for *Viva Zapata*. But Tennessee Williams was insistent. As Kazan writes, 'I really resisted Williams like hell,' the reason being that he didn't want to play around with the same material all over again. But, as he admits, he had no way of knowing that the movie would turn out to be a masterpiece. *A Streetcar Named Desire* became an immortal piece of art in the history of English literature and cinema.

Sir Lawrence Olivier had carried the play over to London from Broadway which he directed, with Leigh playing Blanche. The Blanche of Kazan's play was Jessica Tandy. But the producers wanted a better-known name for the movie, and the opportunity went to Vivien Leigh.

When the shooting began, Kazan did not much care for Leigh's presentation of the character. She was delivering dialogues the way Olivier had taught her to do for the London stage. When Kazan had had enough, he reminded her that she had to do it his way. Leigh was a very hardworking actress. She amazed Kazan with the amount of labour she put in. He stated in an interview, later, that while both of them worked very hard towards creating a beautiful piece of art, his respect for her had doubled.

The movie opens with a shot of New Orleans, as the railway train makes its sinuous way from a distance, belching smoke, and rolls into the station. The marks of the Second World War is still quite evident. We notice a marriage party having a gala time. A burst of smoke whitens up the screen; and as it clears, we see the arrestingly beautiful face of 30-year-old Blanche (Vivien Leigh), quite like a goddess peeping out of the clouds. She has arrived from Laurel, Mississippi, on a visit to her younger sister Stella Kowalski. She is a woman who has cut herself off from the world of reality and lives in her own cocoon of dreams—an enigmatic, out-of-the-world personality. With this very first frame she establishes the image of a dominant personality.

Her rendition of a schizophrenic Southern woman, who touches the lowest depths of character is so beautiful that it hurts. Her emotion-churning, haunting Blanche holds the mind for a long long time. The *New York Times* saluted Leigh as the greatest actress of England and she bagged the Oscar for her portrayal of Blanche, exactly eleven years after she had got the Academy Award for playing Scarlet O'Hara in *Gone with the Wind*.

With Vivien Leigh playing Blanche and Marlon Brando as Stanley, two strong actors with mutually contradictory styles of acting, the duet was unparalleled. Marlon Brando was barely 24 when he walked the boards for *A Streetcar Named Desire*, and in the prime of his youth when he faced the cameras. When he portrayed the compactly-built, youthful, boorish, aggressive, knavish, yet likeable Stanley Kowalski, Brando truly embraced immortality. The medium of the movie carried this electrifying character to every nook and cranny of the world.

That this role should have landed in the lap of a 24-year-old novitiate was a gift from heaven. When he first met the director Kazan and the producer Irene Selznick, they both thought him too immature for the part. The producer, indeed, did show him the door. She wanted a heavyweight Hollywood star with an established reputation. In fact, she had already decided to offer the role to John Garfield.

Probably with the intention of giving him a soft heave, Kazan advised Brando to have an audience with Tennessee Williams, who was at home in Provincetown, Massachusetts. What kind of reception did he get at the farm house? The playwright's toilet had sprung a leak which Brando helped him fix. Post that they sat together and Brando read out a few lines from *A Streetcar Named Desire*. Williams was absolutely stunned by the rendition.

He immediately wrote to his agent Audrey Wood that Brando's arrival was a godsend. What reading! He had never heard reading like that before! He was certain that this new actor would lift his play to really great heights. The arch Williams imagined Brando erecting on the stage was certainly not within the ability of any other actor, including Garfield. Along with his talents, he had also the physique that fitted Stanley's role very well. Williams wanted Wood to ensure that the role went to nobody else.

Brando had had occasions to observe rough characters from close, in whose image he sculpted Stanley. In an interview, Brando confessed that dramatists like Shakespeare and Tennessee Williams were such masters of dialogue that they left no scope for actors to improvise. Their genius in the choice of words was adequate enough to lift the actor to the desired spot.

Brando shook Broadway with his phenomenal performance. Young theatre-goers would go around the theatre imitating his lustful call of 'Stella! Stella, sweetheart! Stell-lahhhhh!' The body-hugging, round-necked T-shirt that he wore for the movie became an instant craze worldwide. His resonant voice and polished body language left the audience delirious, and particularly mesmerised the young girls. He writes in his autobiography that when he returned to the greenroom after a night's performance there would be at least eight to ten girls waiting for him with stars in their eyes. The 24-year-old Brando would sweep his eyes across the waiting bunch of cooing young pigeons, signal to one with his eyes, and spend the evening with her.

Marlon Brando, however, had his knives out for Leigh. In his autobiography *Songs My Mother Taught Me*, he turns mean, and says that Leigh was quite the original Blanche in many ways. She was by far more attractive than any other actress of her times. But her life too was not different from the wounded butterfly of Tennessee Williams. She went to bed with pretty nearly everyone, and like Blanche, she was falling to pieces emotionally. He claims to know for sure that Lawrence was aware of his wife's escapades, but like other husbands in a similar situation, he had no choice but to pretend ignorance.

Kazan was tremendously impressed by Brando's performance. He writes that Brando was an acting genius. During shooting he was always ready for his role. His personality, his histrionic arsenal, his ambition, his extraordinary efforts were so intense that as a director he never needed to worry about this actor. Whenever he told Brando about what he wanted in a certain character, or acted it out, he never imitated him. Frequently, he came up with something of his own, often radically different, fresh and unusual, which Kazan found more attractive.

With his role of Stanley, Brando brought in the Stanislavski School of acting called dramatic naturalism, or method acting, which revolutionised the world of cinema. The American theatre too saw a significant shift away

'What is straight? A line can be straight, or a street, but the human heart, oh, no, it's curved like a road through mountains.

Marlon Brando as Stanley and Vivien Leigh as Blanche, in Elia Kazan directed *A Street Car Named Desire* (1952). COURTESY: WWW.DOCTORMACRO.COM

from melodrama and toward dramatic naturalism. There were some who tried to imitate him, but fell flat on their face. Some critics, however, found his performance rather loud. In 1951 *A Streetcar Named Desire* received twelve nominations for the Oscar, and finally won four. Vivien Leigh won it for the Best Actress, Kim Hunter got it for Best Supporting Actress, and Karl Malden got it too for Best Supporting Actor—that made three out of the four awards for acting. Brando alone missed it for acting. What he did not miss one bit was the overwhelming appreciation of the audience.

While the play begins with Stanley on the stage, the movie begins with the beautiful face of Blanche emerging from the smoke of a steam engine on the railway platform. This introduction of Blanche's character, Kazan says, came to him from reading Tolstoy's *Anna Karenina*. The screenplay for the movie was prepared by streamlining the dialogues and scenes of the play. Two scenes that didn't exist in the play were added towards the concluding part of the movie. The entire episode had to be written fresh for the movie.

The filming has been largely done with eye-level shots. Not much use has been made of any trick photography. There are not many movements in the screenplay anyway. Kazan has taken some shots on a slow dolly. The major focus has been on the building up and portrayal of the characters by the actors. The lighting visualisation of this black-and-white movie is unmatched.

The set erected for the Stanley household, both for the stage as well as for the screen, has been acknowledged a great piece of art: a dilapidated two-room apartment with a kitchen in front, with a folding bed and a table, and bedroom behind. The table is where Stanley and his friends cramp in regularly for a hand of poker. The wallpaper is either torn or peeling off, smudgy and lustreless. Blanche is quite taken aback at first sight, and wonders how she will survive in this dinginess

A Streetcar Named Desire confirmed Elia Kazan's place in the ranks of the greatest directors in the world. A native of Istanbul, he was fortunate to have landed dramatists of the calibre of Arthur Miller and Tennessee Williams from his earliest days. He had a third great writing for him, the novelist John Steinbeck, whose novellas *Viva Zapata* and *East of Eden* were converted into very successful movies later. Among his many great achievements is his introduction to cinema of such all-time greats as James Dean, Warren Beatty and Marlon Brando.

Over the years Kazan acquired the reputation of a perfectionist—a director who fully exploited his artistic sensibilities and never left anything missing. His movies are a boiling cauldron in which Karl Marx and Sigmund Freud dissolve. In his opinion life is a play, and dramatic conflict is the essence of life. All his characters look at life as the fountainhead of violence, and give extraordinary, overriding importance to emotion. Even his second rung characters are as inflammatory and combustible as the leads. His scripts accorded as much importance to villains as to the protagonists. For a little while he moved over to the writing of novels. He spent a few years there, meeting moderate success. When he returned to the cinema, he was not as successful as he had been before; but he remained the magician he was at seeking out the relationship between the outside character and the demon that resides inside.

Whether in a play or in a movie, both Williams and Kazan were, in their different ways, intent on delving into the depths of the animal called man. The substance of their conversation was that the people of the world do not have the equipment to see others with an unerring or realistic eye. They see others through the holes in the tattered veil of their own ego.

THE BRIDGE ON THE RIVER KWAI

AUTHOR Pierre Boulle **PUBLISHED** 1952
DIRECTOR David Lean **PREMIERED** 1957

'Do not speak to me of rules. This is war! This is not a game of cricket!'

The conflagration of the Second World War has given birth to a number of stories big and small. Its destructive flames had spread to the war frontiers in the jungles of South East Asia too. During 1942–43 the Japanese army was laying down a railway track from Bangkok to Rangoon. This was before Netaji Subhash Chandra Bose reached there. For this enterprise the Japanese had forcibly conscripted a large number of Indian citizens and prisoners of war (POW). During its construction, approximately 13,000 POW died, and were buried along the railway track. An estimated 80,000 to 100,000 civilians also died in the course of the project, chiefly forced labour brought from Malaya and the Dutch East Indies, or conscripted in Thailand and Burma (Myanmar), prompting many historians to christen this track as the 'Death Railway'.

It is around this historical setting that Pierre Boulle wrote his largely fictional French novel *Le Pont de la Rivière Kwai* in 1952. The small 200 page novel created an immediate stir, and was translated into English by Xan Fielding in 1954.

The Bridge on the River Kwai takes as its title from one of the line's main engineering feats, the bridge across the Kwae Yai river, north of Kanchanburi. Boulle was an engineer serving as a secret agent with the Free French in Singapore, when he was captured and subjected to two years' forced labour in this project.

This book caught the attention of the well-known producer Sam Spiegel, and the wheels began to spin. It was eventually immortalised in David Lean's 1957 film.

The movie begins with a bird's-eye view, well, more precisely a falcon's-eye view of the scenario. The very first frame is occupied by a falcon soaring in the sky with the camera on its wings, for a stunning aerial view of the land: the dark green of a dense tropical forest somewhere in the Far East.

The camera descends on a POW encampment, Camp No. 16, under the command of the Japanese Colonel Sa'ito (Sessue Hayakawa). 'There is no barbed-wire, no stockade, no watch tower,' the commandant informs his prisoners. 'They are not necessary. We are on an island in the jungle. Escape is impossible. You would die.'

Strongly built, 55-year-old Col Sa'ito is a strict disciplinarian, a terror by himself. Out there in the jungles are other terrors: blood-sucking leeches and venomous snakes, malaria, beriberi and diarrhoea, carnivorous wild birds, which, according to the POWs, have, together with Sa'ito, taken a heavy toll on human lives. Sa'ito's discipline is unrelenting—a sentry should stay at his post even with ravaging storms and torrential rains pouring over his head!

The POWs working on the 'Death Railway' are a pitiable sight: scrawny, skin-and-bone cadavers, more like dry, tall reeds than like human beings. The unrelieved company of starvation and the debilitating forces of nature have worn them down threadbare. The drill-sergeant has no teeth left, and all he can manage is to splutter out barely comprehensible commands through a collapsed mouth.

Surrounding the camp on all sides is a veritable forest of crosses that marks the graves of their companions, the crosses merely a pair of rotten bamboo sticks held together, transversely, by coir thongs. Nearby, stands a bare, skeletal bamboo-and-grass hospital under the charge of medical officer Major Clipton (James Donald). American officers like Commander Shears (William Holden), of the US Navy, pilfer cigarette lighters and other trivia from the pockets of dead soldiers, which they use for bribing junior Japanese officers for an extended stay in the hospital. The entire camp and its surrounding wilderness are under the sole command of Col Sa'ito.

Into this community arrives Col Nicholson (Alec Guinness) with his battalion, and sparks off his first confrontation with the Japanese colonel. Col Nicholson is a slim and impressive six-footer, with 28 years of service in the British Army behind him. A discipline-

'We can teach these barbarians a lesson in Western methods and efficiency that will put them to shame. We'll show them what the British soldier is capable of doing.

loving officer of the highest quality, he cares greatly for the honour of the men who work under him. For adversary he has Col Sa'ito of the Imperial Japanese army, a soldier of the old school who believes in unquestioning obedience to his superiors, and is ready to lay his life down at their command.

The instructions from the Japanese High Command are that the bridge on the river Kwai should be ready for the railway to begin by May 1943. Towards this end, Sa'ito puts not only the POW soldiers under the harrow, but issues orders for the officers to be sent for physical labour too. These orders, Nicholson tells Sa'ito, fly against the provisions of the Geneva Convention, which clearly protects officers from being used for manual labour.

Before the movie reaches midway, the conflict and tension between Sai'to and Nicholson have reached their extreme. Lean has given this stand-off far greater space in his script than is found in the book. The episode takes this extraordinary turn clearly on account of a clash of temperaments between two adversaries who refuse to compromise with their respective principles, a battle of personalities worthy of conception by powerful dramatists like Anouilh or Shakespeare.

Next day on parade, when Nicholson pulls out of his pocket the Geneva Convention booklet, Sa'ito flings the booklet into the dust. 'Cowards' code!' he barks, and gives Nicholson a back-handed slap, drawing blood. Nicholson, however, is the kind who would rather die than let go of his principles.

To make an example of Nicholson's insubordination, Sa'ito trains a machine gun on him, and gives him time to surrender till he counts three. Before the third count, Dr Clipton leaps in, and challenges Sa'ito, 'Is this your soldier's code, murdering unarmed men?' Shamed and frustrated, Sa'ito fumes off towards his logs-and-bamboo office. Shamed, yes, but pacified? Not a whit. While the rest of the soldiers set off to work on the bridge, Nicholson and the other officers are made to stand under the hot sky, right through the day.

The rebellious Nicholson is then cooped like an animal into a rusty, cramped, 5 x 5 x 5 ft box-like structure made of sheet-metal, which stands in a patch enclosed by a barbed-wire fence, commonly referred to by the soldiers as the 'oven'. The rest of the officers are incarcerated in a punishment hut. Before sending Nicholson in, Sa'ito tries to break his spirit by administering a bashing and smashing his legs. His soldiers are deeply impressed by the man's resilience and courage, and as he is marched into the coop, they break out in unison with 'For he's a jolly good fellow.'

Taking advantage of the confusion that prevails in the camp, the American prisoner Shears slips out with two others. While he manages to escape, his fellow escapees are shot down. Sa'ito is obsessed with the mission of getting the bridge ready within the specified period. He threatens to reduce the rations of the British soldiers and to pull the sick out of their hospital beds and set them to work. All of Dr Clipton's efforts to bring about a rapprochement between Nicholson and Sa'ito are futile. As he stands out in the sun with the two sparring inside, he wonders aloud, 'Are they both mad? Or am I going mad? Or is it the sun?'

The soldiers at the construction site keep throwing up endless obstacles, and Sa'ito turns frantic. He drags Nicholson out of his confinement and gets him into his cabin. He spreads out drinks and delicacies before him and tries to reason with him, and tells him that he is not asking for a major and above to go to work, it's only the duty officers. In an effort to win his sympathy, he admits that if the bridge is not up in time, he would be left with no alternative but to commit ritual suicide. Nicholson, however, is unmoved. Sa'ito flies into such a rage that he screams, 'I hate the British! You are defeated, but you have no shame! You are stubborn, but you have no pride! You are injured, but you have no courage! I hate the British!' In his fit of anger he stabs his knife deep into the wooden table-top.

The winds of war begin to change. One day Sa'ito invites Nicholson over with considerable geniality and informs him of the orders of amnesty he has decided to grant. Officers would no longer be compelled to work, and Nicholson and his officers are set free unconditionally. The British soldiers instantly break into celebrations, and felicitate the colonel by carrying him around on their shoulders. Col Sa'ito locks himself up in his office and cries inconsolably like a child. Once he has won his battle for dignity, Nicholson throws himself heart and soul into the business of erecting the bridge. The Japanese engineers had selected a bad site for the bridge. Nicholson identifies a new spot and work begins with a new zest. He tells his men, 'We will show them what the British soldiers are capable of doing.'

'A word to you about escape. There is no barbed wire. No stockade. No watchtower. They are not necessary. We are an island in the jungle. Escape is impossible. You would die.

From Left to Right: Allec Guinness as Colonel Nicholson, William Holden as Shears and Jack Hawkins as Major Warden, in *The Bridge on the River Kwai*, directed by David Lean (1957). COURTESY: AUTHOR

His engineer Reeves tells him, 'The trees in this forest are very similar to elm, and the elm part of the London Bridge lasted for 600 years.'

'Six hundred years, Reeves?'

'Yes sir!'

'Six hundred years!' mutters Nicholson, as he bids them goodnight, 'That would be quite something!'

Meanwhile, Shears somehow makes his way into a British hospital in Ceylon where he has been enjoying his recovery with a blonde nurse. Here he runs into Major Warden (Jack Hawkins) of the British Army. The Allied High Command had received intelligence about the laying out of the Bangkok-Rangoon railways by the end of May, and that the Japanese were using the forced labour of the Allied POWs to erect a big bridge across the River Kwai. The bridge, if it were allowed to come into being, would be a huge asset to the Japanese, already a powerful enermy, and Major Warden has been assigned the task of blowing it up. He invites Shears to volunteer for a Commando mission to destroy the bridge.

Walking back into the dense steamy jungles, from which he had barely escaped with his life, is an insane thought for Shears, and he vehemently rejects the offer. But Major Warden knows his secret: he is not really Shears but merely an enlisted man from the cruiser *USS Houston*. He had switched uniforms with the dead Commander Shears after the sinking of their ship 'to get better treatment'. Faced with the prospect of being charged with impersonating an officer, Shears has no choice but to volunteer; Warden gives him the 'simulated rank of major.' The problem is how to cart the explosives through those dense diabolical jungles! Major Warden resolves it by having himself and his team para-dropped into the combat area. Immediate casualty results when one of the team gets entangled in a branch and chokes to death. The jungle odyssey for the remaining three—Warden, Shears, and Canadian Lieutenant Joyce (Geoffrey Horne)—begins.

The jungle is under round-the-clock Japanese patrol. To dodge them Warden takes a rather circuitous route from the east. To help them through this ordeal are the guide Khun Yai and his gang of lungi-clad young women porters who traipse through the jungles, nimbler than mountain goats. It's a treacherous journey with knee-deep ditches brimming with sludge; turbid rivers overflowing with leeches; tall, precipitous cliffs; roaring, tumultuous waterfalls!

Warden is suddenly wounded in the leg in an encounter with a Japanese patrol. Beset with leeches, with his wounded leg refusing to bear his weight, he drags himself on the make-shift crutch, but refuses to let his team relax. He simply cannot afford to stop midway. He hobbles for some time and is later carried on a litter.

Back at the POW camp, once Nicholson has taken over responsibility of the bridge, he leaves no stone unturned. He, who had resisted with might and main the conscription of officers for manual labour, the same Nicholson flouts the Geneva Convention with abandon. To ensure the timely completion of his mission, he takes his fellow officers through the grind. He even goes running to Dr Clipton looking for sick-bay recruits. He happily persuades semi-unwell patients to come over. They could be used for light assignments, he tells the doctor.

The eve of 31 May. The bridge is ready. Col Nicholson and Col Sa'ito are seen promenading along it, with an air of deep satisfaction about them. Time and again they look at the bridge and utter only one word: 'Beautiful!' At this very moment Major Warden and his demolition team are sitting concealed behind a dense bush along the river bank.

Nicholson looks at the bridge and tells Clipton, 'One day the war will be over, and I hope the people who will use this bridge in years to come will remember how it was built, and who built it. Not a gang of slaves, but British soldiers, Clipton, even in captivity.' With dusk settling, as he looks at the darkening waters of the river, he voices the thought how in life too there crop up certain moments when a person realises that he is nearer to the end than to the beginning. These words, that would have graced an epic, are loaded with such dramatic irony that they stun the sensitive viewer.

In the evening there are wild celebrations in the camp accompanied by songs, dances and skits. Out there along the black river, Warden's men are busy laying out the dynamite sticks at strategic places under the bridge. Early next morning the whistle of a steam engine comes piercing through the jungle, and then the low rattle of an approaching train. Suddenly, at a distance down there, Nicholson spots something unusual glinting above the water.

During the night Warden had concealed the wire under the water; but by dawn the water level had dropped, exposing the wire connecting the explosives to the detonator. Nicholson brings it to Sa'ito's attention. As the train is heard approaching, Nicholson, with Sa'ito in tow, hurries down to the riverbank to investigate. Joyce, hiding with the detonator, breaks cover and stabs Sa'ito to death; Nicholson yells for help, while attempting to stop Joyce from reaching the detonator. Shears and Warden yell for Joyce to kill Nicholson, but Joyce is killed by Japanese fire. Shears then swims across the river to fulfil the mission, but is shot just before he reaches Nicholson. Recognising the dying Shears, Nicholson snaps out of his bridge-obsession and exclaims, 'What have I done?' Warden fires his mortar, mortally wounding Nicholson. The dazed colonel stumbles towards the detonator and falls on top of it as he dies, just when the train steams across half the length of the bridge. There is a huge explosion as the bridge collapses, and the train comes hurtling into the river below.

Tossing in the gushing, rumbling water one can see mutilated bodies, innumerable chunks of what once constituted the bridge, and a sodden wooden plank proclaiming the labour of the British POWs that went into its construction. As he witnesses the carnage, Clipton shakes his head exclaiming: 'Madness...Madness.' The last frame is of a falcon flapping its wings as it loses itself in the sky.

The question that remains with the script is Nicholson's attitude towards the bridge. After all the commitment, the energy, the labour that Nicholson puts into the bridge, who was going to reap the benefit? Who else but the arch enemy, Japan? Many critics have roundly condemned the character for being blinded by the short-term passion for quality as a hallmark of British efforts, and completely missing out on the long-term mission of winning a war. I, however, disagree with this negative assessment. I see Nicholson as a creator who is faithful to his creative urges even in the middle of a war. One may legitimately say that the passion of creation does not recognise the limitation of nationality or space or time. The blowing away of the bridge both in the novel and in the movie is, indeed, poetic justice. But the bridge did not disappear thus, in reality.

The novel neither glorifies war nor outrightly condemns it. At its core are strong characters of Shakespearean proportions who are locked in mortal conflict with each other. It was reason enough reason for David Lean to have gravitated towards it.

Stephen Spielberg, one of the acknowledged masters in world cinema today, had well-publicised differences with David Lean. But over and over again, he has declared himself as a devoted student of Lean's films, and worships him as a trendsetter in movies. Spielberg is particularly fond of Lean's *The Bridge on the River Kwai* and *Lawrence of Arabia*. His works have the quality to mesmerise the greatest of artists. While Lean himself received the Oscar twice for Best Director, his movies have garnered as many as twenty-eight Academy Awards through their actors and technicians. *The Bridge on the River Kwai*, an immortal epic on celluloid, is the product of his magical directorial skills and boundless labour.

Lean is known particularly for creating spectacular magnum opuses out of great novels. Other than the two Charles Dickens novels *Great Expectations* and *Oliver Twist*, his list of novel-based movies carries such heavyweight names as *Ryan's Daughter*, *The Bridge on the River Kwai*, *Doctor Zhivago* and *Passage to India*. Lean had made it a practice to commit a good few years to preparation before he began production: research on his subject, travel and heaps of paperwork. There are numerous others, even today, who go in with this kind of comprehensive preparation; it is in the execution of their plan that most of them fall short. Landing one's dreams on the desert sand of hard fact and reality is, indeed, a difficult job. This also requires the delicate art and technique of committing the entire unit to a tough grind, which only rare moviemakers possess. David Lean is rare among those rare ones.

Lean was born on 25 March 1908 at Croydon, Surrey, now part of Greater London, England. His chartered accountant father was a disciplinarian, and as a child of this strict Quaker family, Lean was not allowed to see movies. They had a maid, though, who loved films and rarely missed out on any. She would hold little Lean spellbound with her dramatic narrations; she often picked up a supple cane and gave a terrific impersonation of the Charles Chaplin waddle. Lean took his first lessons on the cinema from this maid.

Lean was a half-hearted student with a dreamy nature who was labelled a 'dud'; he left school in his mid-teens and entered his father's chartered accountancy firm as an apprentice. Bored by his work, Lean spent every evening in the cinema, and in 1927, at the age of 19, after an aunt had advised him to find a job he enjoyed doing, he went to Gaumont Studios where his obvious enthusiasm earned him a month's trial without pay. He was taken on as a tea-boy, promoted to clapper boy, and soon rose to the position of third assistant director. By 1930, he was working as an editor on newsreels.

In a later interview, David Lean advises ambitious young people to seek out the company of knowledgeable and gifted people. Breathing the same air as them makes one grow. He advises people to be ready for any kind of sacrifice if it helps them learn from the wise.

A director of the calibre of Guru Dutt first came to Pune to join Prabhat Studios merely as a dance director. But once there, he kept his eyes open and ears cocked. Greatness came to him in a steady stream as a result of his devotion. Lean first earned for himself a reputation as an editor. People would often address him as the 'great cutter'. Snipping other people's obese, unwieldy film reels with unfailing instinct, and trimming them into shape

Director David Lean

came easy to him. No wonder he was also called 'doctor of films'. In his early years Shakespeare too would set right other people's unhealthy plots, and was known as a doctor of plays.

Before he sat on the editing table, he would commit the movie's script to memory, and he would read the dialogues from the sound frame. His career in feature films began with *Freedom of the Seas* in 1934 and *Escape Me Never* in 1935. His first work as a director was in 1942 in collaboration with Noel Coward on *In Which We Serve*.

Lean was busy with his movie *Summertime* when Spiegel contacted him. Since then his hawk eyes began scanning the jungles of South East Asia for a suitable site. Lean loved performing on an epic scale.

Lean has been known to shoot his movies on the very locations where the events are supposed to have occurred. While *Doctor Zhivago* was filmed in the freezing cold of the Russian ice fields, *Lawrence of Arabia* was shot in the face of singeing, violent dust storms in the deserts of Arabia. For *The Bridge on the River Kwai*, however, the Thai Government refused to grant permission, and there was no recourse except to hunt out a close enough substitute. This was located in the jungles of Sri Lanka, where Lean went on to construct an authentic wooden bridge across the river that ran through it. The awe-inspiring scene of coaches tumbling over it into the valley below was filmed with authentic railway carriages. Money flowed like water.

In order to capture the grandeur of the jungle with its mighty mountains and steep abysses, Lean undoubtedly brought all the resources of his talent, imagination and stamina into play. Discussing his technical style in an interview, he says that he began his scenes with a wide-angle composition. From there he went into the focal lens, and finally picked out whatever items fell into focus.

A scene from the nightmarish journey through the jungles exemplifies this strategy. The camera frames a delightful panoramic view of a slope of a mountainside about one and a half kilometre away. It is sunset, and in the dusk are silhouetted the porter girls trudging up the slope with their loads. From the right side in the same frame hobbles in Major Warden on his crutch, and occupies the foreground.

Visualise this mind-blowing composition: Major Warden on right foreground, with the rest in a panoramic long shot of the porter girls scaling up the dense, sunset-tinted mountainside! The frames within this master-shot

'One day the war will be over. And I hope that the people that use this bridge in years to come will remember how it was built and who built it. Not a gang of slaves, but soldiers, British soldiers, Clipton, even in captivity.

keep changing, but the ethereal beauty is never broken. We have had Bimal Roy and Nitin Bose who were masters at framing too. But the felicity with which Lean balances a frame delicately inside another frame, well, that can only be Lean! The lighting scheme changes according to the mood of the scene, and the camera movement picks up accordingly. There are times when the camera trolley moves slower than an ant!

Lean has presented the jungle through precise, slick and the minimum of scenes. Look at these episodes and you realise what a detailed study this great director would have made of the jungles of the South East, what travails he would have suffered, and what labour he would have committed to this study!

In another splendid composition from the same journey, Warden's unit enters the frame from the right through the tall grass, hacking branches to clear the way. Out there, from around the trunk of a massive *peepal* tree arrive Shears and the Siamese girls, dead tired, and ready to collapse. Shears leans listlessly against the trunk, and the girls squat on the ground on the far side of the frame. Into the same frame limps in Warden from behind, reaches foreground and slides to the ground. The visual question: What is more twisted and tangled? The roots of this gnarled old tree, or the inter-knotted vicissitudes of an excursion gone mad? Propping himself up, Warden pants out, 'You go on without me, that's an order!' Shears gets back at him, 'I won't obey that order. You make me sick with your heroics! There's a stench of death about you!… You and that colonel Nicholson, you're two of a kind! Crazy with courage! For what? How to die like a gentleman, how to die by the rules, when the only important thing is how to live like a human being. I'm not going to leave you here to die, Warden, because I don't care about your bridge and I don't care about your rules. If we go on, we go on together!' And then, signalling to the girls, 'Come on!' At which the girls come up with the bamboo-and-thong litter, deposit Warden forcibly into it and get moving. Packing this action within the dimensions of a single scene and a single frame is nothing short of genius.

The Bridge on the River Kwai proved to be a runaway hit, and broke many box-office collection records. It stunned the cinema critics, earned for itself eight Oscar nominations, and finally walked away with seven awards: Best Picture—Sam Spiegel; Best Director—David Lean; Best Actor—Alec Guinness; Best Screenplay—Michael Wilson, Carl Foreman, Pierre Boulle; Best Music—Malcolm Arnold; Best Editing—Peter Taylor; Best Cinematography—Jack Hildyard. The nomination that did not convert into an award was that of the talented Japanese actor Sessue Hayakawa for Best Actor in a Supporting Role. At the age of 68 he had essayed the role of the 55-year-old Sa'ito with considerable elan.

Even today, the memories of this great film are fresh in the mind. Alec Guinness playing Col Nicholson, tall and erect, obstinate, resolute, resilient; his eyes that cannot withstand the sudden flood of sunlight when the sheet-iron door of the notorious 'oven' is opened after days of confinement; his mind that does not drop its alertness despite the physical tortures! One learns with a shock that Alec was not the first choice for this role! It was first given to Charles Laughton. But the discomforts involved with roughing it out in Ceylon—its intense heat, its jungles, its ants—were more than Laughton could stomach as an actor, let alone as a soldier. He was in bed all the time! The way people like Alec Guinness walk, talk, think, the manner in which they carry themselves on the screen, it would appear that they have been lifted straight out of a military camp and placed before the camera.

Extracting high-quality work out of great actors is by itself a delicate art in the repertoire of a director. Lean was a daddy of a champion in this area. It was Guinness's constant crib that Lean never wanted him in the role of Nicholson. Lean kept him on heat all the time, and got him to deliver a performance worth its weight in gold. He never ordered his cast about in the presence of others. On the contrary, he would place his arms around the shoulder, take them aside and whisper friendly tips into the ear.

No director gets the actor of his dreams. Guru Dutt had written the central role in *Pyaasa* with Dilip Kumar in mind; Mehboob had Nargis in his mind when the script for *Aan* was being readied; Lean had wanted Marlon Brando for his *Lawrence of Arabia*. He would always say that Peter O'Toole was rather young to play the role. But with Alec Guinness's rendition of Nicholson he was completely bowled over.

One will always find some mean-minded detractors who will question and envy success. Be it literature or movies, these nit-pickers gather together like frightened birds on trees to clamour through the day. Lions like Lean, however, have the confidence of their abilities, and they romp across the jungle to strike awe and fear across their territory. There existed an entire caucus of film critics in America whose mission was to punch holes in Lean's movies and run him down as a moviemaker of no great merit. There were mischief-makers who did all they could to cause him mental distress. But after so many years have rolled by, a director of Spielberg's calibre declares with pride that before starting a new venture he watches Lean's movies again and again. The shadow of *The Bridge on the River Kwai* lies dense on his *Saving Private Ryan*.

The actual bridge remained functional till the final year of the War when it was blown out of existence by the Allied Air Force bomber craft, say history books. It is believed Netaji Subhash Chandra Bose had travelled over this bridge on his way to Rangoon. While I was on a tour of Bangkok in connection with the novel *Mahanayak*, I decided to take a guide and visit the site of the bridge which was a hundred kilometres away. I couldn't start till late in the afternoon, and by the time I reached there it had turned pitch dark. Hence I had to return disappointed without getting a good view of the bridge. What was then a cause of regret turned out to be a blessing in disguise. I have seen Lean's immortal creation frame by frame, over and over again. The arch of Lean's work is far taller and stronger than the bridge of reality.

THE GODFATHER

AUTHOR Mario Puzo PUBLISHED 1669
DIRECTOR Francis Ford Coppola PREMIERED 1972

‘I’ll make him an offer he can’t refuse.’

The tinsel world of cinema has never run short of astrologers and crystal-gazers; not now, not ever. It would have been impossible, however, to draw a horoscope for *The Godfather*. It ran quite an obstacle race before it reached conception and delivery. An abortion would have been a tragedy for the world of cinema. We would then not have had a director of the calibre of Francis Ford Coppola. The superstar Al Pacino would have continued to languish as a second-rate actor. The famous Gordon Willis School of Cinematography would perhaps not have come into being.

The Godfather is the story of Vito Corleone, a gangster who rules the American underworld. It tells of his efforts at retaining his supremacy over his mafia kingdom; it is a study of his personality, his highs and lows, the study of a gangster as a human being.

Our Don, the Italy born Vito Corleone, has just turned sixty. He is broad-built, stocky and gruff voiced. His bulldog jowls and homely turnout make him look more like a farmer than a city slicker. But he is sharp, very sharp, very observant and very alert. He never talks on the telephone for fear that it could be tapped. His father had been brutally done to death in his native village of Corleone, and the killers were keen to rule out the possibility of vengeance by snuffing the brat out too. Young Vito, therefore, had migrated to the safety of America.

The family of the Don has been elaborately sketched out in the book. He has three sons: the eldest is the 6-foot-tall Santino, called Sonny; the second is the hedonistic Fredo, who has already been declared a softie and a wastrel by the family; and the youngest is Michael, who has recently returned with a gallantry award after battling the Japanese in the Second World War. Mike wants to have nothing to do with his family's nefarious activities. He detests their work ethics, and is even considering changing his surname to distance himself from their influence. His dream is to live a proper middle-class life somewhere as a professor of mathematics.

The underworld is controlled by five powerful families, among whom the Corleones have established a unique and predominant place for themselves. For Vito, friendship is the bulwark of this structure. If a person has been accepted as a friend, he would sell the shirt on his back for him. The anxiety of the petitioner at the Don's door is his own anxiety. All that he needs to do is to acknowledge Vito as his godfather, and the Godfather will stand by him through the toughest ordeal. Be the person strong or weak, rich or poor, Godfather dispenses affection with an even hand. It is also in Vito's nature to talk straight.

The novel, as well as the movie, begins on an August day of 1945, with a party thrown to celebrate the Don's daughter Connie's marriage. The venue is the spacious lawns in the Corleone villa on Long Beach, New York, where a large number of his friends, admirers and protégés are having a gala time. They carry envelopes full of dollars, to offer the bridal couple as a token of their submission to the overlord. Despite it being his daughter's wedding day, Godfather has made himself available for private audience in his study. He occasionally withdraws from the celebrations to step into the study, and listens to people's grievances. This is an auspicious day, the supplicants know, and he is not likely to turn down their petition.

One of his admirers is the singing star, 'Johnny' Fontane, who has flown across 3000 miles to be with his godfather. In his early days Johnny had been trapped in a rather vexatious contract. The remedy was simple. Some of the Don's men visited the bandleader and made him an either-or offer. Either his signature or his brains would be on the contract. Johnny now wants a role in a certain movie, but he has been firmly turned away. He wants Godfather to help. Godfather will, too. But the old man also gives him a dressing down about the way Johnny has been ignoring his wife and children, and spending time with a bimbette.

Among others is one Amerigo Bonasera, an undertaker by profession. His darling daughter has been cruelly used by her boyfriend. 'Two months ago he took her for a drive, with another boyfriend,' he tells the Don. 'They made her drink whiskey and then they tried to take advantage of her. She resisted. She kept her honour. So they beat her...like an animal. When I went to the hospital her nose was broken. Her jaw was shattered, held together by wire. She couldn't even weep because of the pain.... The judge sentenced them to three years in prison, and suspended the sentence. Suspended sentence! They went free that very day! I stood in the courtroom like a fool, and those two bastards, they smiled at me.' He begs the Don to uproot the thorn from its very root. Vito can't do that. That wouldn't be fair; his daughter is still alive. He promises to give him justice in exact measure, and true to promise, he gets the boys crippled and sent to hospital.

There are some wonderful character portraits in the novel. Puzo does not allow the story to leave the human frame to zoom off into too many flights of imagination. The opening wedding celebration episode is full of typical party chit-chat. Sonny's roving eye rests on his sister's bridesmaid Lucy Mancini; while he is measuring her up, his wife Sandra is discussing him and his philandering with her friends. She says she knew of his profligacy within a year of their marriage, had heaved a huge sigh of relief and offered a candle at the church. This confession titillates Lucy no end, writes Puzo, and she sends positive responses to Sonny's amorous signals. Easing themselves out of the company outside, they meet indoors and indulge their passion.

Fontane desperately wants this role in Jack Woltz's movie, so Vito dispatches Tom Hagen, his consigliere, to deliberate with the studio head. Jack is a tough cookie, with a weakness for young girls and race horses. He takes Tom around for a walk to his stable, and shows off his prize-horse Khartoum, worth millions of dollars. Boor that he is, he points at the horse's penis and laughingly wishes he had a weapon like that! As for offering Johnny a break, he rejects the request outright. 'Let me lay it on the line for you and your boss, whoever he is! Johnny Fontane will never get that movie!'

One night, the arrogant Woltz wakes up in his bed with a terrible start, as if he has snapped out of a nightmare. He pats around, and finds his hands dripping with blood. Then his eyes fall upon the severed head of his favourite Khartoum. He shrieks like a mad man, calls up Tom instantly, and lets loose a torrent of abuses. But the message has reached him. For all the guards and security that surrounds him, he is not safe. He announces the selection of Johnny Fontane to play the central part in his movie.

Vito Corleone, the gangster, created by Mario Puzo and presented on celluloid by Coppola, is altogether out of the ordinary. He has the muscle to spill blood and spread terror, but he also has breadth of heart and benevolence of mind. He possesses instruments of violence which he uses mercilessly when the occasion demands; but for the ordinary sufferer he has sympathy and succour. And he has a very, very sharp brain.

Tom Hagen came to him as an orphan and grew up with the Corleone family as an adopted son. After getting himself a degree in law he does not attend court, but functions as Don Vito's confidante and advisor—a consigliere. His life begins and ends with the Corleones. For all his extreme intelligence, he is no match for the Don, and is happy to be his acolyte. Many of America's judges and senior police officers are on Godfather's rolls. The weight that he carries in the police department, and the justice that he delivers, none of the other families can even remotely match.

Vito is also a master at convincing. At the discussion table he has no competition. Tom has often witnessed marathon sessions where the Don has held counsel for eight continuous hours, without getting irritated, without getting angry, laying out his points and plodding on coolly with persuasive arguments. If the occasion demands he swallows insults, absorbs threats, but labours on till he finally emerges as the winner. It's quite another thing that those who constrict or obstruct manage to die in a hurry.

Vito Corleone's hands are bathed in crime. If it serves his needs to slit open a person's throat, he does so with complete nonchalance and no compunction. At the same time, he does not want his own children to inherit this kind of life. He so much hopes that his son Michael will become a really important person like the governor of a state, or a senator.

A poison tree can only bear bitter fruits. Sonny is a living example of this adage. From his student days he had begun walking into his father's footsteps. As a very young boy he had witnessed his father bump off the local enforcer Falucci. Still later, when some Irish rebels had pumped bullets into Vito's chests, it was Sonny who had held the band together. He had eliminated plenty of rival shooters on his own. The father-son duo exploits the uncertainties of war time and strengthens its finances, its violence and its overall dominance. Sonny's reputation for violence is so notorious that his very name makes rivals shiver.

Narcotics is the emerging field of activity in gangsterdom, because the profits are huge. But the police and the legal departments come down particularly strongly on these activities. The other families are aware of Vito's oft-stated desire for cooperation. Also knowing how well connected he is, on behalf of the others, Sollozzo offers Vito a very lucrative deal. Vito turns it down on two counts: (a) he believes selling narcotics is sinful, and (b) he is sure his connections would never approve of it. As a result, he is gunned down in the marketplace. Despite the many bullets lodged in him, the Don survives, and is immediately hospitalised.

Violence, for the Mafiosi, is part of business. They turn upon one another, they let blood flow, and unleash unbridled violence without infringing their moral code. It is all

'A friend should always underestimete your virtues and an enemy your faults.

From Left to Right: Al Pacino (Michael), Marlon Brando (Don Vito Corleone), James Caan (Sonny) and John Cazale (Fredo) in *The Godfather*. COURTESY: WWW.DOCTORMACRO.COM

business. The youngest son, Michael, goes to the hospital to see his father. From the way things are laid out, indications are clear that the enemy is going to mount another attack on his father's life. With great courage, secrecy and dispatch he gets the old man shifted to another room. There he runs into Captain McCluskey, the police officer who has been bought over by the enemy. There is a small altercation and McCluskey punches Michael so hard that he breaks his jaw.

Crises keep mounting upon Michael and his father. The despicable, near-fatal attack on his father and the corruption permeating the police force transform Michael. He flips from being a god-fearing person with middle-class ambitions of professorship to a fearful don-in-the-making. To inaugurate his new life he kills both Sollozzo and the redoubtable McCluskey, and escapes to Italy.

There have been many occasions when Vito Corleone has jumped into waves of violence, and sometimes also initiated them. There have been other occasions when the waves have come rolling in at his doorstep—unprovoked and unexpected. The Don keeps his daughter Connie's husband Carlo Rizzi away from his business. Wherever there is power, whether legally acquired or snatched by force, there will always be people who want a share of the benefits; and not just the immediate family, but relatives, close and distant, friends and sundry acquaintances, all would want a piece of the cake, and feel upset if denied.

Carlo badly wants a big slice, and resents being deliberately kept out of the game. Once he beats up his wife, and Sonny happens to see the black eye he has given her. Despite his sister's protestations, he goes up to Carlo and gives him a merciless thrashing. Sonny has always been a flint in the eye for his business rivals. They utilise Carlo's grievances against Sonny, learn about his movement, waylay him at a check-point, and riddle his body to a sieve with machine-gun fire. Puzo has painted a gripping word picture of this episode in his novel, which Coppola has converted with equal impact for the screen.

The naked violence comes home to roost for the Don. He cannot find the courage to show his firstborn's shredded body to his wife. It is his undertaker friend Amerigo Bonasera who is called in to do some cosmetic work on the corpse before the mother can see it. His eldest son cut down in the prime of youth; his second son Fredo a pleasure-loving softie; his youngest, Michael, in forced exile in Italy—Vito does not have the strength of his youth now to absorb these shocks, but he battles on with fortitude.

Having gone underground in Italy, Michael falls in love with a shepherd girl named Apollonia Vitelli, and after duly proposing for her hand, gets married to her. Puzo has given this love story such a dream-like quality, located it in such a romantic haze and used such honey-laced language to narrate it that it needs to be read in the original. The entire episode has been covered in the movie; but only on experiencing both the versions does one realise the limitations of the cameraman's eye in reproducing the gossamer, ephemeral atmosphere created by the words. Michael's enemies, however, have traced him up to his sylvan den, and planted a bomb in his car to blow him up. While Michael escapes, the stunningly beautiful village belle, Apollonia, becomes the unintended victim of the explosion.

The novel goes into great details on Vito's moves to get Michael back home. He runs well-planned press stories to reveal to the readers the nefarious side of the murdered police, Captain McCluskey. He locates the case of a criminal who has been sentenced to death. After satisfying himself that there is no saving him from the gallows, Vito offers him a deal: he should take upon himself the responsibility of having killed Sollozzo and McCluskey, in return for which the Don would take good care of his family. Accordingly, the man confesses in court to having killed the two, which the court accepts. Michael is now officially absolved of the crime, and a major roadblock to his return is removed.

Vito Corleone is keenly aware that Michael is going to face the heat from his rivals on his return to America. To bring down the temperature, he calls for a secret conclave of the five families of the crime world. There have been numerous imitations of such gang-lord meetings in Hindi films, even to the extent of creating 'Families'. It has to be clarified that this conclave is not of petty thieves, but of their controllers, their overlords. The participants in this one discuss the bad name their community is earning on account of young, frivolous upstarts getting into the field. The bad-old days of flaunting weapons are over. The need is for them to turn smart and cunning like entrepreneurs in other professions.

'You talk about vengeance,' Vito addresses them. 'Is vengeance going to bring your son back to you or my boy to me? I forgo the vengeance of my son. But my youngest son had to leave this country because of this Sollozzo business. So now I have to make arrangements to bring him back safely cleared of all these false charges. But I'm a superstitious man. And if some unlucky accident should befall him, if he should be shot in the head by a police officer, or if he should hang himself in his jail cell, or if he's struck by a bolt of lightning...then I'm going to blame some of the people in this room...and that, I do not forgive. But, that aside, let me say that I swear, on the souls of my grandchildren, that I will not be the one to break the peace we have made here today.' The peace offering as well as the warning sinks in. The book devotes 24 pages to this episode, while the movie covers it with a few well-chosen words and shots extending over a few minutes.

Michael gets to know of the complicity of his brother-in-law, Carlo, in the killing of Sonny. He is in a cold rage. He has also committed himself to become his sister's child's godfather. Matters move much faster and far more grippingly on the screen than they do in the book. There are fascinating montages, juxtaposed against one another. On the one side is the swift elimination of Carlo and of rivals like Barzini and Tattaglia, all orchestrated by Michael; on the other side is the baptismal ceremony of Carlo and Connie's son, with all its associated rituals and innocent fun.

Mario Puzo wrote the *The Godfather* in 1968, sketching out numerous aspects of the underbelly of American society—the struggle for dominance, corruption, organised violence, self-deception, destruction.

An Italian by birth, Mario Puzo grew up in the New York district of Hell's Kitchen. His mother had wanted him to become a clerk in the railways and earn a decent living; but from the age of sixteen, there was only one thing he wanted to be—a writer. The mother was convinced that her boy was heading towards being a wastrel. With the coming of the Second World War, Puzo joined the US Air Force and was posted in the South-East Asian theatre of the Second World War. Later he also spent some time with the German Air Force.

His first novel, *Dark Arena,* was published in 1955. His next work, *Fortunate Pilgrim* came a full decade later. He then took a stroll in the area of youth literature. But there was neither recognition nor popularity, and therefore no money coming his way. He had accumulated a debt of $20,000, and, as a result, had to display a good lot of enterprise in ducking friends, relatives and sundry other lenders, and responding to bank notices. No wonder, morale was running low.

At 45, he began realising that he was not likely to turn out any classic to place him in the ranks of Tolstoy or Dostoyevsky. So how about becoming practical, and trying to turn out stuff that would fetch him some money? His *Fortunate Pilgrim* had the character of a gangster, and his friends thought that was where his strength lay. He could put that character as a central figure and write something different, they suggested. He took in hand the writing of a novel which he tentatively named *Mafia*, the story of an Italian Mafia that had created a powerful criminal empire. Ideas came rushing. He belonged to a community of Italian immigrants, he had heard about the deeds of many, there

'I don't trust society to protect us, I have no intention of placing my fate in the hands of men whose only qualification is that they managed to con a block of people to vote for them.

were the newspaper reports and his own research. He wrote on furiously. In the frenzy of writing, he has no memory when the name changed from *Mafia* to *The Godfather*.

In 1968 he handed over the first hundred pages of some very crisp writing to his literary agent and left with his family for a tour of Europe. When he returned, there was a shock waiting for him—a pleasant one. A publisher was impressed enough with those hundred pages to offer him a fee of $410,000 as advance payment for paperback rights. It was an eye-popping figure, never before offered to any author, that too for only the paperback rights!

The book became an instant hit. Since the book also delves on the influence that the underworld exercises on the Hollywood cinema industry, immediately after the book was published, tongues began wagging about the similarity between one of its characters, Fontane, and the singer-actor star Frank Sinatra. Although Puzo was at pains to insist that the character of Johnny Fontane was NOT based on Frank Sinatra, many assumed that it was, and Sinatra was furious; when he met Puzo at a restaurant he screamed vulgar terms and threats at Puzo.

For sixty-seven consecutive weeks it remained on top of the *New York Times* bestsellers list. A delightful translation of the book has been done in Marathi by Ravindra Gurjar, which also has gone into many editions.

Spawning imitations of *The Godfather* has become a kind of cottage industry. Ram Gopal Varma's *Sarkaar*, where an effort has been made to present a number of *The Godfather* characters in native Indian ambience and apparel is a poor imitation of the original classic.

The original movie alone has done business worth $268 million worldwide. When combined with its sequels *The Godfather II* and *The Godfather III*, it has grossed $3.5 billion. On the one hand, it smashed box-office records created by *Gone with the Wind* and *The Sound of Music*; on the other, it is now ranked as the second greatest film in American cinematic history—after *Citizen Kane*. There are many examples of classics being converted into successful, popular movies. But the book *The Godfather* was no classic; it was a regular crime-thriller—pulp fiction! Examples of popular fiction giving birth to a classic cinema are rare!

This extraordinary story of a gangster's life was tailor-made material for making a money-spinning movie. But when this nugget of gold landed in the hands of a gifted director like Francis Ford Coppola, he brought all his skills into play and brought out an invaluable, imperishable work of celluloid art. Paramount Studios then was going through a lean period, and wanted the movie to be produced with the minimum of expenses. A number of top-flight directors had turned down their offer. When the offer was first made to Coppola, he too read the first fifty pages of the book and did not find it exciting enough, and rejected it. The young man felt deep inside him that he would bring out a classic someday, soon.

Meanwhile, the novel went on shooting up the popularity charts. Coppola himself was going through financial difficulties. Surprisingly, Albert S. Ruddy, a producer in the Paramount stable, once more got back to Coppola with the *The Godfather* question.

Coppola went back to the book again, this time with greater commitment. Sure enough, as he read on, he discovered the pith, the essential substance that lay in the depths of the story. The story is not about one powerful gangster and his shenanigans. It is the story of a family, its thirst for power, its lines of inheritance. If the extraneous stuff surrounding the kernel could be shaved away, there would be material left for a great movie, felt Coppola. He later confessed that the primary reason for his accepting the movie was the desire for money. But what came along with the flower was also its heady fragrance. Coppola's genius transformed a commonplace thriller into a work of art.

The Godfather became a vehicle that propelled a thirty-two-year-old director named Francis Ford Coppola and seated him among the ranks of the greatest directors of the world. Who was this Coppola? What contributions had he made to this domain before *The Godfather* arrived? At the time, Coppola had directed just a few barely noticed feature films, the most notable of which was the adaptation of the stage musical *Finian's Rainbow*—although he had also received an Academy Award for co-writing *Patton* in 1970.

As with Mario Puzo, Francis was born in an Italian-American family at Detroit, on 7 April 1939. His father Carmine was a flautist with the Detroit Symphony Orchestra. Along with being a flautist, he looked after the administration of radio programmes. Two years later Carmine joined the NBC Symphony Orchestra, and the family moved to New York City. At age nine, Francis was struck by polio, on account of which he was compelled to stay confined to bed for large periods of his childhood.

The polio confinement brought benefits too. During those days he watched large numbers of TV serials and movies. He even picked up an 8 mm camera and shot himself a few movies. He was deeply impressed by the works of the Russian master, Sergei Eisenstein. As a young man he took to scriptwriting. *Reflection in a Golden Eye* was his script, although it was not acknowledged as such in the credits. He was happy enough that the great Marlon Brando was mouthing his words. That he would work with him to create celluloid history with *The Godfather* was still ten years into the future. Coppola loved Shakespeare's *Julius Caesar*. As a young actor Marlon Brando had played one of the central roles of Mark Antony in the screen version. At the death of Julius Caesar, Antony addresses the Romans from the Senate steps. This speech has long been acknowledged as the greatest piece of address ever composed. Watching Marlon Brando deliver that peroration is enough to give goosebumps to any lover of literature. It is this histrionic magic of Brando that would have planted a seed somewhere in young Coppola's heart; and made him insist upon getting the thespian to portray Vito Corleone in *The Godfather*.

Paramount was very keen on making a low-budget movie on the Puzo book, and appointed A.I. Ruddy as the producer. Ruddy was determined to have an Italian-American direct the movie, and finally zeroed in on young Coppola. Coppola had just collected for himself an Oscar for Best Screenplay for *Patton*, and it helped the young man to come to the notice of people who mattered. Once he had taken the project in hand, Coppola set about immersing himself into the story. In his next meeting with Ruddy he presented his script in the form of a play. He pitched strongly and insistently to the assembled board of directors on exactly how he proposed to mount the movie. Ruddy realised that while Coppola was a relative newcomer, his concepts were very clear. Here was a director who would stand up to the studio bosses and not let them dictate terms. It was in September 1970 that Paramount announced the name of Francis Ford Coppola as the director of their next venture—*The Godfather*.

Although Coppola was an accomplished scriptwriter, it was a challenge for him to encapsulate into a few screen-hours what Puzo had taken 446 pages to roll out. The dark underworld of the American Mafia—its blood-curdling violence, the terror it spread over whatever it touched, the betrayals and sell-outs, the stark fear that accompanied like a shadow, the chilling suspicions—was a world as dangerous as the tip of a sharp sword. Coppola and Puzo put their heads together and, after much hacking, slicing and paring, came out with a manageable 150-page document.

A novelist never has the constraint of expressing himself within a couple of hours. His tendency is to spread himself out in luxurious ease. Hence the belief in Hollywood is that a novelist can never be a good scriptwriter, and the unwritten rule is never to entrust the job to him. Ruddy, therefore, was made to answer a lot of questions when Puzo was taken on board for writing the screenplay. Ruddy's logic was that a writer who could hold millions of readers spellbound would certainly have the magical sensibility to turn out a good script.

During their joint venture with the script Coppola and Puzo became good friends and developed a fine understanding. They both belonged to Italian-American families, and had a first-hand understanding of Italian traditions, cuisine, values and style of life. Meanwhile, word had spread about a Mafia movie being made, and many Italian-Americans were worried that the movie would show their community in a negative light and bring them a bad name. Many citizens' groups organised protests across cities in America. Coppola and Puzo, however, turned a blind eye and stayed immersed in locating contacts in the underworld.

During the casting, Paramount had announced that it would provide opportunities to new faces; as a result it received thousands of photographs of struggling wannabes hoping for a break. There was considerable curiosity across the country about the central role of Don Vito Corleone. A number of senior actors like Danny Thomson were very eager to land the part: on one hand a cruel and violent gangster Don, on the other a humble and simple,

'Never hate your enemies. It affects your judgment.'

deeply caring family man. Although his appearance on the screen is about forty per cent of the time, his influence is such that his power and his spirit brood over the other sixty per cent. The portrayal of the character certainly required histrionic talents of the highest order, as also worldwide acceptance through sheer force of personality—in other words an actor with an established reputation for forceful performances. Coppola could imagine no one else fitting the bill as well as Marlon Brando.

Before the arrival of *The Godfather*, the name Marlon Brando would conjure up for the movie-lover the image of a handsome romantic lover or a red-blooded rebel. Came *The Godfather*, the movie, and the thespian portrayed the Mafioso Don Vito Corleone with absolutely stunning credibility. The degree of identification he acquired with the character is unprecedented, and probably unsurpassable. When he died, people could hardly think of him in any other image than the bulldog-faced don.

Long before Brando was brought on board, Puzo had sent him a copy of his book, but the response was cold. Brando's colleague also pitched in with a strong recommendation. Here was an opportunity that had come walking to his doorstep. Puzo too continued with his efforts, assuring him that he alone had the talent to realise the character of Godfather on the screen.

Brando was already a legend with scores of hits and critically acclaimed films like *On the Waterfront* and *A Streetcar Named Desire* behind him. But during the sixties he had accumulated as much notoriety as fame. His private life was no less full of colourful episodes, fairy-tale happenings and enigmatic aura than that of a Mafia don. He held a fatal attraction for his large army of women admirers, some of whom are reputed to have committed suicide in a fit of passion. The cavalier tendencies such immeasurable fame brought with it were frightening. He indulged in all the vices associated with super stardom, such as reporting late on the sets, gross indiscipline and scraps with directors. The Executive Vice-President Paramount Studios, Stanley R. Jaffe is known to have shouted his colleagues down saying that he would not tolerate so much as a discussion of the undependable Brando's name in his Studio, let alone consider offering him a role. 'Marlon Brando will never appear in this motion picture', he declared. After much pleadings, Coppola was allowed to cast Brando only if he appeared in the film for much less salary than his previous films, perform a screen test, and sign a bond saying that he would not cause any delay in the production (as he had done on previous film sets).

Coppola now had the problem of persuading the phenomenon named Brando to take a screen test! Fortunately, Brando too was enamoured of the vast histrionic dimensions of playing Vito Corleone. When Coppola reached him video camera in hand, Brando was in a kimono, hair tied up in a ponytail. He stuffed tissue papers low in his cheeks and gave Coppola a sampling of the bulldog-jowled Don that we now so well know. With some make-up, the forty-seven-year-old actor had transformed himself into a sixty-five-year-old patriarch.

Al Pacino, who rode to superstardom on *The Godfather* has an equally absorbing casting history. Coppola could visualise Al Pacino as the dreamy-eyed young Michael with middle-class tendencies metamorphosing himself into a cold-blooded gangster. But a great many people at Paramount simply didn't like his face. During the shooting there would be snide comments: 'What kind of an actor is this?'; 'He will take the movie down with him!' Pacino had been struggling for this break for the last decade-and-a-half or more. He had quit high school, chasing his dream of Hollywood movies. He slept on cots lent by friends, and managed to eke out a marginal existence on the strength of a dream. When he was put through repeated tests, his heart sank for fear that the role was slipping out of his hands. But as the footage began assembling on the editing table, the winds began changing. The wife of a board director told Coppola to instantly perish the thought of replacing Pacino. His manner of looking alone had the power to strip a person naked!

The movie began with an initial budget allotment of two million dollars. But even before the shooting began, it was revised to six million. The expenditure for a day's shooting was $40,000, i.e. $5,000 per hour. Make-up man Dick Smith laboured for 90 minutes each day fixing Brando as the Don. Flesh coloured acrylic mouthpieces, specially prepared by a dentist, were stuffed into both his cheeks and fused to his teeth; a padding was tied over his belly; his shoulders were padded up too, making his neck look stodgy; his shoes were loaded with weights to make his gait slow and heavy.

Coppola put in a year of hard work before the shooting began. Starting a good five months later than scheduled, it took the cast and crew to Manhattan, Las Vegas, Long Beach, New Jersey and Sicily. Dressed in loose clothing, the 32-year-old Coppola would report on the sets much before anyone else, and was always the last to leave. There seemed to be no end to the back-breaking ordeal that he had invited upon himself. The earliest scenes filmed were Brando's going to hospital and a few other passing shots. The rushes did not impress many, and vicious whispers started circulating. Conjectures were being made on who would be booted out first—Coppola or Pacino. Coppola would hear nasty remarks come wafting out of the toilets: 'Which stupid ass got this person to be the director?'; 'What can even a master actor like Brando do with an incompetent director?' The dissatisfaction of the senior management at Paramount also began surfacing. As a result, the atmosphere prevailing on the sets would be tense and disturbing.

Another piece of news bubbled up on the sets one day: the famous director Elia Kazan would take over as director! Who did not know the equation that existed between Kazan and Brando? Even the spot-boys were loudly and audibly sure that Kazan alone could do justice to Brando's talents. Two of Coppola's assistants would carry a daily supply of vicious tales to their masters at the Studio. Despite his resilience, Coppola began to feel the disheartening pressure of these unsavoury goings-on. He reported later that he once dreamt that Kazan had arrived on the sets and snatched away the director's baton from him.

An interesting tale that did the rounds was that the spirit of the horse whose head had been used was haunting the sets. Coppola was getting desperate with insecurity. It was Brando who burst his dam one day. In the middle of a shot he growled at the detractors that they could report to their dumb bosses at the Studio that if they removed Coppola as director, he would pack his bags and leave too. Coppola couldn't hold his tears back at hearing these words of support from his idol.

Slowly but surely, the tide began to turn for Coppola. As more and more scenes began arriving in the lab, it started getting evident that a most unusual movie was in the process of taking shape. Coppola's personal life also began changing for the better. While the shooting was on, he became the father of a girl they named Sofia. It was also around this time that the

Oscar announcement was made declaring him as the Best Screenplay writer for *Patton*. The Paramount bigwigs began sensing the unusual strength that lay in their director. He did not go to Los Angeles to receive his first ever Oscar, as if to suggest that he knew next year he would be fetching the same award for Best Movie and Best Director. In the end neither Coppola went out, nor did Al Pacino. Those who were shown the door were the two detracting assistants.

Both Coppola and his cameraman Gordon Willis were determined that they would come out with something way out of the ordinary. Before he landed *The Godfather*, Willis had been with the movie medium for about two years. Before that he had done some internship in still photography and documentaries. The two of them took some deliberate, conscious decisions. The sets would be low on colour and low on light. Large portions of the movie have been shot in tight close-ups with 40 to 75 mm close-up lenses to create the dark, secretive world of crime.

While the rest of Hollywood was chasing flash and glitter, Willis was busy carving his own realistic groove. There was no Oscar waiting for him for *The Godfather.* In fact, for the next seven years, the various films that he shot received as many as forty Oscars in one department or the other, but never for cinematography. The judges did not much understand his style. 'What kind of cinematographer is this, who does not have the sense to throw a simple spot on Brando's eyes?' They didn't realise that, to begin with, Willis was forced to use overhead lighting for Marlon Brando's scenes because of his make-up. He and Coppola then decided it created a sinister ambience too, not letting his eyes reveal what was cooking in the Don's mind. They decided to extend it throughout, which is one reason the movie is so dark.

Willis went on to make *Manhattan* in black-and-white which showcased his cinematographic class. The recognition by the Oscar Academy, however, took a long time coming. He was later nominated twice, once for his inventive recreation of 1920s photography in Woody Allen's *Zelig*, and then for *The Godfather Part III* (1990). In 2009, at the inaugural Governor's Awards, the Academy chose Willis as the recipient of the Academy Honorary Award for his life's work. Today he runs a flourishing school of cinematography.

While planning the filming, both Coppola and Willis were strongly conscious of its being a period film. The zoom lens was thus discarded, and the two masters staked their talents at composing each frame as if it were

‘Great men are not born great, they grow great...

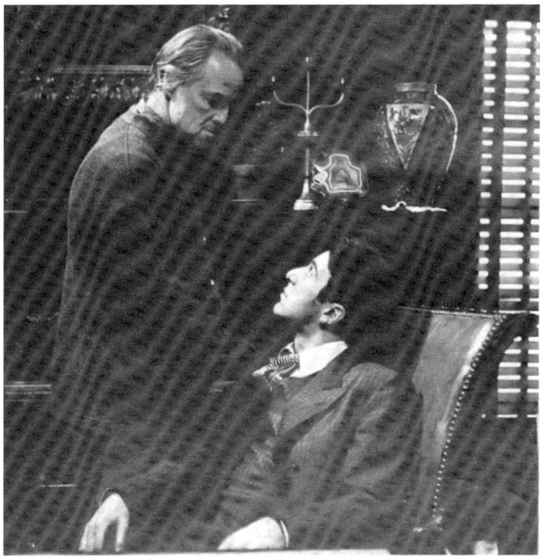

Marlon Brando and Al Pacino in *The Godfather* (1972), directed by Francis Ford Coppola.
COURTESY: AUTHOR

a painting. Their partnership flourished right up to *The Godfather Part III*. During the shooting of the original, though, they were notorious for their frequent scraps on the sets. Coppola would frequently change the angles that Willis had set, forget the discussions held earlier, and send Willis into paroxysms of fury. Coppola would then scream and shout and leave the set to sulk in his room. Willis would promptly march off and sit fuming in his van. Once Coppola so lost his temper that he kicked the door of his room hard and brought it off its hinges. Brando, observing these battles, often joked about them with his colleagues. ‘I thought only the film is about gangsters!’ he had quipped.

Some very interesting facts come out when one reads the biographies and interviews of the cast and crew of *The Godfather*. The quarrel between Coppola and Willis was of course a clash of personalities. But those who knew them say that with this mechanism each squeezed out the best that was in the other. Amazingly, the man who carried the biggest notoriety of being undisciplined, Godfather Brando, behaved like a saint all through. On the first day he had missed his flight, but after that he never gave the crew any cause for complaint. He had got the Paramount people to sign a contract that would entitle him to pay $40,000 of compensation for every week of work beyond the schedule. The production did overshoot the schedule, but Brando did not claim the compensation. He seemed to have realised that what was being created here was an extraordinary piece of art.

While writing *The Godfather*, Mario Puzo had stated that a hundred gun-toting criminals do not get as much for their effort as a lawyer carries away in his briefcase. Puzo, of course, simply narrated the story of the gun. Coppola, however, brought out the human souls that lie hiding behind the steel. James Caan as Sonny, Al Pacino as Michael and Marlon Brando as Don Corleone, Coppola managed to extract the best that these actors had to offer.

Woltz's discovery of the severed head of his horse is easily the most jolting scene in the film. Paramount had suggested that Coppola should make do with a rubber head. But Coppola was assured of procuring a real head from a New Jersey slaughterhouse. It was delivered to him by a dog-food company. The shooting of this episode is said to have so shaken John Marley, who plays Jack Woltz, that for the next few weeks he could not sleep!

The Godfather may well be considered as a festival of histrionics. The second of the series, *The Godfather II*, is regarded by many critics as the superior of the two.

After the unprecedented success of *The Godfather*, Coppola advised one of his assistants that if he really wanted to be a successful director, he should ensure three things. First, he should have a complete, perfect script in hand, allowing for a minor adjustment here and there. Second, he should work with technicians on whom he has complete faith. He should work with a unit that offers him a sense of deep satisfaction; it should preferably be a unit with which he has worked before. The third important advice was that he should always keep his cast happy and contented, which would guarantee their sincerity and commitment.

The assistant was delighted with these pearls of wisdom. But as he was shaking hands with his mentor, Coppola turned grave, put his hands upon his assistant's shoulder, and confessed that when he was making *The Godfather*, he did not have even one of the three factors working for him.

The great Marlon Brando passed away in 2004. In his library was a manuscript of *The Godfather* that he had acquired during the making of the movie, which was littered with markings and margin notes. When this historically significant manuscript was put up for auction in 2005, it fetched a whopping sum of $312,800, the highest price ever paid for a manuscript. It is not as if crime and violence have not been depicted on the screen before. It is just that the swollen, ugly human face of this dark world has been more efficaciously delineated than ever before in *The Godfather*—the novel as well as the movie.

SCHINDLER'S LIST

AUTHOR Thomas Keneally **PUBLISHED** 1982
DIRECTOR Stephen Spielberg **PREMIERED** 1993

'The List is Life.'

The Second World War that so blighted human life, and the unbridled savagery it brought upon the hapless Jews have formed the subject matter of hundreds of books the world over, and have spawned heaps of movies too, like: *The Diary of Anne Frank* and *Life Is Beautiful*.

The twister winds of the War turned round later and uprooted the mighty oaks of Hitler and Mussolini, razing to the ground their murderous regimes. While the war years were ruinous for the common citizen, there were many who exploited the turbulence of the times and made massive fortunes. It was festival time for Schindler's tribe of profiteers and extortionists.

Oskar Schindler, a member of the Nazi party was a wheeler-dealer who had amassed a vast fortune for himself. But remarkably, he also became the unlikely saviour of the lives of 1100 Jews in the Kraków ghetto in Poland. The story of this unusual person was the subject matter of Australian writer Thomas Keneally's book *Schindler's Ark* (later published in the US as *Schindler's List*). The novelty of the central character brought the book immediate success, and it also bagged the Booker Prize for best fiction in 1982.

'[T]he war…brings out the worst in people, never the good, always the bad, always the bad!' Schindler says at a moment of exasperation. Except that it was this war that brought the best out of him. Thomas Keneally's fact-based novel *Schindler's Ark*, chronicled, through first-person accounts, the amazing story of the *Schindlerjuden* literally translated as 'Schindler Jews'. Roughly 1,100 of them saved by Oskar Schindler during the Holocaust.

At a full six feet height, with a wide brow, his small, beady eyes, Oskar Schindler exuded an enigmatic persona. These are features that strike us at first appearance in the movie, where we see him hovering around a railway station near Kraków, Poland, where over 10,000 families arrive every day from the countryside, for relocation, to the Kraków ghetto. Orders have been given for the construction of a new forced labour camp at Płaszów on the outskirts of Kraków, where these Jews would be, eventually, incarcerated. While a 24-member Jewish Council (*Judenrat*) oversees this relocation the entire work progresses under the eyes of the feared and utterly merciless SS (*Schutzstaffel*) Guards.

Here, Schindler makes the acquaintance of Itzhak Stern (Ben Kingsley), who, he believes, would be of great use to him. He has finalised plans of starting a factory for enamelled utensils, and intends to use Jewish labour for the purpose, as it will come cheap and help him make enormous profits.

Schindler has not an iota of knowledge about the enamel industry, but he does have a sharp eye for people. He appoints Stern as his accountant and has him gather the incarcerated Jewish traders surreptitiously at the gates of the ghetto. He gets the reluctant traders to invest in his enterprise by reminding them of the circumstances in which they are placed. The labour—Jewish; the capital—Jewish; the massive profits, however, would be Schindler's, except for a small share of the profits to the investors. He picks out eighteen smart young Jewish girls as his secretaries, and supplies them for gratification to German Nazi officials to keep them happy. He enrols a large number of Polish Jews as workers, restarts an old, abandoned factory, and starts making hefty profits. The early image of Schindler is of a lecherous, hedonistic, tippling, eccentric profiteer. All he cares for is raking in money, by hook or by crook.

The arrival of SS Lieutenant, Untersturmführer Amon Goeth (Ralph Fiennes) on the scene results in an immediate rise in atrocities on the Jews. Both, the book as well as the movie, paint him out as utterly wicked. He is in fact a noxious animal. The coming together of Schindler and Goeth, their confrontations, their underhand machinations to promote their own individual agendas, leave one speechless.

There are similarities as well as differences between Amon Goeth and Oskar Schindler. They both love their drinks, both are womanisers and love to philander. For

Goeth the greatest satisfaction lies in slitting people's throats and killing them. Schindler, in contrast, exploits Goeth's gerrymandering tendencies, keeps him supplied with women, and manages to save hundreds of lives.

As soon as the Płaszów Camp is completed in March 1943, Goeth orders the final liquidation of the Kraków ghetto, and Operation Reinhard[1] begins, with hundreds of troops emptying the cramped rooms of their inhabitants and arbitrarily murdering anyone who protests, or appears uncooperative, or is elderly or infirm

At one point, while they are drinking together, Goeth tells Schindler, 'Control is power, that's power.' Schindler asks Goeth, 'Is that why they fear us?'

'It's that we have the f***ing right to kill this way that they fear us.'

'They fear us,' responds Schindler, 'because we kill arbitrarily.'

It is in exercise of this untrammelled right that Goeth indulges his bloodlust. Six hundred years ago the Jews had come and settled in Kraków. Goeth's instructions are—they should be gathered back into history in six hours! And he gets it done! The Nazis let loose a reign of terror upon the entire Jewish community—big and small, rich and poor, young and old. Schindler has the privilege of watching it from a ringside seat and it affects him profoundly. The barking of ferocious dogs; the belching of orders from excited German officers; the tramp-tramp-tramp of army boots; frozen with fear carefully hidden young kids, popping out from everywhere.

A young boy is shown trying to escape! A German trains his rifle on him! The father screams, and is instantly shredded! The boy is of course caught and killed too! To save them humiliation and physical torture, nurses and doctors serve poison to their patients. The soldiers spray them with bullets anyway to ensure that they are dead!

How far does one run? Where does one hide from these German hordes? In the toilet, up in the attic, down the manholes into the flowing gutter, inside the cavities of beds? Timid, hesitant kids look frantically around! The spaces behind the planks, under the floorboards, on the lofts have already been taken! A mother comes running with her girl. A woman from inside screams, 'I can take the girl, but not you!' Mother and girl separate. A person is trying to hide inside a wooden cabinet on the upper storey. He steps upon the piano key. The sound travels, and the Sten gun carrying soldiers trample up the stairs. There, in the narrow spaces they sense life, and let loose a volley of bullets. Festival time sparklers dance in the air, and human beings come tumbling down from every cranny!

---

[1] Operation Reinhard marked the most deadly phase of the Holocaust with the introduction of extermination camps.

At the Płaszów Camp, men and women are housed separately. Since the young and attractive among the women are picked out for other purposes, some daub themselves with shoe polish to look ugly, and some rub blood on their cheeks and lips in an effort to look healthy. These are the poor, helpless unfortunates that Schindler is losing his sleep to save. Whatever wealth he has accumulated, he puts it all at stake for his mission.

In one last ditch effort at saving as many Jews as he can from being shipped for the Final Solution[2] to Auschwitz, Schindler proposes to start an artillery shells factory in his own home of Zwittau-Brinnlitz in Moravia, Czechoslovakia. To get the prisoners under his charge, he empties literally cases upon cases of Reichsmarks at Goeth's feet. But the artillery shells factory at Brinnlitz is for pulling wool over the eyes of the German authorities. In the seven months of its existence it does not produce a single shell! What it does do is to keep its workers alive. Millions upon millions of Reichsmarks, however, are spent in bribing Nazi officials and buying shells from other companies.

The Second World War gets over, and the destruction and genocide come to a stop. The German regime surrenders to the Allies, and the Jews are overwhelmed with joy. Schindler stands before his 1,100 Jews in a victory stance. They have come out with their lives, but Schindler's own problems might just be beginning! He takes up an elevated place to deliver his address to his workers, with the SS Guards standing on the balcony behind. 'At midnight, tonight, the war is over,' he tells them. 'Tomorrow, you begin the process of looking for survivors of your families. In most cases, you won't find them. After six long years of murder, victims are being mourned throughout the world. We've survived....I'm a member of the Nazi party. I'm an ammunitions manufacturer. I'm a profiteer of slave labour. I am a criminal. At midnight you'll be free and I'll be hunted. I'll remain with you till five minutes after midnight, after which, and I hope you'll forgive me, I'll flee.'

During these moments of great upheaval, Schindler shows himself to be a true, upright person possessing a deep wellspring of love. The soldiers who crushed and lacerated the hapless prisoners are right there on the balcony. 'You could leave,' he tells them, 'and return to your families as men instead of murderers.'

A factory worker named Gerath, meanwhile, has melted his gold dental bridge and made it into a ring. It carries the Talmudic quotation, 'Whoever saves one life saves the world entire' engraved on it in Hebrew. This ring is gifted to Schindler as a mark of gratitude, along with a letter proclaiming that he is not a criminal.

---

[2] The Final Solution was formulated in procedural terms in January 1942, at the Wannsee Conference in January 1942.

'Today is history. Today will be remembered. Years from now the young will ask with wonder about this day. Today is history and you are part of it.

Itzhak Stern (Ben Kingsley) taking orders from a SS Guard, in Stephen Spielberg directed *Schindler's List* (1993). COURTESY: AUTHOR

Some extremely arresting events towards the end of the novel have been left out of the movie. While Schindler is dressed in a suit as he bids goodbye, in the book he and his wife Emilie have the POW shirts on their backs. The SS Guards of the movie are allowed to go back to their families, but the book, drawing from its records, says that the Jews take the Commander under their custody. After his pleas for mercy, Schindler intervenes and gets him released. In the movie Schindler is seen as departing alone with his wife in his Mercedes. In reality he was given a proper escort of eight men who followed the couple in their van which also carried his household effects. The movie finishes off on a poetic note. Chapters 37 and 38 of *Schindler's Ark*, which cover the leave-taking scenes, have also been beautifully crafted.

There are a number of minor sub-stories in the novel which have not found place in the film. For instance, Amon Goeth has two bitches named Shulf and Rolls who are utterly ferocious and bloodthirsty, just the kind of animals that a flint-hearted person would relish owning. He loves to let them loose upon the defenceless prisoners and watch the animals shred their prey to ribbons. There is this unspeakably gruesome event of a woman's breasts being torn out of her chest.

The 400-page book was very well received both by lay readers and critics. It could not, however, gain the stature of a classic of the likes of *Anna Karenina*. It is more in the form of a documentary, replete with evidence, attestations, notes, documentations and such other stuff which does make reading heavy. But the nature of the experiences it records is so riveting and extraordinary that it keeps the reader spellbound.

Among the Jews who escaped with their lives due to Schindler's unparalleled effort was one Poldek Pfefferberg, one of the *Schindlerjuden* (Schindler's Jews) who had conspired with his benefactor in saving his brethren's lives. Pfefferberg was very keen that the story of this extraordinary messiah, the saviour of 1100 Polish-Jewish lives, should not remain unsung. It had to be announced to the world, preferably through a movie. As early as 1963 he had tried to get M-G-M interested in the enterprise, but he hadn't quite succeeded.

Pfefferberg ran a leather goods store in Beverly Hills which Keneally happened to visit while looking for a briefcase. Learning that Keneally was a novelist, Pfefferberg related to him a quick synopsis of the Schindler story and showed him his extensive files on the man, kept in two cabinets in his back room. After 50 minutes of entreaties, Pfefferberg was finally able to enthuse Keneally into writing the book.

Keneally, of course, did not limit himself to Pfefferberg's experiences, and embarked upon a detailed research on the subject. He drew up a worldwide itinerary, and went hunting for the Jews of Schindler's time. At the end he had fifty first-hand witnesses, people who had worked on Schindler's project with him. To bring the time period alive, he visited each of the places associated with his hero. This exercise took him to Płaszów, the site of the notorious forced labour camp outside Kraków in Poland, and also the infamous Auschwitz concentration camp. Pfefferberg, who had attached himself to Keneally as his advisor, accompanied him untiringly on this sojourn. Once the research work was over, Keneally finished writing with alacrity. The book *Schindler's Ark* was published in 1982. It was received by the readers with great enthusiasm, and got itself another feather in the shape of the Booker Prize, as the best novel of the year.

One of Spielberg's assistants read the book and sent it with strong recommendations to his boss. Spielberg, however, could not find the time to go through it till a small bout of ill-health created the opportunity. The book hit him hard, so hard that this explosive, unprecedented subject scared him.

As a living legend in the world of cinema and as a director, Spielberg had already established himself as a supreme authority over the medium, by the time he looked at Schindler's List. He had straddled the last two decades of the 20th century with runaway hits like *Close Encounters of the Third Kind, The Poltergeist, Jurassic Park, The Jaws* and *Saving Private Ryan.* The earlier Spielberg movies were replete with scenes of high adventure, resplendent colours, dazzling spectacles; the play of mysterious, superhuman powers, and their mesmeric, sometimes ghoulish hold on the audience that kept them nailed to their seats. His formula for success was simple—pump in extravagant quantities of money, and then line up the wagons to cart it back home from the box-office. A magician who wafted across the deep blue sky on wings of glorious, bizarre, mysterious imaginings!

His first identity was that of a producer-director who gave his audience money's worth. Therefore, when Spielberg announced his intention of converting *Schindler's Ark* into a movie, there were many book lovers who were deeply sceptical. The story had for its background the Holocaust—the inconceivable atrocities let loose upon the Jews by the Nazi regime of Germany during the Second World War and they feared that Spielberg would convert an exceptional novel into melodramatic pulp.

Spielberg himself could not find the courage, initially, to translate this intense novel into silver screen. From the day he finished reading the book, he was hounded by one question: how did an unprincipled, profiteering pleasure-lover like Schindler transform himself into a messiah, a saviour of humankind? What, exactly, were the reasons for this metamorphosis? As Keneally had done before, Spielberg too raised this question with the Holocaust survivors. A predominantly large number of them responded, 'There is only one way of looking at this issue. It is not important to know why Schindler did it; what he did is all that matters.'

Eleven years drifted by during which he looked for other more mature directors who, he believed, could do justice to the subject. He first contacted Roman Polanski, who he knew was himself a survivor of the Holocaust, and Spielberg expected him to find intimacy with the subject and connect well. Polanski, however, was not ready yet to open wounds that had not yet healed. His memories of the Kraków ghetto were still raw, as was the memory of his mother who had been killed at Auschwitz. Later, in 2002, Polanski did make *The Pianist* on the Holocaust theme. Subsequently, Sydney Pollack, Martin Scorsese and Billy Wilder also came into the frame, but nothing came of those meetings.

With the release of *Schindler's List* in December 1993, Spielberg virtually rewrote the grammar of film-making and created for himself an indelible image of a director of genius. *Schindler's List* bagged the Oscar for Best Movie. But more importantly, it became a new school of cinematic learning with its own course of study.

The movie *Schindler's List* runs for 3 hours and 16 minutes, and works an out-of-the-world chemistry on the screen. During the course of the Second World War, as many as 6,000,000 Jews were exterminated. But a more penetrating, a more shocking, a more heart-rending presentation of their afflictions is unlikely to be encountered. There is infinite pain here, immeasurable sorrow, flagrant torment; but there is also the ability to withstand—extraordinary determination, the will to battle, and extreme resilience. From the day the cameras started rolling there were many who followed Spielberg's effort, mounted on a budget of $25 million, with hawk eyes. Spielberg had seemingly erased his producer identity. What he held closest to his heart was the painful awareness that he was by birth a Jew, and the savagery inflicted upon six million of his brethren had to be picturised.

The first punch that Spielberg delivered was to make it in black-and-white. The last Oscar to be awarded to a B&W movie was in 1960, and nobody clamoured for this colour scheme any more.

The first shot of the movie however is in colour—a pair of candles lit by a family in Sabbath prayer. The candles gutter out, and the smoke takes us into black-and-white tones, and transforms into the smoke belching out of a steam engine bringing the Jews into Kraków for resettling.

Towards the end of the movie, where Schindler is about to depart and all his *Schindlerjuden* gather around him, many critics have found it melodramatic, especially when he goes up to Stern, takes him in his embrace and cries without restraint. Like the survivors of a thunderstorm, they bid each other an overwrought goodbye. But there are several other scenes which are cinematically unforgettable.

In one of the scenes Schindler is seen standing on the upper balcony of his factory, looking grim. Down there in front are heaps of utensils. The next shot frames only the utensils, one upon the other; dark, silent utensils, signifying the transience of life. This violent dance of death had to be Schindler's moment of truth. In the pitiable scramble for life during the Kraków massacre, Schindler had noticed a six- or seven-year-old girl (named Red Genia in the Internet Movie Database). In the entire B&W stretch of the movie, she is the only spot of colour with her red frock, a red dot in the gloom that permeates the narrative. After the bodies of the Kraków massacre are exhumed, the corpses of the slaughtered are carted in wheel barrows like bales of grass. And there, loaded on top of the heap in one cart, he again sees little Red Genia being rolled out for incineration.

Another scene, which shows the foundation for the new barracks being built for the army is immensely shocking. Diana, the young Jew engineer is seen complaining to Commander Goeth about its structure, which she fears will collapse if not rebuilt. That a lowly Jew should have the temerity to teach things to a person of the superior Aryan race is unacceptable to Goeth's sick mind. He orders that she be shot instantly, right there. Freezing with terror, the poor woman squeaks, 'I am only trying to do my job!' 'And I'm doing mine!' snaps Goeth. She is gunned down in the presence of everybody. As her blood oozes out into the snow, he does not so much as turn to look at her, and instructs his men, 'Bring it down. Redraw it, rebuild it, like she said.'

The scene capturing Goeth's peculiar psychopathic disposition at his tall villa is equally powerful. Goeth is seen out there one morning on his third-floor balcony, bare-chested, in his pyjama trousers. He picks up a long-barrelled rifle and places it across his shoulder. He jiggles himself and stretches his limbs. Down yonder is spread out the Płaszów forced labour camp. To give himself some practice, he sets the rifle against his shoulder, takes aim at the weary, innocent stragglers and simply shoots them down. Quite like mischievous kids throwing stones at chicks, he kills human beings for distraction.

When Schindler finally comes up with an idea to save his Jews, he puts Stern in charge of drawing up the list. Stern is in a flutter, and is seen steadily increasing the list for the Czech factory, and Schindler is in a sweat, as he rushes with his money cases to Goeth's villa for buying off a few more Jewish lives. In the movie Spielberg makes this episodes race. 'These people are my people. I want my people!' Schindler declares to Goeth. Not unaware of the resonance there, Goeth turns sarcastic, 'Who are you, Moses?' The trains for Czechoslovakia are jam-packed. The list refuses to stop swelling, and Schindler is now almost broke. Meanwhile, Goeth has taken a shine to his young Jewish maid Helen, and refuses to release her. 'I want her to come to Vienna with me. I want to grow old with her,' he says. Schindler sits with Goeth for a game of cards. Loses heaps of money, but brings Helen over.

The listed men and women are loaded on separate trains. The women's train loses direction and steams into Auschwitz. A boy standing outside sends the women a mimed message by running his finger across his throat. They can see huge billows of smoke spewing out of a tall, dark, foreboding chimney. They are lined up, given a shearing, stripped, and marched into a big, windowless hall. In absolute terror, they wait for the tell-tale hiss and puffs of poison gas to come steaming in. The lights go out suddenly, triggering involuntary screams of fear. Within moments, a cold shower descends upon their heads. It takes them time to register, but they do. It is water! Water! They are being given a shower! They have come back from the mouth of death, and the sense of relief is uncontrollable! They cry, they laugh, they embrace each other. Meanwhile,

Schindler arrives and retrieves his lost train-load of workers after bribing the right pockets. The entire episode has been beautifully captured on film.

The number of episodes in the novel as well as their spread is very large. While writing the screenplay, Steven Zaillian did considerable hacking and pruning, but he did not allow its essence to be distorted. *Schindler's List* is a resonating example of what magic can be wrought when a first-rate director and a sharp, hardworking scriptwriter come together. Running three meaning-laden scenes simultaneously through inter-cutting, and carrying them forward in parallel lines without ever confusing the audience, this is the kind of virtuosity Spielberg and Zaillian have put on display here.

Schindler's journey, from a dissolute, irredeemable knave to a messiah with a restless conscience, was a huge challenge to portray for the best of actors. This role was obviously the very keel of the ship, and some of the best names were vying to bag it. Spielberg had closely examining the prospect of casting Warren Beatty in the role first. But Beatty would not be able to fit neatly inside Schindler's skin, he realised. For one he would not be able to disguise his accent and then he would bring into the character his 'movie star baggage'. It is very difficult for a popular stars to shake off this image which was exactly what Spielberg did not want.

Spielberg had first seen Liam Neeson perform in Anna Christie on Broadway. He was never listed among the front-rank actors in Hollywood and he seemed to be the right choice. Liam Neeson allowed Schindler to permeate into his personality through every pore. In every frame, in every scene, nay, in every breath that he took, he exuded Schindler. In a scene towards the end, when the train carrying the women prisoners gets accidentally redirected to Auschwitz, Schindler makes a dash for Auschwitz, and bribes the camp commander to release his women for travel to Brinnlitz. When a few boorish Nazi officers try to hold the children away from their mothers, he rushes in shouting 'Hey, what are you doing? These are my workers, they should be on my train!'

The role of the humane, forbearing, Jew Itzhak Stern has been played with remarkable finesse by Ben 'Gandhi' Kingsley. Schindler's closest associate in the entire enterprise, he responds to his inner voice alone. The character of the wicked, misanthropic, scheming Amon Goeth has been realised by a stage actor of the Royal Shakespearean Company, Ralph Fiennes. As on the stage, so on the screen, he carries an aura about him. His implacable scorn for the Jews, the utter coldness with which he dispatches them, his performance reveals the tremendous strength and talent of the actor. Fiennes has an impressive screen presence, quite like a beautiful, sleek but menacing snake that would bite on touch. Goeth is infatuated by his attractive Jewish maid Helen. While he uses her to satisfy his lust he feels ashamed that he, a member of the superior Aryan race, should descend to the depth of cohabiting with a lowly Jew. Conveniently accusing her of being a succubus, he beats her mercilessly. With the power of his histrionics, Fiennes makes this scene unforgettable.

The light composition of this B&W movie is fascinating, haunting. Forty per cent of the film was shot with hand-held cameras. Spielberg says that he 'got rid of the crane, got rid of the Steadicam, got rid of the zoom lenses, [and] got rid of everything that for me might be considered a safety net.' Such a style made Spielberg feel like an artist and grow as an artist. With the penetrating abilities of the hand-held cameras, the audience gets the feel of participating in the flow of the homeless destitutes as they cross the barbed wires to get deep into the concentration camps.

Spielberg was one of many crew members who did not look on during the shooting of the scene where aging Jews are forced to run naked through the slush while being selected by Nazi doctors to go to Auschwitz. The audience see it in B&W, but as he was filming the scenes of the emaciated, broken bodies and the German authorities who were humiliating and grinding them down, it was in the colours of nature, and it pained and disturbed him deeply.

In an interview, Spielberg says that his film should not been seen within the narrow scope of being only a story of the barbarity inflicted by the Germans upon the Jewish community; it is the story of the hatred that exists between man and man, the base instincts, the meanness, the jealousies. This movie brought about a revolution in his life. He had the reputation of being a hugely successful creator of expensively mounted, high-tech extravaganzas that brought in rakes full of money. But with *Schindler's List* he took courage in both hands and ventured into another genre altogether.

He wasn't sure at all how the audience would receive this markedly different effort that focused on pain and anguish; the debasement of one community by another. He doubted whether the movie would recover the investments ploughed into it. His fears, however, were ill-founded, and the movie was a resounding success. On an investment of $25 million, it earned more than $300 million. A huge part of the profits Spielberg gave over to Jewish charity organisations. It brought him unprecedented financial success and stability. More importantly, it created a permanent seat for him among the first-rate directors in world cinema.

Not all the critics were happy with the product. Some proud Germans were deeply offended by its message, and accused Spielberg of making this movie with the deliberate intention of propagating the worst aspects of the Nazi regime. Wasn't there a single good official in all of Germany? Through the entire length of the movie, the German soldiers have been shown as only barking and shouting. The scenes of naked young women, are they there to underline Nazi barbarity, or for filling box-office tills by providing the audience with vicarious titillation? The smoke-stacks and the conveyor belts shown for incinerating the countless corpses are not true to facts. The facts are only a few—a few persons like Goeth and Schindler, and a few place names like Kraków and Płaszów; for the rest, the movie is a fiction, based upon an imaginative piece of writing. It is a pack of lies to say that Schindler went completely broke, as shown at the end of the movie. On the contrary, he vanished from the scene with bags loaded with money. A number of such 'defects' were highlighted by the naysayers, in an effort to show Spielberg in poor light and undermine his success. The provocation was to get square with the outsider who was exposing their fathers' sins in public.

Nevertheless, Spielberg can be justly proud of having presented to the world an exquisite gem in *Schindler's List*. A deeply ironic tale of his student days needs to be mentioned here. Spielberg had wanted admission to learn film-making in a certain Film Institute, but he was turned back for not possessing enough talent. He was left with no choice but to do a programme in English Literature from the Long Beach University. Today, any Film Institute across the world worth its name has *Schindler's List* on its curriculum. The Spielberg phenomenon multiplies.

The movie has, however, created a peculiar problem for its maker and that is to keep the flag fluttering higher than ever. Surpassing its high benchmark is likely to be a major challenge. While *Saving Private Ryan* fetched him 10 Oscars later in 1908, and Lincoln fetched him 4, none has been comparable to the 17 Oscars he had won for *Schindler's List*. ✡

'It's in our nature to want to watch our human frailties played out on a huge, epic canvas. Ancient societies had anthropomorphic gods: a huge pantheon expanding into centuries of dynastic drama: fathers and sons, star-crossed lovers, warring brothers, martyred heroes. Tales that taught us the danger of hubris and the primacy of humility. It's the everyday stuff of everyman's life, but it's writ large, and we love it.'

TOM HIDDLESTON

ACROSS BORDERS

II

THE HUMAN MIND

THE IDIOT
DEVDAS

'The causes of human actions are usually immeasurably more complex...' *THE IDIOT*

There have been many great stalwarts who have graced the Hall of Fame of literature, and suffused it with their fragrance. Fyodor Dostoyevsky set the trend for his age, and his *The Brothers Karamozov* is acknowledged as a magnum opus. His other great masterpiece is *Crime and Punishment*.

As it happens, between two peaks lies a valley replete with springs, waterfalls, herbs, birds and beasts. So lies his novel *The Idiot*, a creation of extraordinary power and beauty. Whenever I meet the simpleton of a hero of this novel, Prince Lev Nikolayevich Myshkin, Saratchandra Chatterjee's Devdas invariably comes to my mind.

The subject of the two novels—*The Idiot* and *Devdas*—and the culture they project are not the product of the same soil, but the depth of the human mind they explore their inner music, the thread that binds their narration,t these are quite the same. There are a number of other parallels, besides. I have read both these novels one after the other, over and over again. You visit the Ajanta, gaze at the art that lies encrusted on the walls of the Buddhist caves, nestled in the steep valleys, and return with a sense of deep fulfilment. You then head towards Verul (Ellora), get stunned by the grandeur of the Kailasa temples and the stupas; wind your way to your heart's content, in and out of the countless sculptures, and experience the limits of ecstasy. This is the state to which the reading of these two books brings you.

Devdas is not much more than a novella, as against Henry and Olga Carlisle's English translation of *The Idiot*, which runs into 632 pages. But being small does not in any way cramp its scope. Its weave, like the French novels, is unitary and compact, and it soaks up effortlessly the chemistry of life. *The Idiot*, on the other hand, is a Russian novel, after all. Its canvas is huge, as huge as the Russian steppes. But Dostoyevsky, as its writer, sits forcefully on the saddle, and his feet are firmly in the stirrup. This is the reason why he gallops across these vast spaces with such consummate ease.

Prince Myshkin, the hero of *The Idiot*, is the last remnant of one of the oldest aristocratic families of Russia. Prey to epileptic fits since early childhood he becomes the target of the world's scorn, an 'idiot' by traditional norms. His heart and mind, however, overflow with compassion for the same world that ridicules him.

The novel[1] begins at a juncture where Prince Myshkin is seen returning to Russia from a sanatorium in Switzerland where he has spent four years to recover from his illness. He is on his way to St. Petersburg, to the house of a distant cousin, Lizaveta, the proud survivor of the Myshkin family, and the wife of General Yepanchin. They are the only surviving relatives he knows, and he hopes they would help him find some anchor in life.

In the railway coach Prince Myshkin meets Parfyon Semyonovich Rogozhin, the son of a Russian aristocrat. It is he who shows Myshkin the photograph of the beautiful Nastasia Philippovna (the heroine of the novel). Rogozhin is infatuated with her and wants to possess her. Later, Myshkin too falls deeply in love with her. This triangulation forms the crux of the novel.

Semi-educated, guileless and innocent, when the handsome young Prince Myshkin presents himself at the palatial mansion of his cousin he has just a bundle under his arm, emphasising his country bumpkin looks. The bundle represents the pile of sorrow with which he has set off on his journey of life. Idiotic, innocent, naive, callow, these terms have been as if imprinted permanently on Myshkin's brow. However, his innocence, his complete transparency and his unaffected laughter win everybody over, and he is instantly accepted as a part of General Yepachin's family.

The general has three daughters, all very educated, pursuing arts, and very pretty—particularly the youngest, Aglaya. The simpleton Prince Myshkin and the dreamy Aglaya

[1] The translator referred to the English translation of *The Idiot* by Julius Katzer

'I am a fool with a heart but no brains, and you are a fool with brains but no heart; and we're both unhappy, and we both suffer. *THE IDIOT*

feel a strong emotional pull for each other. As Paaro felt for Devdas, Aglaya too wishes to become the Prince's partner for life.

The heroine of the novel, Nastasia Philippovna, gets into the story trailing a heart-rending background. Her father, Philipp Alexandrovich Barashkov, owned substantial lands in one of the central gubernias of Russia. He is singularly dogged by misfortunes that send him deeper and deeper into debt. His property goes on shrinking till he is left with just a small patch of land, which he farms to keep himself and his family going.

Once, when he is in town to meet one of his principal creditors, his steward arrives with the shattering news that his house has been destroyed by fire; his wife has perished, but his two daughters are safe. This is a shock that even Barashkov, inured as he is to the blows of fortune, cannot withstand; he goes out of his mind, and dies of brain fever a month later.

The neighbouring landlord Afanasi Ivanovich Totsky takes charge of the two little Barashkov girls, aged six and seven, and places them with his bailiff's family. Shortly afterwards, the younger child dies of whooping cough, leaving the elder child, Nastasia, quite alone in the world.

When she is about 12, Totsky, who is on a visit to his lands, notices her, and is immediately struck by her extreme beauty. A connoisseur in these matters, he decides to use her for himself when she blooms in the near future. Towards this end, he shifts her into comfortable settings and appoints a Swiss governess for educating and grooming her. When he returns four years later, she is ready to be taken over as his mistress, which he does.

Totsky, at 55 years of age, now wants a legitimate wife as well and negotiates with General Yepanchin for his eldest daughter Alexandra. Nastasia, however, is determined to prevent Totsky from bringing in any bride, and stands in his way like a wrathful cobra with hood distended. Yepanchin and Totsky though, are old at this game. Totsky secures the services of the young, ambitious and vain assistant of the general, named Gavril Ardalyonovich Ivolgin (nicknamed Ganya), and promises him 75,000 roubles if he marries Nastasia. When Totsky offers Nastasia 75,000 roubles to step out of his way and marry

Ganya, she scornfully rejects the money, despite knowing of the notoriety she carries for being Totsky's mistress, and that she is not likely to find herself a decent suitor.

When Myshkin discovers this he declares openly, 'I love you, Nastasia Philippovna, and would die for you.' Nastasia has implicit faith in Prince Myshkin, but she is fiercely conscientious, and cannot think of exploiting his goodness of heart for her own benefit. 'Won't you be ashamed when you're told your wife was Totsky's kept woman?' she asks. To which the Prince responds, 'Nastasia Philippovna, I told you just now that I would take your consent as an honour, and that you would be doing me the honour, not I conferring it on you.'

Nastasia, determined to discourage him, tells him, 'You don't need a wife, you need a nurse to care for you.' In a state of delirious excitement, she wails, 'Thank you Prince, no one has spoken to me like that before. I've been bid for, but no man of probity has ever asked me to marry him.' But why should she accept the offer of this innocent young man if not for causing his ruin.

On the morning of her wedding to the Prince, Nastasia looks 'as pale as a corpse'. As she steps out of Darya Alexeyevna's house, her large black eyes blazing like burning coals she recognises Rogozhin in the crowd. She runs up to him like one possessed, and catches both his hands, 'Save me!' she cries, 'Take me away! Wherever you wish, at once!' For the sake of saving her beloved Prince a dismal future with her, she has taken this fatal step.

The Prince instinctively knows which way the birds would have flown, He waits patiently through the day and sets off for St. Petersburg next morning. He makes repeated visits to Rogozhin's house through the day, but is unable to gain entry. Finally, he books himself in a hotel that Rogozhin knew he always stayed in. Sometime after sunset, as he comes down to the street, Rogozhin taps him from behind and says, 'Come along with me. It's urgent.'

'Is Nastasia Philippovna at your place?'

'She is.' They walk the distance to Rogozhin's house, and he leads the Prince furtively up to his study. 'Go in!' he tells the Prince,…'Go up close.' In the darkness inside, someone is lying on the bed in the alcove behind heavy silk hangings. The sleeping figure is covered from head to foot with a white sheet. All about, at the foot of the bed, on the armchairs and even on the floor, clothes lie scattered—a magnificent gown of white silk, flowers and ribbons. From a stand at the head of the bed comes the glitter of diamonds. On a heap of crumpled white lace at the bottom of the bed, the toes of a naked foot can be glimpsed from under the bedsheet—chiselled out of marble and frightfully motionless.

The two spend the night in the makeshift bed Rogozhin spreads out on the floor. Both are in a state of raging delirium. 'Let her lie here now,' he blathers, 'next to us, next to you and me.'

'Yes, yes,' the Prince agrees like a zombie.

'So we shan't say anything and won't let them take her away.'

After a lot of incoherent conversation, the Prince asks, 'What did you do it with? A knife?' Rogozhin makes affirmative noises. Then, after some dilation, 'The blade went in about two-and-a-half inches...under her left breast—and there wasn't more than half a tablespoonful of blood on her chemise—not more.'

The next day, the door is broken open and the murderer is found in an unconscious state, in a raving fever, with the prince completely unhinged, sitting in a state of stupor. In court, Rogozhin makes no effort to defend himself, and is sentenced to 15 years of penal servitude in Siberia. The prince is so totally deranged that he is sent back to Dr Schneider in Switzerland, where the doctor is convinced that his malady is beyond cure.

This theme had been hijacked a few years ago by the Hindi cinema for a movie named *Yug Purush*. But an actor with an aggressive image like Nana Patekar was fundamentally unsuited to play the role of a childlike simpleton. The gold was real; but the producer-director, in his eagerness to conceal the heist, had carried it to the village goldsmith to be melted and re-fashioned, and brought it back seriously adulterated. Such is the consequence of plagiarism. Great writers of the world have embellished many splendid monuments with gems and pearls. All that a petty plagiarist can filch, I have always believed, is a bauble or two.

In the scroll of honour of Dostoyevsky's powerful works, *The Idiot* is viewed as a masterpiece of lyrical beauty. What is so remarkable about this novel? Dostoyevsky began writing *The Idiot* in 1867, when he was 46 years of age. In the biting cold of Switzerland then, he was harrowed by epileptic fits that caused him great misery. Coupled with this divine curse, his own intemperate tendencies must also have contributed to wrecking his personal life. In the mornings he would swear on his dear child's head that he would stay straight, but come evening his reprobate legs would drag him incontinently towards the dark and narrow lanes where stood gambling houses and bar rooms.

This supreme artist was not only insolvent, but was also under a load of debt. His wife's pregnancy, his own delicate constitution, nothing, nothing served as deterrent for his profligate ways. But in the middle of these wretched, obnoxious times, along with the many sins of commission and omission, he continued with one meritorious deed with clockwork regularity—he sat and wrote. Be it day or night, he committed thought and word to paper, and little by little, *The Idiot* began to emerge.

As during the writing of *Crime and Punishment*, this time too he underwent great anguish. By the time the book finally went for print, Dostoyevsky had churned out as many as eleven drafts, big and small. In the manner of Flaubert's *Madame Bovary*, the inspiration for *The Idiot* sprang from a contemporary event. In the region of Tula, there lived a 15-year-old girl named Olga. Disgusted with the ill-treatment meted out by her parents, she flew into such a rage one day that she burnt their house down.

Also, Dostoyevsky was incessantly researching through seemingly inane notings of criminal proceedings, their arguments and counter-arguments, and gleaning out big and small characters from their maw. Each draft set off fresh sprouts of imagination, caused characters to bloom, and shook away half-ripe or rotten growths. The tree, on the whole, went on gathering girth and height.

Dostoyevsky had wanted to create 'a beautiful individual', a perfect character who would be virtuous and truthful, the possessor of an attractive personality. In a diary entry of 2 August 1868, Dostoyevsky, who was quite ill then, wrote that if he could work out a good draft of the novel he wanted to write, if he could put it down well on paper, he would rid himself of his strange illness and all his mental agony. If he couldn't, that would be the end of him.

He had two idiots in mind when he began with the novel. But as the writing progressed, the second idiot disappeared in the process and was replaced by Rogozhin. The labour pains were racking. His house overflowed with shelves as his shelves overflowed with paper containing notes, comments and jottings. It was as if Dostoyevsky had thrown his all—his energy, his intellect, his skills, his genius—into this effort.

Prince Myshkin—the fallen angel was quite the apple of Dostoyevsky's eye. The Prince was forever striving to dispel the darkness, to stand with the unfortunate and the dispossessed. Life for the Prince was a perpetual, unequal struggle with a superior adversary. This is epitomised by his ragged, weather-beaten overladen sack, splitting here as you darn it there. To function as a counterfoil for the Christ-like Prince Myshkin, Dostoyevsky created the character of Rogozhin. While the Prince was the pure, innocent, artless, idealised picture of a human being, Rogozhin had no redeeming good quality, and was a calculating, lust-driven go-getter. For the first-time reader, the Prince and Nastasia are strongly evocative of Christ and Mary Magdalene.

Myshkin, for all his infatuation with Nastasia, loved Aglaya too. This triangulation of a set of people ready to suffer so much for each other is well portrayed in both *The Idiot* and *Devdas*. As with Dostoyevsky, Saratchandra too searched for the gold dust of essential life experiences in simple stories. His *Devdas* is an extraordinary story that deals in the simplest of words with subjects of the widest import.

Neelkanth Chakravarti's daughter Parvati, alias Paaro, and Narayan Mukhopadhyaya's son Devdas have been childhood friends. As neighbours, they have grown up together, entangled with each other as a pair of vines, bound to each other with bonds of love. Paaro grows up with the unarticulated understanding that Devdas alone has a claim upon her. The latest version of *Devdas* on celluloid, by director Sanjay Leela Bhansali, represents the undying love of the girl through the symbol of a faux earthen lamp that never dies out. The earlier representations of Paaro had no such lamp, but Devdas did live in her every pore, her every breath, every beat of her heart.

Trouble arrives with the arrival of puberty, when Parvati turns thirteen. Her grandmother visits Devdas's mother with the proposal that since both the young people have borne such deep affection for each other since earliest childhood, they should be tied together in marriage for the rest of their lives. The problem is that the Mukhopadhyaya family considers the Chakravartis as inferior in class, and so rejects the marriage proposal on grounds of Paaro's lower social status.

Deeply humiliated, Paaro's parents commit her for marriage to a rich landlord who is a widower. For the young lovers, though, the thought of living without each other is inconceivable. Despite her betrothal to another man, Paaro continues to worship Devdas's image in her sanctum sanctorum as husband and master.

Blinded by her love for Devdas, she ignores the restraints of culture and tradition, and presents herself at the doorsteps of Devdas's mansion in the middle of the night.

Devdas is aghast. 'How did you dare to visit here at this hour of the night? What will society say?' he enquires in agitation.

Fixing her beloved in the gaze of her sad, limpid eyes, she answers, 'If I hadn't been certain that you would protect my honour, I would surely have lowered my head in shame.' She goes on to ask, 'The river is in such flood. Isn't its water enough to wash away my taint?' She rests her head at Devdas's feet and beseeches over and over again, 'Give me a place here.'

Till late in the night, almost till the cusp of dawn, she stays parked at his gates, but draws a blank. The next day Devdas collects the courage to present himself to his parents and stammers out the subject of Paaro. When he is roundly upbraided, in a state of great agitation he leaves for Kolkata the same day. 'Get the misconception out of your head that I was ever in love with you,' he writes to her from Kolkata, in the hope of projecting himself as a dry, stone-hearted person. But immediately after consigning the letter to post, he can hold himself no longer, and drags himself irresistibly towards his village, towards Paaro.

In the river-bank scene, in Chapter VIII of the novel, Saratchandra seems to have touched the apogee of sensitive portrayal. Paaro arrives at the bank with a pot on her hip to collect water. Preparations for her marriage are in full swing. Devdas appears swinging a fishing rod in his hand. Abraded of heart, ridden with guilt, he goes up to her shamefacedly and offers profuse apologies. 'I will do whatever it takes, but I will get my parents to agree to our marriage,' he says.

Paaro, who is livid, casts a withering glance at him and asks, 'Are you the only one with parents? I, of course, have grown without shade or support, huh? Wouldn't I need my parents' consent?' One word leads on to another, her hurt pride keeps pricking at her deepest emotions. They spill out in an uncontrollable torrent, as she says, 'The person I am getting married to, is rolling in wealth. My parents know very well what is good for me. Why would they want to tie me to the apron strings of a cruel, careless, stupid person like you? Go away!'

'Such conceit!'

'And why not? If you have your pride, so have I. You may be handsome, but you are not virtuous. I possess both beauty and virtue. Your family may be landlords, but we are not paupers either!'

If the argument had stopped here, Devdas would not have lost his cool; but when she adds, 'You are free to defame me in the village,' his patience snaps. Twirling his fishing rod, he snarls, 'Paaro, people should not possess such beauty that it turns their head and

‘Main toh peeta hoon ke bas saans le saku
(I drink only so that I may be able to breathe) *DEVDAS*

makes them so conceited. Step up, so that I may blemish your beauty a little bit.’ With this he raises the fishing rod and brings it swishing down on her brow, and draws blood.

The next instant he removes his shirt, tears it into strips and hands them over to Paaro for bandaging the wound. ‘From here on, every time you look into a mirror, you will remember me, yes?’ Overtaken by contrition and sorrow, he places his hand affectionately on her head and says, ‘Lady, your choice is quite proper. What comfort could I have provided to you, after all? But don’t forget this either, dear—if you had become mine, Devdas would have held all of heaven in his left fist.’

Devdas ends on a sombre note, with its lead characters falling victims to a callous social system. Towards the end, Saratchandra writes, ‘If you ever come across a hapless young vagabond like Devdas breathing his last, please do pray for the salvation of his soul.’

Where does the sorrow-stricken wretch not wander, riding his litter of misfortune; from Kolkata to Allahabad, and then to Chunnilal at Lahore, with just his faithful old retainer Dharmdas and, indeed, his strange visions and fevered dreams for company!

Chandramukhi...Paaro...Chandram...Paa...the two float in and out of his mind’s eye, like a pair of friends giving him constant but alternate company! Devdas hits the bottle, and hits it hard. Lahore to Mumbai! Floating directionless in the endless sky like a snipped kite!

‘Let’s go to mother, at Varanasi,’ begs Dharmdas. But how can he go to mother in such a miserable state? His rickety frame is racked by relentless bouts of coughing. His hair has fallen rapidly, with just a tuft left trailing over the brow. More travel! Raging fever and delirium!

Bimal Roy has made inspired use of the railway train as a motif for Devdas’s futile, purposeless drift across the country. The furious rattle of its wheels, the streak of blinding light cutting across the black screen, the hiss of steam and the piercing whistle combine to externalise the storm that is ravaging Devdas’s ulcerated mind and body. Sanjay Leela Bhansali goes whole hog too in lifting Bimal Roy’s concluding scenes frame by frame.

Devdas is not fated to meet his mother. The train has shot past Varanasi and is standing at a wayside station named Pandua in the middle of the night. There has been a drizzle, and the air is wet. Devdas stirs himself, caresses the fast asleep Dharmdas on the forehead, and clambers out into the biting cold. His destination now is Hathipotha, the abode of his beloved Paaro, a promise to fulfil.

Sensing his imminent end, he gets desperate. The bullock-cart speeds up and goes bumping along the narrow, infrequently used cattle-track. His childhood comes flooding into his febrile mind—the pranks he played on little Paaro, their boisterous fun times; and then Chandramukhi—Chandramukhi who had abandoned a flourishing career of a danseuse and lived in a small hut in an unknown village, like a hermit

There is slush everywhere, and rain-wrought puddles. The bullocks are periodically whipped mercilessly into a trot, and then allowed to amble awhile. The macabre journey stretches on. The fever begins to mount as evening descends. The wind sharpens its fangs and begins reaching his bones. 'How far away...uh...the village?' he croaks at the cart-driver from time to time. He is overtaken by violent, uncontrolled shivering. Blood trickles down his nostrils, and he can taste it oozing off his gums too. His breath keeps getting locked in his throat. And then the litany of the incoherent gasp, 'How much longer?'

Around midnight, the cart creaks to a halt outside Paaro's gate. A dense blanket of silence envelops the place. The forecourt appears to be in deep slumber. Scraping the barrel, Devdas gathers strength for one last pitch. He fishes out a hundred-rupee note and deposits it with gratitude in the cart-driver's hand. The poor man wraps a shawl tight round the master's scorching body, dims the hurricane lantern, and sits at his feet, waiting for daybreak. With the first streak of light arrives the first person, and soon the second, the third and a few more. They gather around the peepul tree, gawking at the strange sight. Among the assemblage is Paaro's husband, Bhuvan Babu. The tongue has thickened too much now, and no sound escapes Devdas's gullet. His eyes peep out through heavy lids as he weakly surveys the gathering. They stare back at him in perplexity. Who is this apparition? Expensive shawl, high boots, diamond ring on finger! Who could he be related to? Helpless tears trickle down his cheeks. A doctor is summoned, who mutters, 'A few minutes left, maybe.' 'Poor wretch!' they mumble.

Paaro is on the balcony. Word reaches her that some unknown gentleman is breathing his last there under the peepul tree. 'Poor man!' she sighs. Ritual demands the pouring of some water into a dying person's mouth; somebody does this too. Devdas turns a beholden eye towards him. He chokes, lets out two painful hiccups, and lets his head fall limp—forever.

A poster of *Devdas* (1955), directed by Bimal Roy. COURTESY: AUTHOR

The question remains—who is this person? What his caste and what his creed? What funeral rites to be performed? The police arrive and locate two letters in his pocket. There is also his name tattooed on his left wrist. The unclaimed body is handed over to the *dom*, the professional cremator. The man carries the corpse to an old, unused algae-ridden pond outside the village, chops it up into pieces for quick burning, and sets it alight. The half burned pieces are then flung over and across the pond. Devdas, the star-crossed scion of an affluent Brahmin family—spread out as a feast for crows and vultures, dogs and wolves!

The expensive items on his person are recorded and deposited in the police locker. Paaro's maid exclaims, 'What an unfortunate individual! Born somewhere, and driven by wretched fate to die somewhere else!' Her stepson pipes in, 'Mother, it was someone from your village, it seems, someone called Devdas Mukhopadhyaya... '

On hearing the name Paaro goes berserk. Screaming his name, she runs insanely down the staircase. In a bid to prevent her from harm her relatives restrain her. She swoons in their arms and is carried to bed. She is not destined to get a glimpse of her Devdas's mutilated body. The next day, when she regains consciousness, she asks her maid, 'Had he arrived here in the middle of the night?' And then, 'All night he lay there...!' she wails inconsolably.

This is the extraordinary end Saratchandra accords to his hero. No moviemaker has yet been able to capture in any great depth the ardour, the billowing love, the agonising lamentations, and the sinister vein of calamity that runs through the novel. The novelist, of course, has done all this and more within the brief space of a hundred pages.

Contrary to appearances, *Devdas* is not the tragedy of a dispossessed drunkard. In its pages one runs into extraordinary experiences of life at every turn. Each of the three corners of the *Devdas* triangle—Devdas, Chandramukhi and Paaro—has been created out of solid, real life experiences. The character of Devdas is a subtle coming together of Saratchandra's own self-image with the images of other moonstruck youngsters. Paaro has evidently grown out of the author's schoolmate Dheeru, who had a crush on him. While nothing came of it, this event did leave a deep mark on him; the emotions that suffused this juvenile, giddy-headed, unsuccessful romance constitute the motif of the Paaro-Devdas relationship.

As for the intoxicating Chandramukhi, the prototype swept through the young author's life like a storm. Saratchandra had to miss his school-end exams because he had no money for the fees. As an impecunious and directionless young boy, he got into the company of Rajendranath, or Raju, the profligate son of a rich father. With money to blow, they debauched themselves with visits to theatres and musical soirees and dancing girls. One such courtesan was Kalidasi, who had made her pile in her profession, and operated out of her glittering two-storey house in Mansurganj. She was beautiful, talented, and blessed with a mellifluous voice. She had a repertoire of devotional songs too. The two young men were very often her guests.

Saratchandra has often recounted a particular episode to Maharshi Dileep Kumar Rai and others about visiting her one evening in the company of a friend who worked for a landlord. This friend had been entrusted with the responsibility of handing over Rs 3000/- to someone, and he carried this money to the dance hall, tucked on his person. The rupee, then, carried far greater buying power than now, and living was inexpensive. A single rupee took care of a month's meals even in a city like Kolkata. Hence squandering a few thousand rupees in a dancing girl's parlour was extravagance of the highest order.

Both drank heavily and went on posting one request after another. Finally, completely sozzled, they both keeled over and lay on the floor like empty liquor bottles. Next day, the friend got up with a start and felt his pockets; his three thousand rupees had vanished. 'Where the devil do I get the money from? How do I save my job?' He howled disconsolately. The danseuse was nowhere around either. Could she have disappeared with the money?

In a little while Kalidasi walked in with a laugh. 'You guys lost your head, or what?' she enquired coolly. 'Walking into a bordello with such thick wads of money! Five bucks here are reason enough to draw a contract killer! And the way you were pulling out and displaying your wad in your pickled state! Good you got knocked out here. When I came to put pillows under your heads, your wealth was all out in the open. I gathered it all up and put it safe. But that was a good thing to happen, and certainly averted a catastrophe.'

'What was?' asked Saratchandra.

'That you two passed out here. So many in the gathering had taken note of the money you were flaunting. There were some roughnecks who lay in wait for you to emerge all night right outside the door down there. I had to mount guard on you and stay awake all night with this tiny lamp for company.'

Here, in this dark, dingy hall of disrepute, Saratchandra sighted the incomparable Kalidasi and her awesome heart. How many epics would have spilled over the curved banisters of such whorehouses the world over! How many plays would have enacted themselves in their tarnished saloons! Saratchandra says, 'About my Chandramukhi I have written that these dance houses, these parlours, these brothels—for the labouring class, for the lost humanity, for the down and out, they are veritable houses of worship.' When 26-year-old Saratchandra was writing the early draft of *Devdas*, Kalidasi would often meet him, and ooze through his pen over to paper in the shape of Chandramukhi. His biographer Vishnu Prabhakar endorses this story.

Saratchandra in *Devdas* has wrought a novel that is the story of the ordinary people living in the many villages and towns of India. This is not the story of a certain Devdas. It is a mirror in which millions have seen their own reflection, read their own hearts. Devdas is not the embodiment of an alcoholic, but of diffident youth. We find his kind everywhere, pining for the beloved; dreaming fanciful dreams of setting up a happy nest for two. But as for finding the courage to declare love to her, the mere thought is enough to send shivers down the spine. Even handing her a decently drafted letter is way beyond the sparse resources of spirit. Inevitably the day comes when the poor girl herself steps up and hands over an envelope. 'My wedding invitation. Please do come.' *Finis!* End of story!

Some, of course, are a little more intrepid. An occasional rendezvous behind trees, some pigeon flying. But when the crunch time comes, when she announces, 'There are some people coming home tomorrow to see me,' paralysis of tongue results.

Reasons, there are many—social, economic, familial! There is unemployment; there is the joint family; responsibility of younger brothers; a sister to get married; what will people say; responsibilities towards parents; the burden of gratitude! Enough reasons to break the back of the stoutest Devdas! He frets, he stumbles, he is petrified! Many a Paaro has had the spunk to confront her Devdas, but in the face of such pusillanimity, buckled under circumstances, damming her flood of tears, she has walked away with an unknown man, to turn the conjugal mill.

In the eyes of the world, Devdas was gutless, while Prince Myshkin was naive, unbalanced and epileptic. They were neither rich nor well-employed. They were vagabonds, really. Why, then, did Aglaya and Nastasia, Chandramukhi and Paaro coo over them like lovesick pigeons? Why should these startlingly beautiful women stake their youth on weak, star-crossed, 'good-for-nothing' swains? Why do they reject handsome sons of Mammon and deposit their fate in tattered sling bags? It seems that young women of this kind have fountains of affection inside them that gush for the weak and hapless. Wealth and affluence move them not, and true divinity for them is found among the Lords of the Rags.

An important hallmark of both these novels is their strong women characters. Dostoyevsky had for long been nursing the idea of writing a woman-centric novel, with Nastasia to play the lead character. Deprived of parental shelter, brought up in a stranger's house, abused time and again by the world, young Nastasia is an unusual character. The cowherd who had reared this poor calf turns out to be a butcher. Her hide too he puts up for sale in the marriage market. Her experience with the mental and moral sickness of this 'wise' world warps her personality; she considers it prudent to wear the mask of madness herself.

Nastasia, in spite of her love for Prince Myshkin, rejects him for his own good. Chandramukhi too tells Devdas, 'Poor Paaro hasn't caused you any harm; you yourself are responsible for the dissipated state to which you have reduced yourself.' These two women clearly belong to the same tribe.

Quite like Paaro of *Devdas*, the character of Aglaya has also been beautifully delineated. She is beautiful, virtuous, and she loves Prince Myshkin. If Nastasia is a flaming torch, Aglaya is a happy little earthen lamp that glimmers on for love. She senses the Prince's stellar moral qualities, his intellectual strength and his infinite compassion for people. Nevertheless, she has her self-esteem and pride. She smoulders with resentment when she sees the world exploit his simplicity as he lets them exploit him without any resistance.

While moviemakers have fleshed out Paaro's role more, I personally find Saratchandra's Chandramukhi stronger and a more unforgettable character. Interestingly, both Chandramukhi and Nastasia are older than Devdas and Prince Myshkin respectively, and both are acutely concerned about the safeguarding the future of their respective heroes.

Quite like Urdu writer Mirza Haadi Rusva's *Umrao Jaan Adaa*, Chandramukhi is a courtesan with strong principles. She insists that Devdas should marry, after which she would be willing to serve him as his housemaid. On the subject of man-woman relationship, she declares, 'I believe women have unreasonably been branded as whimsical and giddy-headed. When it suits men, women are flattered silly and raised to the skies; then one fine day these same women are branded as wicked and pulled down from the altar. This is typical masculine misdemeanour. Women, however, do not suffer from such passion-induced blindness as men do, and do not get carried away.' She further observes, 'If a woman expresses compassion for a man, it is so readily misconstrued as love. If in her innocence, the poor thing opens up emotionally, you instantly revile her as untrustworthy and of loose morals.'

The distinguished doyenne of Hindi cinema, Meena Kumari, had a pronounced taste for Bengali literature; and regaled herself with Saratchandra's novels again and again. Once while shooting at a Mumbai studio she learnt that Bimal Roy was shooting *Devdas* on another floor right there. She froze. 'Who is playing Paaro?' she asked excitedly.

Bimal Roy had personally visited her film-maker husband Kamal Amrohi, with the offer of Paaro's role for her. The Mumbai film-makers, however, had been considerably rattled by the increasing prestige of this Bengali gentleman on their turf. Meena Kumari would grow in stature as an actor with that role, Amrohi did not mind that. What did bug him was the thought that Roy himself would then get into the elite club of top-notch directors, which, as a member of that club, Amrohi was loath to allow. He had, therefore, sent Roy packing. When Meena Kumari was informed that Paaro's role had come walking to her doorstep, tarried there awhile before walking away disappointed, she was heartbroken. She packed up shooting for the day, stumbled home and cried through the night.

Bimalda had wanted Nargis for his Chandramukhi, but the good lady feared that her character would be completely overshadowed by Paaro, and she turned down the offer. Finally, it was Suchitra Sen who played Paaro, and Vyjayantimala who essayed Chandramukhi, and they put up stellar performances. But Bimal Roy never quite got over his regret. 'In Dilip Kumar I got the Devdas I wanted,' he would sometimes mutter to his assistants, 'the movie was a hit too. But what if..., what if I had got my choice of Paaro and Chandramukhi?' Yes, what if? What heaven would he have scooped up?

Sanjay Leela Bhansali has given his *Devdas* a modern look. While in Bimalda's *Devdas* it was the thespian Dilip Kumar who realised the lead character with consummate skill, in Bhansali's version, it is Aishvarya Rai who takes the palm for her superb rendition of Paaro. It is quite obvious that she had soaked herself in the trauma of Paaro's existence to enable her to give such a power-packed performance.

The cameraman for the very first *Devdas* (1936—produced by P.C. Barua) was Bimal Roy himself, with K.L. Sehgal playing the lead. The wonderful frames and compositions of the second, Bimal Roy directed, *Devdas* were carried over into Bhansali's *Devdas*. His cameraman Binod Pradhan had an excellent sense of lighting and the advantage of the latest equipment, which he utilised it to the hilt to once again establish his suzerainty over his domain. Money, for the creation of the Bhansali edition, was never an issue—it flowed like water.

An Art Director worth his salt is required to enter the very soul of the subject before he can hope to visualise and create the physical structures for the enactment of the story. John Box was one such Art Director, who went on to create such magnificent sets for David Lean's classics like *Dr Zhivago* and *Lawrence of Arabia*. Another craftsman who goes deep into his subject matter is Nitin Desai, whether it is for decking up his cast in the glittering wardrobe of Bhansali's *Devdas*, or for creating the ambience of rural India in *Lagaan*. No wonder the magic of Nitin's art infuses into his movies such strength of character.

Saratchandra wrote his *Devdas* in 1903, and a hundred years have not dimmed its freshness. 'Age cannot wither her, nor custom stale her infinite variety.' *Devdas*, within its few pages, displays its understanding of sensitive human beings grappling with circumstances. The same intensity of feeling, the same compassion Dostoyevsky pours into his narration as he relates the story of a certain Prince Myshkin in *The Idiot*. Writers of genius leave their great works behind, a treasury of immortal creations; a revisit to these holy sanctums by later generations leaves not just ordinary readers, but great artists too in a state of blessedness.

THE CALL OF THE EARTH

THE GOOD EARTH
THE GRAPES OF WRATH
MOTHER INDIA

'Land is one's flesh and blood.'

THE GOOD EARTH

A lovely aroma comes floating in, not merely from the farms but from the village plains too, when the crops begin to sway during harvest time. While here, in the Maval region of Western Maharashtra, people dance to the *lezim*, in faraway Assam they celebrate the harvest festival as *bihu*. In every village, on every threshing floor, groups of young boys and girls dance to the beat of drums all night through. In our land of poetry, from the songs of poet Kazi Nazrul Islam in distant Bengal, to Vitthal Wagh's celebration of the black soil of Warhaad in the Vidarbha region of Maharashtra, nature joins in the merrymaking.

Be it Russia, America, India or China, the call of the earth is of identical note. The story of its children, sweating it out in the lap of mother earth, has been immortalised by many in literature and cinema.

The American novelist Pearl S. Buck had invested a lot of passion in sketching the story of Wang Lung in *The Good Earth*. When it was published in 1931, it stirred the hearts of readers across America and across the world. Irving Thalberg, an executive producer with M-G-M was so deeply moved by the novel that he was determined to make it into a movie someday. He prepared a detailed proposal for its production and presented it to the M-G-M boss Louis Mayer, but he was brushed away with scorn. Mayer reminded him that when the moviegoers didn't care for the travails of American farmers, why would they ever be interested in watching the woes of a Chinese farmer on the screen? Thalberg, however, was determined to do the impossible, and he did it.

As the wheels of history turn, people change their opinion on works of art, often determined by self-interest. An artistic creation may drop out of memory by mere lack of mention. When the movie *The Good Earth* hit the screen in 1937, not just America but the entire world screamed hoarse in appreciation. Both Paul Muni, who played the Chinese peasant Wang Lung, and Luise Rainer, who played his hardworking wife, O-lan, were heaped with praises. Many wrote that a copy of the movie should be sealed in a time capsule and buried as a gift for posterity. But as China began emerging as a competing world power, the Americans began looking at China and all things Chinese with suspicion. Consequently, in the decades that followed, *The Good Earth* has become the victim of deliberate amnesia.

The story of *The Good Earth* starts with Wang Lung's father keen to have his son married. But who would offer his girl to an indigent farmer? The House of Hwangs, however, has a number of girls from poor households working as slaves; a suitable bride can be located there. Preferably, she was not to be beautiful, because beautiful girls get despoiled in rich households; all that the father desires for his son is that she should not be cleft-lipped or pockmarked.

On the appointed day Wang Lung gives himself a vigorous scrub, puts on his best clothes and goes to the landlord's mansion. The old landlady is in an opium trance, while the landlord is still busy with his bedroom escapades, and nowhere to be seen. The landlady gets a slave girl from the pantry, and hands her over to Wang. Wang pays her price, lifts his wife's heavy trunk on his shoulder, and marches off with her.

Tall, pallid, slit-eyed, O-lan is just as determined and ambitious as her husband. Her arrival in the Wang household brings prosperity. The harvests are good, and each year brings an addition to his family. He keeps buying little plots of land too. He has three sons one after another. When the fourth-born is a girl, he is quite upset, and ascribes it to somebody's evil eye. His state, however, steadily improves, till he begins dreaming of buying out the Hwang lands and palatial mansion one day.

‘Hunger makes thief of any man.’

THE GOOD EARTH

Both Wang and O-lan labour day and night. They have the blessings of the two stone gods standing on their farm. But the good days do not last. Famine hits their land. People begin to die of starvation. Wang's malicious uncle incites the villagers against his nephew, suggesting that while the villagers are dying, he has been hoarding food. The villagers march up to his house, but find not a grain in his house. They are dumbstruck when they find O-lan is boiling the dry roots of a tree. As in the movie, the scenes of famine have been portrayed with frightening authenticity. When Wang's child dies, and he sees a dog gnawing at the corpse, he breaks into uncontrollable sobs.

In the movie, the director has filmed the buffalo episode with great sensitivity and power. O-lan's children are starving and emaciated. There is no option left but to slaughter their only male buffalo. The rumour is that men are eating other men, and in an effort to save his children Wang walks into the barn, knife in hand. But when he looks at the limpid-eyed animal, he cannot see it as another dumb creature, but as a dear friend who has laboured with him on the farm. The knife clatters on the floor, and he sits down and bawls in anguish. But when the children's survival is at stake, the soft-hearted O-lan turns hard, and slaughters the animal. From a simple, compassionate woman to a tough-as-nails person, Luise Rainer traverses the entire range as O-lan, and scales such heights as a performer that it is difficult to believe that it is an American doing it, and not a Chinese.

Both Wang and O-lan are completely devoted to their land. The uncle comes up with the proposal that they sell their land instead of letting the famine crush them. But Wang decides on retaining his land, and opts for temporary migration. Caught in the abyss of famine, thousands have moved to the city for shelter and survival. It is so hugely overcrowded that neither man nor his labour has any value. Wang pulls a rickshaw and his wife and children beg on the streets. One day, one of the sons brings in some meat. When Wang learns that the boy has stolen it from somewhere, he throws it away and thrashes the boy. The practical O-lan, however, picks up the flesh and it becomes a day's sustenance for the starving family. When they are reduced to selling their little girl for survival, Wang cries inconsolably; it is O-lan again who tries to pacify him. She reminds him that she too was sold by her parents to tide over a similar state of famine. If they have to return to their village, they will need the money for travel. The dilemma for Wang is, what should he lose? Child or land?

The city is in transformation. The trumpets of revolution are being blown everywhere, but nobody knows what the revolution is, and who it is for or against. It is really anarchy masquerading as revolution, and shops, houses and palaces are being looted. The pangs of hunger convert Wang into a thief too. In one such melee of looting O-lan too is sucked in. In the press of thousands of people rushing, she gets bulldozed into a massive mansion. She loses her balance and falls, and loses consciousness under the feet of the milling crowd. The director has filmed the stampede scene with great command and assurance. It is an amazing piece of cinema to watch.

When O-lan regains consciousness she finds lying before her a small purse, which, she discovers, carries invaluable gems. She tucks the purse in her clothes, but within minutes she is rounded up and taken outside the palace. A number of people have been tied to posts and are being shot dead. She is tied up too, with the gems on her person and a gun lined up to dispatch her. At the last minute the whimsical soldiers abandon her and move elsewhere.

Riding on their luck, they return to their village and use their newfound wealth to good purpose. Wang supplies seeds to other farmers and collects his own harvests. Little by little, he buys off all of the landlord's farms, and a day arrives when he makes the Hwang mansion his own too. He is now the new landlord, with his own retinue of slave boys and girls.

The wicked uncle intervenes again and takes the nephew to visit a slit-eyed danseuse by the name of Lotus. Smitten by Lotus Wang brings her home as his mistress, and sets her up in her own new apartments. He begins to find fault with the worn-out O-lan and also gives O-lan's pearls to Lotus to gain her affection.

With their own sons ready for marriage, O-lan is shattered at her husband's behaviour. She agonises over her husband's philandering on the one hand, and her children's future on the other. When young Lotus makes advances towards Wang's younger son, Wang asks him to leave home. Storm clouds once again gather over the family, and the farms are invaded by locusts. O-lan is hit hard by these developments, and takes to bed.

There are a number of small characters and episodes which are dealt in great details in the novel. The director, given the limitation of a movie, found it impossible to find space for them all. The movies ends with everyone uniting to try to save the crops. Just when all seems lost the Wang household is saved from a near-disaster. Wang Lung, back to his senses, reconciles with his younger son and also returns the pearls to O-lan before she dies.

'It is the good land that has made you something better than a farmer's lad. *THE GOOD EARTH*

The Good Earth brought Pearl Buck the 1932 Pulitzer Prize. Bringing this widely acclaimed novel on to the silver screen was a big challenge. Within a year of its publication, the writer duo of David and Owen Davis converted it into a lovely play. It was staged immediately thereafter in 1933, on Broadway, and it met with instant success. It was on watching this play that Irving Thalberg decided to produce it as a film. While preparing the screenplay, the director Sidney Franklin used the stage script to the hilt.

It is, of course, the story that constitutes the spine of the movie *The Good Earth*. But it is the superlative acting of the great actors—Paul Muni as Wang Lung and Luise Rainer as O-lan—that really breathes life into the film. Thalberg had initially decided to use mainly Chinese actors for his cast, but with modern make-up technology at hand, it became possible to give the American actors a Chinese appearance.

Rainer, a native of Germany, had made a name for herself on European stage before she migrated to America. She gained fame as Isabella in Shakespeare's *Measure for Measure*, and also in the title role of George Bernard Shaw's *Saint Joan*. M-G-M Studios had brought in Rainer to pit her against Greta Garbo of a rival studio. A year prior to the commencement of work on *The Good Earth*, she had played the lead in *Escapade*; a year after her Academy Award for best actress in *The Good Earth*, she brought in another Best Actress Oscar with *The Great Zeigfeld*. The Academy, of course, honoured her for her superb rendition of O-lan. Along with Katherine Hepburn, she is the only other Hollywood actress to win two consecutive Oscars.

Paul Muni was also a renowned actor who has been nominated as many as six times for the Oscar, and that places him in the same exalted category of great actors like Sir Lawrence Olivier, Jannings, Gregory Peck, and Marlon Brando. He won his Best Actor for *The Story of Louis Pasteur* 1936, the year before the making of *The Good Earth*. He was born to Phillip Weisenfreund, a Jewish stage actor who toured from town to town with his company. The father wanted Paul to get into music rather than acting, but an episode in early life in their drama company tipped the scales for him. On the day of the performance an important character fell ill. To see the difficulty through Paul got his face painted. That paint never peeled off for the rest of his life. A mere adolescent pasting beard on his face playing out the character of an old man with such aplomb marked him out as a great actor.

Valiant was his first movie and he played the role of a convict on death row. He did it with such conviction that his very first role brought him his first Oscar nomination as Best Actor. He deliberately went for variety. In *Scarface* he played a notorious American goon, while in *I am a Fugitive from a Chain Gang* he played an innocent person with equal felicity, and won another nomination. He would study deeply each role that came his way—that was his hallmark—and was often pulled up for his obsessive commitment in studying a character. Be it in *Black Fury* where he was cast as a miner working in a colliery, or for the stage performance as old Willy Loman in *Death of a Salesman*, or in the role of the great novelist in *The Life of Emile Zola*, he exhibited the same penchant for perfection to immortalise each role.

It was inconceivable, then, that Paul Muni could just sit back and relax when he landed the challenging role of a Chinese peasant in *The Good Earth*. For months together he visited the market place at China Town in San Francisco. He would sit there closely observing the way of the Chinese; how they walked, talked and carried themselves. When on the set, once he was made-up as Wang, he *became* Wang, whether the camera was rolling or not. The finer aspects of his portrayal become evident when we watch the movie: Wang on the farms, Wang among the cattle, Wang who migrates to the city during the famine, the slogging farmer fighting his battle for survival, Wang who loses his balance at the arrival of prosperity, and finally Wang who answers with a resounding 'Coming!' when his locust-hit land calls for help. Paul Muni lives out Wang with all the passion he is capable of.

Producer Thalberg was also very keen to give his movie a thrilling climax, and worked very hard towards it. They chose the locust episode for it. It is not where the novel ends. In fact, it occupies only three-and-a-half paragraphs in Chapter 23. The movie, however, dwells on it for a good 12 minutes, and presents a stirring conflict—a conflict no other movie has ever carried—between nature, as represented by the locusts, and the unrelenting, courageous farmers.

The producer and the director have captured the pull of the land that shakes Wang out of the lap of luxury and idleness, rather well. The wife is on the sickbed when a cloud of a million locusts arrives from over the hillock and spreads over the crops like a dark, inky shadow. Wang walks out with the villagers to confront this calamity. Gongs are beaten to frighten the pests away; kerosene torches are set alight; trenches are dug round the fields and flooded with water; fires are lit up at intervals. Sound, water, fire, and finally the welcome wind that runs in to help, all of these weapons are thrown against the invaders, and Wang finally wins the field. At home, though, the ailing O-lan gives up the ghost. The two big pearls she had held in her fist roll out of her limp hand. Exhausted, Wang goes to his farm, lifts up a handful of earth, and cries out in anguish, 'O-lan, you are my true Mother Earth!'

Shooting the locust episode turned out to be an arduous task. Ink marks were tried on a blank screen. The M-G-M technical team ran out of ideas; the special-effects people were at their wits' end. Producer Thalberg and Director Franklin had more or less decided to abandon the scene when news arrived that a swarm of locusts had descended on the crops in a neighbouring state. They rushed to the site and managed to get enough live footage of the invasion.

The Good Earth turned out to be an extraordinary movie. The movie depicting the struggles inherent in a farmer's life reached such heights that it did not remain the story of one individual Chinese peasant. Not just the farmers of the world, but all workers everywhere saw themselves reflected in Wang Lung.

Time did, though, raise a welt on the body of the runaway success of the movie. The person who dreamt up this unprecedented movie and converted his dream into reality, Executive Producer Irving Thalberg did not live to see his magnum opus screened. He died just a few days before its release.

The celebrated American novelist John Steinbeck wrote the modern classic *The Grapes of Wrath*. Many other beautiful novels rolled out of his prolific pen. Pearl Buck, too, wrote a number of novels after *The Good Earth*. Despite going on to write more than fifty books apiece, they could never again reach the heights they scaled with these two respective books.

John Steinbeck was a spirited and skilful writer. He has written a diary that records the creation of *The Grapes of Wrath* and the events as they occurred to him. It records his travel with the migrants, his experience of his

A still from *Mother India* (1957), directed by Mehboob Khan. COURTESY: AUTHOR

A still from *The Good Earth* (1937), directed by Sidney Franklin. COURTESY: WWW.DOCTORMACRO.COM

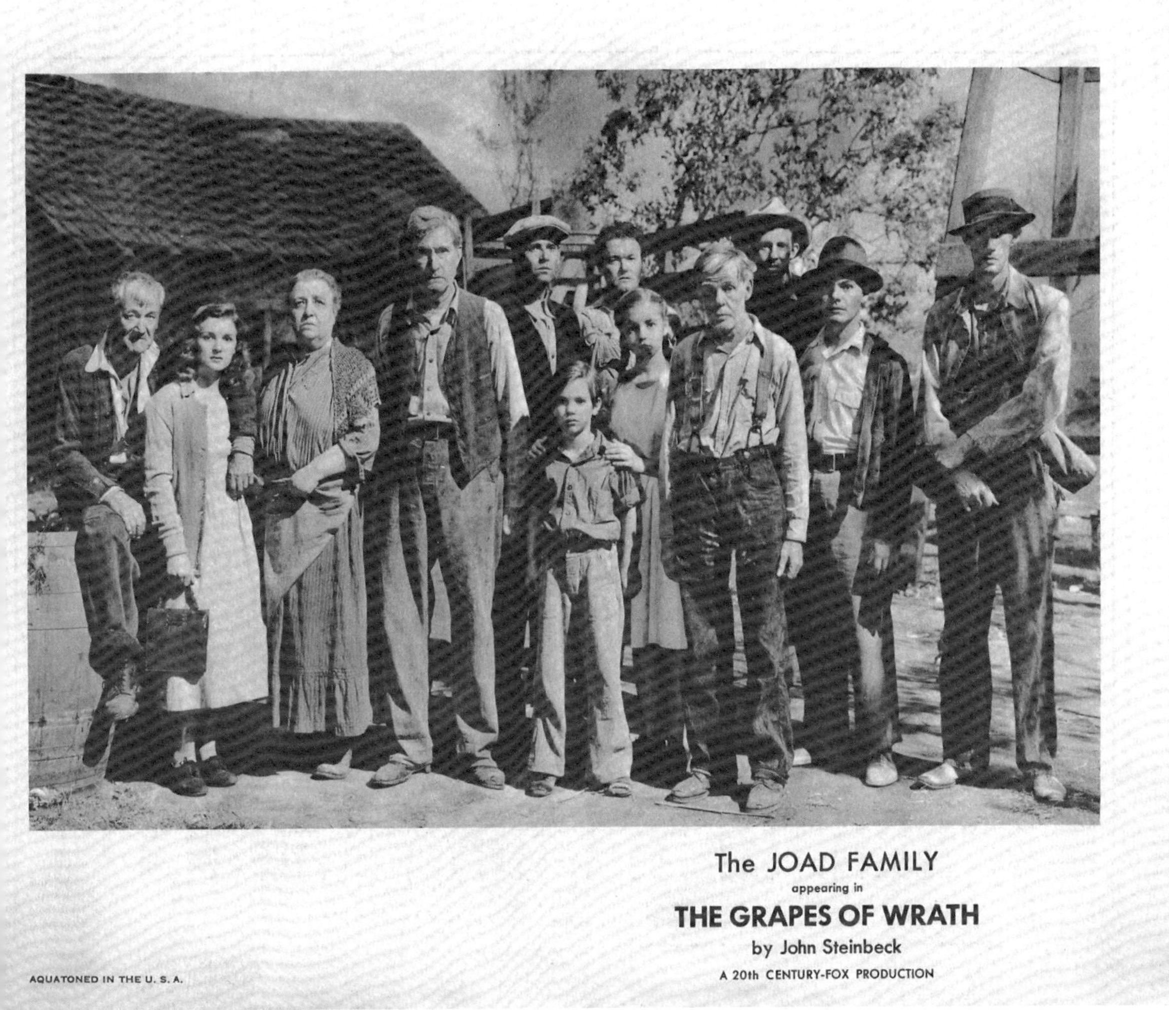

A poster of *The Grapes of Wrath* (1940), directed by John Ford. COURTESY: WWW.DOCTORMACRO.COM

pilgrimage with the displaced. He had to get a first-hand feel of it; therefore, before his pen calloused his fingers, he had picked up the shovel and joined the ranks of the labourers. He had become a part of their struggle, a part of their pain. It was this total commitment that bore fruit had brought forth a masterpiece. Steinbeck later went on to write many wonderful novels like *East of Eden*, *The Pearl* and *Of Mice and Men*, but the pennant of *The Grapes of Wrath* has always fluttered highest.

The Grapes of Wrath came trailing a storm from the day of its birth. Not since the slavery-related *Uncle Tom's Cabin* had any book stirred up such widespread discussion. Steinbeck's rendition of the 'dirty thirties' when tens of thousands of families were forced to abandon their farms, was so impactful that it created an uproar across America. The eight years of drought from 1930s had seen massive migration with a lot of people from Oklahoma migrating to California, only to find that the Great Depression and hit all and sundry. Steinbeck writes the story of one such migrant family, the Joads and their pathetic bid to survive amidst all of it. *The Grapes of Wrath* is the story of their days in exile.

The Joad family migrates from Oklahoma to California. The movie begins with a long shot of young Tom Joad (Henry Fonda) covering the distance on the highway. He had been sentenced to seven years in prison for murder, and is out on parole after having done four years, heading for his family and home in the country. During a ride on the lorry he meets Jim Casy, a former preacher, who joins him on the journey. Casy gave up preaching when he realised that holiness resides in all humankind. When they reach Tom's homestead, they find that it has been abandoned. All that remain are empty, crumbling houses and deserted fields. Muley Graves, the dim-witted village bumpkin is the sole inhabitant left, only because he is determined to live his life out in his birthplace, even if he has to live like a farm rat. He informs Tom that after the Great Depression, the banks and corporations and their agents had descended on the countryside, and blown the settlements away. Homes were bulldozed, and the peasants were pushed out by force of law, with barely a pittance as compensation. Tom's family too had disappeared.

When he finally traces them at a relative's they are already getting ready to embark on another journey. There are jobs aplenty in faraway California, the advertisements claimed; mines laden with dollars. So before their little money ran out, the Joads wanted

'On the highways the people moved like ants and searched for work, for food. And the anger began to ferment. *GRAPES OF WRATH*

to reach California. Old Grandpa Joad refuses to budge from his native land at first, and bellows like a barn animal. He has to be drugged before he can be moved. Tom's younger sister Rose of Sharon, married while Tom was in jail, was pregnant. The Joads, however, saw no alternative but to dump all their belongings on their rattletrap lorry and move on.

They do not go far when Grandpa Joad is cut down by high fever. They don't have a white shroud to cover the corpse. They make do with a borrowed bedsheet, and just move on. The journey is an ordeal. As they cross one vast desert after another, Grandma Joad shrivels. One person who stands up to the fight and becomes the family's ultimate support is Tom's courageous mother. She meets every calamity with an unyielding front. They run into a number of toll booths and insensitive police officers. When they come to an octroi post in the desert, Ma Joad begs her way through by pointing at her ailing old mother-in-law. It happens that the old woman had already died but the fact is revealed to the rest of the family only after they cross the desert. There is no money to give her a proper burial, and she is interred in an unmarked pit.

The long journey through the desert nights has been very imaginatively filmed by John Ford. The superimpositions of the shadowy deserts upon the pictures of the terrified travellers have been beautifully composed.

The Joad family rolls into a transit camp, a concentration camp, if ever there was one. The camera is placed on the front seat of the lorry. As the vehicle turns into the camp, it is followed in by the staring eyes of hungry, wraith-like children. Here, Casy prepares to lead the inmates on a strike against the injustice of the camp authorities. The moneybags, unfortunately, succeed in having him killed. In a frenzied effort to protect Casy, Tom kills one of the camp guards. When he returns to camp with a gash across his face, Ma Joad tells Tom to leave camp and disappear.

Cotton picking gets over, and it begins to rain. Water floods into the camp. Rose of Sharon, resting in the box car, gets into labour and delivers a stillborn child. Ma Joad wades through the slush with great resolution, and they hit upon a track. There, in a barn, they come upon a man on the verge of death. For six days at a stretch he had gone without a grain. In an effort to save the starving man, she pleads with her daughter, Rose of Sharon, to suckle him on her milk-laden breasts. The girl obliges. Ma Joad is the epitome of sacrifice and forbearance. She wears herself out to the bone in an effort to keep the family together.

The Grapes of Wrath, as one of the greatest novels of world literature, compares with the works of Tolstoy and Dostoyevsky. As with the best Russian novels, this book also stands witness to natural calamities like storms, hurricanes, floods and famines, with detailed descriptions of such episodes, not related to the main theme of the book, fitting snugly into the vast canvas of the narrative.

The twelfth chapter of the novel is an excellent example of great writing: the waves of migrants coming together for a night; the camps erected for an overnight halt; the provisional rules and regulations for better management; the young and old of different regions in interaction with each other! Come daybreak, the camps are dismantled, and the human wave moves on towards its next halt. The manner in which Steinbeck has brought to life the episode of a tiny tortoise caught under a truck, no cinematographer can ever hope to reproduce it on celluloid.

Within a month of its publication, the filming rights of *Grapes of Wrath* were bought by Twentieth Century Fox. The Executive Producer Darryl Zanuck wrote out a cheque of $ 75,000 for the rights, an unheard of figure for those times. When news broke that the Twentieth Century Fox had hired the world renowned director John Ford for the enterprise, the people of California—particularly its entrepreneurs and traders under the California Chamber of Commerce—drummed up huge public opposition to the plan of converting the novel into a movie. They feared the movie would hang out the tatters of their prestige to the scrutiny of the world. They went to the extent of threatening a boycott of all Twentieth Century Fox movies if it went ahead with this project.

Ford was, however, keen to bring to life the thousand-mile journey from Oklahoma to California and the travails suffered by the migrants along this long march. He wanted to capture the hardships suffered by the peasants during the Great Depression, but there was another reason too. A similar, ruinous famine had occurred in the middle of the 19th century in faraway Ireland, causing thousands of families to abandon their homes and property, compelling them to migrate. Many had relocated themselves to the American continent across the Atlantic. John's parents were among those who had arrived on the continent with barely the clothes on their emaciated backs. The blood of these migrants ran through John's veins and he held close to his heart the pain of the poor and homeless. That was why he looked at *The Grapes of Wrath* with a different perspective.

John Ford the director was not an individual but an institution. From 1917 to 1966, from being the jewel of the silent era to becoming the king of the talkie, he stretched his suzerainty across almost half a century. He was a master at locating the core of a literary work. That was why he could create a memorable movie called *Stagecoach* based on a short story. From *The Grapes of Wrath* and *How Green Was My Valley*, based upon great novels, to *The Iron House*, *My Darling Clementine*, and *The Quiet Man*, he went on turning out one great movie after another, and proved his mastery as a director over and over again. He loved stories that showcased the grandeur, the loyalty and the extraordinariness of human actions. He has portrayed the large-heartedness and resilience that exist among all kinds of people. As evident from Abraham Lincoln of *Young Mr Lincoln* and Tom Joad of *The Grapes of Wrath,* John Ford was gifted with the insight to locate the drama and quality of life. A large number of his subjects had a poetic underpinning. No wonder, then, that his movies are steeped in the same kind of poetry as Kurusowa and Satyajit Ray.

The subject matter of *The Grapes of Wrath* was particularly close to Ford's heart. Capitalism flourished immediately following the Depression years; while companies moved from strength to strength, the common people were stripped of the clothes off their backs. What fell to their lot was nothing but the grapes of wrath, the sour grapes of dispossession and misery. Alongside is the message of hope, the desire to surmount all obstacles and live on. As Tom Joad says, '[W]herever there's a fight, so hungry people can eat, I'll be there. Wherever there's a cop beatin' up a guy, I'll be there.'

Determined to make a powerful movie on this outstanding novel Ford went ahead with readying the screenplay, contracting the competent **Nunnally Johnson** for the job. While giving the novel a fine reading and during discussions on the screenplay, Ford was assailed by doubts himself: was the plight of the farmers truly as shocking as presented by Steinbeck? To resolve the issue, the producer and the director set up a fact-finding committee. The members made an undercover trip to Oklahoma and California, and submitted a secret report that confirmed the veracity of Steinbeck's presentation. With the eyewitness report removing all doubts, Ford got busy with the movie in right earnest.

Twentieth Century Fox was under a lot of stress, and all its movies and their exhibition were under threat. Many elder statesmen of the industry advised patience, and the suspension of this enterprise. But producer Darryl Zanuck and director John Ford were equally adamant. To allay the storm they played a ruse. They gave the movie a new title, *Highway 66*, and let out that they were working on a different project altogether. The filming continued.

Ford got Gregg Toland to do the camera work for *The Grapes of Wrath,* and he did a beautiful job of capturing the note of melancholy that runs through the film. A year after this came Toland's *Citizen Kane*. The cinematography of this movie reached such dizzying heights that *Citizen Kane* is even today presented to students of cinematography as the epitome of the craft. The neo-realism of Roberto Rossellini and Vittorio De Sica had still to arrive before *The Grapes of Wrath* made its appearance. But John Ford and Gregg Toland had worked their magic five years earlier. It was also in this movie that Henry Fonda made his debut, and went on to become an acting phenomenon.

John Ford had the thin, slim actress Bondi in mind to play Ma Joad. But the producer compelled him to settle for the heavy-built Jane Darwell. This actress, however, so beautifully eased herself into the character, and gave such a flawless portrayal of Ma Joad that she has become an indelible part of the movie.

John Ford is regarded as the guru of the long shot. Close-ups were rare, and only when necessary. His particular talent lay in shooting gorgeous scenes with a static camera. He used a special style of lighting to capture the human tragedy that unfolds in *The Grapes of Wrath*. The novel is undoubtedly great, but the scenes in the movie too come to life one after the other like the turning pages of the Bible. Jane Darwell bagged the Oscar for Best Supporting Actress. The award for the Best Film that year went to Alfred Hitchcock's *Rebecca*, but the jury did not dare to let the Best Director's award go to Hitchcock. It had to go to John Ford for his masterpiece.

When *The Good Earth* was screened at the Metro cinema hall in Mumbai, it attracted a large number of Hindi cinema technicians and artists to gather some new ideas. Mehboob Khan's screenplay writer Babubhai Mehta saw it first, and recommended that Mahboob see it too. Along with their Chief Assistant Director Chimankant Gandhi, the three saw the movie together.

Mehboob hailed from a village called Sarara near Billimoria in Gujarat, and his grand-parental village was Kashipura. As a child in his father's and his grandfather's place, Mehboob had seen life in the village from close. His father Ramzan was the village blacksmith. He was particularly well known for fixing horseshoes. Mehboob grew up observing the misery of peasants groaning under the burden of debt, with their life hocked in perpetuity to the moneylender. He owned some land too. He had experienced how the peasant ultimately fell victim to famine, however hard he worked. It was this personal experience that brought tears to his eyes when he saw the misfortunes visited upon Wang Lung, on screen. When he stepped out of the hall, he announced that he would make a movie on a similar theme, that too, before the year was out.

He barely had enough education, but he knew how to spot and appreciate talent, and collected technicians and artists around him of the highest calibre. Babubhai Mehta, who read English literature extensively, had read Pearl Buck's *The Good Earth,* and another of her novels called *Mother*, which he brought to Mehboob's notice. *Mother* is the story of a Chinese peasant woman who sacrifices her all to look after her emaciated children. She sells her body to the wealthy and saves her children from perishing. But the sacrosanct Sita-Savitri image of womanhood has such a strong hold on the Indian psyche, that the thought of a woman selling her body even in the most extreme circumstances would be unacceptable. That is why the powerful character of Radha is the product of the combined imagination of Mehboob and Babubhai. In *Mother*, a son of the Chinese woman becomes a rebel and finally joins the Communist revolution. Out of this boy emerges the character of the rebellious Birju. For eight to ten days Babubhai sat spinning a screenplay on this theme, and soon shooting began for *Aurat* at National Studio in Mumbai.

Usury has been as much of a curse for the Indian farmer as famine. Famine disappears after some days, but the moneylender and his account book pursue the poor farmer to his grave. The dead farmer's debts settle like a ghost on his children. This explains why even today, in the early years of the 21st century, farmers find suicide an easier way out. Even before he saw Thalberg's *The Good Earth*, Mehboob had been deeply impressed by Baburao Painter's *Sawkaari Paash*, a Marathi film released in 1937. It tells the pathetic story of a farmer named Anyaba, who puts his thumbprint on the moneylender's ledger, and allows his life to be caught, in perpetuity, in the mesh of debts. The character of Chikate, the moneylender, had left a deep impression on Mehboob Khan. It was on his lines that the character of the wicked, fraudulent, dissembling moneylender Sukhilal was created. It was on this theme that Mehboob first produced *Aurat* in 1940, and repeated it with the magnificent *Mother India* in 1957. The main cast that served in *Aurat* was different from the one in *Mother India*. But Kanhaiyalal had portrayed the character of Sukhilal with such perfection that Mehboob did not even think of any alternative to him. Often, during the shooting, he would place his arm on Kanhaiyalal's shoulder and say, 'Pal, it is good that you are still alive.'

The movies that Mehboob made during his early days for Sagar Movietone and others were technically not of the best quality. But as time went on, as he gained experience and knowledge, he steadily went on improving. Cinema was the very air that he breathed. As a child, whenever touring talkies visited his village, he would run to see those silent films, and be roundly caned by his father for his effort. Later, when the lure of the screen pulled him to Mumbai, he had no money; so he had made friends with a Railway Guard named Ismail. Initially he lived in the *chawls* (tenements) close to Lamington Road. The great director, who would later occupy a seat of honour among the sculptors of Indian cinema, often stood in line to be picked up for an extra's role. It was only when *Andaaz*, studded with matinee idols like Dilip Kumar, Nargis and Raj Kapoor hit the screen, the audience realised the true potential of Mehboob.

The foundation of his production company, however, was laid with *Aurat*, in which Sardar Akhtar played Radha. Mehboob married her the same year. While writing the script of *Aurat*, Babubhai and Mehboob dwelt deeply on Indian farming and culture and this led to another great movie of all times—*Mother India*.

Radha's husband Shaam, alias Shaamu, is a traditional farmer. His mother Sundar Chaachi mortgages their farm with Sukhilala to raise a loan for her son's marriage. While Sukhilala's ledger was beyond anybody's ability to read, his head was forever scheming to drown the harassed, adversity-hit farmers in the cesspool of debts. Those who have lived or observed from close, the life of the Indian farmer know very well that ornaments are

'Main beta de sakti hoon, laaj nahi de sakti'

(I can give my son, but not my honor) *MOTHER INDIA*

made not for the women to deck themselves in, but to rest in the moneylender's locker. Aesop's tales talk of only inward going hoof-marks at the mouth of the cave; that is exactly what happens to the gold ornaments that go to the moneylender's house. The house gets swallowed next, never to be seen again. Unable to withstand the pressure, Shaamu just walks out on his family one day, leaving the responsibility of bringing up the children on his wife Radha. Her rebellious son Birju nurses just one dream: to retrieve her mother's bracelets from the moneylender's safe.

Like O-lan in *The Good Earth*, Radha too wears herself out raising her children. She protects herself from the lecherous intentions of the moneylender. When the rains flood the fields, she stops the rest of the villagers from abandoning their farms, persuading them that pearls are where their soil is. Through her words and deeds, she rises beyond being the mother of Raamu and Birju alone; she becomes the mother of the entire village community—she becomes Mother India.

Birju grows up to become a bandit and returns to avenge his mother's woes on the day Sukhilala's daughter is to be wedded. He kills the moneylender and abducts his daughter, only to be spotted by his mother who shoots him down. Birju dies in his mother's arms but before dying hands over her gold bangles that had been pawned to Sukhilala.

While Mehboob Khan had studded his screenplay with a number of conflict-ridden episodes and heart-wrenching scenes, he was searching desperately for a suitably taut finish for his film. In *The Good Earth*, it is just the change of circumstances of the farmers that have been stirringly portrayed. *The Grapes of Wrath* does not carry a sensational climax either. Mehboob wanted a climax for his movie that would elevate it to the lofty heights of an epic.

A childhood friend, who knew of Mehboob's love for groundnuts, arrived with a parcel wrapped in a Gujarati newspaper. As he sat munching, his eyes fell on a news item printed there. It was the sensational story of a peasant mother in Junagadh district who had killed her own son. As she was returning home at dusk, she heard a shriek. She noticed, at the edge of the farm, a young man trying to molest a girl from the village. When she ran towards them, she recognised her own son as the perpetrator of the crime. When after repeated pleas and threats the boy refused to withdraw, the woman swung the scythe in her hand and hacked him to death. Mehboob recognised in this news item the climax he was looking for and it went and fit neatly in his screenplay.

The Birju of *Aurat* was played by Yaqub, a well-known actor of those times. Dilip Kumar was very keen to land the role for himself, but Nargis and Dilip Kumar had had a number of hits as a romantic pair, and it was feared that the audience would not accept them playing mother and son. So Mehboob had to turn down Dilip Kumar's plea. Mehboob had actually decided to give the role to Saaboo, who had lately become very popular in Hollywood movies.

Around this time there was this young man called Sunil Dutt who was eking out a living working part-time at a Mumbai bus depot, and doubling up as an anchor with Radio Ceylon to keep the hearth warm. It was through comic actor Mukri that Sunil Dutt went to meet Mehboob. Mehboob agreed to give Sunil Dutt the role of Raamu, the decent of Radha's two sons. Seizing the opportunity of working under a great director, Sunil Dutt agreed to do the role for free. Meanwhile, it was realised that the bill for housing Saaboo in a five-star hotel would go well beyond the budget. Mehboob bid Saaboo goodbye, and after some dilly-dallying handed the Birju role to Sunil Dutt, and that turned the struggling actor's fortune. Ramu's role was finally played by Rajendra Kumar.

Sardar Akhtar had given a wonderful rendition of Radha in *Aurat*. Radha in *Mother India* would be the very life and soul of the film, and the industry was keen to know who the role would go to. Everybody knew that it was Mehboob Khan who had given Nargis her break in films. Everybody also knew that he would not give her the role of Radha under any circumstance. The reason was that, under the influence of Raj Kapoor and R.K. Studios, Nargis had turned down Mehboob's offer of the lead role in *Aan*. In a huff, Mehboob handed over the meaty role to debutante Nadira. While the movie did well, Nadira was found to lack the requisite acting skills. Mehboob was still sore at having been turned down and having landed a cuckoo with Nadira, and was in no mood to offer Radha to Nargis. The search for a competent Radha was on in full swing. Old timers say that the Marathi actress Sulochana was high on Mehboob's list.

Meanwhile, the winds were changing. Nargis was steadily distancing herself from R.K. Studio. In the company of her mother Jaddanbai, Nargis had seen *Aurat* plenty of times. She knew very well the fire that the role of Radha carried. Destiny alone could help an actress land this incomparable role. Keeping all this in mind, not letting vanity get in her way, she presented herself before Mehboob. The canny director spotted the glitter in her moisture-laden eyes as she pleaded for the role. A woman who would stand up against the tyranny of the usurer, a woman who would save the village from the ravages of famine, a woman who, to protect the dignity of womanhood, would have the stomach to pump a bullet into her own son, portraying such a woman needed passion—and a glitter in the eye. It didn't take long for Mehboob Khan to let his anger dissolve. The role of Radha is the role of a multidimensional woman in head-on collision with the vicissitudes of life. Shakeel Badaayuni has summed up her persona in the movie in just four lines:

Lakdi jal koyla bhayi,
Koyla jal bhayo raakh:
Mai Paapan aisi jali,
Naa koyla bhayi naa raakh
(The log burnt itself to coal,
The coal then burnt to ash;
I, sinner, burnt such
That burnt to coal nor ash)

Nargis breathed such life into Radha that it became the crowning glory of her entire career as an actress. No surprise, then, that the newly instituted Filmfare Award came her way.

Mehboob shot most of *Mother India* outdoors. For a number of days he shot in the Gujarat countryside, including his grandfather's village Kashipura and his father's Sarara. He flooded the open fields near Azamgarh in Uttar Pradesh, and assembled 200 bullock carts and a mob of 1000 men. This is where Nargis's song—*O jaaney waaley naa jaao ghar apna chhod ke*—dissuading the villagers from abandoning the village, is filmed. Some scenes have been shot at Bhuinj in Satara district, and in Kolhapur too.

The filming of the song *Matwaala jiyaa boley piyaa* on a field at village Shiroli near Kolhapur went on for a number of days. Mehboob compensated the farmer generously for the loss to his crop. Additionally, when the film was exhibited at Rajaram Talkies at Kolhapur, he phoned up the proprietor Major Nimbalkar, and arranged for the farmer's family to be brought over by car to see the movie.

Mother India was released in 1957. It ran to full houses across India, and went on running for a long time. In the world of cinema today, the Oscar is regarded as the most authentic measure of quality. *Mother India* was one of the five movies nominated for the Best Foreign Film award.

The nomination for the Oscar brought a sense of pride to the entire nation, including Prime Minister Jawaharlal Nehru and President Rajendra Prasad. The film reached the third and final round, but lost the golden opportunity in this critical round by one solitary mark. In the International Film Festival at Karlovy Vary in Czechoslovakia, it held the audience spellbound, and brought for Nargis the Best Actress award.

Even today, while watching *Mother India*, one becomes forcefully aware of the outstanding directorial genius of Mehboob Khan. One especially remembers his tight close-ups immediately followed by long shots covering extensive details of the scene in cutaway close-ups. He has executed the final scenes of the movie with great effectiveness. When Radha sees her son galloping away with the moneylender's daughter, she aims her gun at him and lets out a loud yell, 'Birjoooo!!!' On the right corner of the frame is Radha, and on the left corner is the horse. When the determined, sweat-bathed Radha shoots her son, she is captured by cinematographer Fardoon Irani in the avatar of the avenging Goddess Kali flaunting her trident.

The scene has been shot during the hot afternoon hour. When the mortally wounded Birju slips off the horse, the dumb animal turns round to lick its master. How, then, could the mother stay away? When she dashes towards her fallen son to gather him in his arms, the camera trolley too runs at the same pace to record the mother-son embrace. When, with shaking hands he pulls out of his shirt the blood-soaked gold bangles to give over to his mother, the blood too bears an uncanny resemblance to the water bursting out of a dam mixed with the red soil of the earth. Another symbol of the hapless lives of the poor, toiling peasants.

A little reflection reveals that while the three movies sprang out of different soils, religions and cultures, they sing paeans to the same mother earth. However much some may shout the slogan of 'Leave the farm', farming culture is the greatest of the world's cultures. The two images of woman and land are often considered as one. New life springs out of the soil.

THE UPRISING

SPARTACUS
BRAVEHEART
LAGAAN

'Death is the only freedom a slave knows'

SPARTACUS

John F. Kennedy was the President of US in 1960, when he heard great reports about the movie *Spartacus* from friends. He insisted on enjoying it sitting among the ordinary filmgoers of the country and walked into a cinema hall in Washington DC. The 196 minute epic on celluloid left him stunned. The little-known 1951 historical novel, written by Howard Fast, had been rendered into an epic by director Stanley Kubrick

The United States abolished slavery in the 19th century. However, it was between 73 BC and 71 BC, roughly 2000 years ago, that an ordinary slave, by the name of Spartacus, first unfurled the flag of revolt against the unjust and cruel system of slavery. The Roman Empire had reached a stage of glory and prosperity, enough to make the gods envious. The stigma it carried was of slavery. Human beings were bred like poultry and pigs and subjected to unimaginable persecution. It was against this disgrace that Spartacus had first hoisted the red flag of revolt.

Spartacus was a mineworker who slogged like an ant in the deserts of Libya, a territory under Roman occupation. His life was nothing more than the perspiration dripping down his body, blood oozing from his wounds, tears damming in his eyes and the sun beating down on his back.

The super-rich and the super-powerful Romans of those times organised plenty of games for their entertainment. One such popular pastime was the gladiatorial contest, where slaves were made to clash against each other. Robust labourers from these mines were sent over to the Gladiator Academy in Capua. These select class of labourers were supplied with good food, drinks, and an occasional girl as reward. As with cockfights, the slaves were thrown into an arena armed with deadly weapons, and they fought till one died. This inhuman contest was watched with great relish by the spectators in the gallery. The dead one was then dragged by his feet and thrown out.

The movie begins with the ambitious, senior general of Rome, Marcus Crassus (Lawrence Olivier), going to Capua with his family to witness a gladiatorial clash. Out of the herd of slaves lined up like animals, they select Spartacus (Kirk Douglas). He is to be pitted against the mammoth dark slave, Draba.

As they wait to be released into the arena, these two contestants look at each other with resignation through their wooden cages. Using a single source of light, the director effectively catches the expressions on their faces—the miseries of existence and the meaninglessness of life and death.

Sharp weapons in hand, Spartacus and Draba charge at each other. Crassus and the other lords and ladies in the gallery watch the combat with great excitement and scream with delight. When Spartacus falls to the ground wounded, Draba places the tip of his weapon on his rival's throat. Overexcited women from the gallery can be heard chanting, 'Kill him! Kill him!'

Overwhelmed with disgust at the bloodthirsty brutality of the heartless rich women, Draba turns round and sends his spear flying into the gallery. He jumps over the barricades with violent intent when a guard's spear gets him in the back. Crassus steps forward and beheads him with one stroke of the sword. Spartacus is moved beyond words at this noble gesture of Draba, of staking his own life to save another, and the spark of rebellion is ignited in him.

The walls of the slaveyard at Capua make Spartacus restless. He has been seeing a young slave girl named Varinia but Crassus, attracted by her good looks has bought her for a handsome price. Bursting with anger at the merciless persecution of his fellow slaves, Spartacus snaps the chains of servitude. He and his co-conspirators smash through the barbed fencing of the Gladiator Academy and escape into the Italian countryside.

They go from village to village inciting the other slaves to rise up and revolt. They form a large army of rebels, under the leadership of Spartacus. The mission is the capture of Rome itself, the fountainhead of oppression. If a sustained war has to be waged against Rome, the rebellious slaves believe they have to head out to sea.

Ordinary slaves fly the flag of revolt, and gather a large army within a matter of six to seven months. The Roman senate is jolted at the turn of events. Through guerrilla tactics, Spartacus shreds the vast Roman army. When out at sea a pirate tells Spartacus, 'Surely you know you're going to lose, don't you? You have no chance.' Spartacus responds, 'When a free man dies, he loses the pleasure of life. A slave loses his pain. Death is the only freedom a slave knows. That's why he's not afraid of it. That's why we'll win.'

'When a free man dies, he loses the pleasure of life. A slave loses his pain. Death is the only freedom a slave knows. That's why he's not afraid of it. That's why we'll win. *SPARTACUS*

There are two streams of thought in the Roman court: one represented by Crassus who wants dictatorship under the guise of freedom; the other by the contemplative, senior senator Gracchus who cares for democracy in its truest sense. The conflict between these two streams brings to mind William Shakespeare's great play *Julius Caesar*. The Roman Empire cannot allow the rebellion to succeed at any cost. As they claim, 'This campaign is not alone to kill Spartacus. It is to kill the legend of Spartacus.'

The political games that Crassus and Gracchus play in their effort to eliminate Spartacus become evident in the second half of the film. When Spartacus is preparing for his last battle, his wife Varinia is pregnant. The love scenes encompassing the joys and sorrows of the two have been beautifully captured. Overcome with the enormity of his mission, Spartacus creeps into the bed beside her one night. 'I love you more than my life,' he tells her. 'Yet, sometimes, even with you here sleeping beside me...I feel so alone. I imagine a god for slaves...and I pray. I pray for a son who'll be born free.'

The Roman senators use everything in their power to annihilate Spartacus. Finally, the vast army of the Roman Empire and the resilient band of Spartacus's soldiers join in mortal clash on the battlefield. At the critical moment General Pompei rushes in with his forces, and with his help the Romans hand Spartacus a crushing defeat. The battlefield is littered with corpses. Stanley Kubrick shot the grand war scenes on a vast plain outside Madrid in Spain, which constitute a major attraction of the movie.

Burning to wreak vengeance upon his foe, Crassus goes hunting for Spartacus among the dead bodies. There he runs into Varinia and her child, and dispatches them to his tent. The six to seven hundred survivors of the rebel band are brought in chains before Crassus. The announcement is made to them, 'By command of His Most Merciful Excellency...your lives are to be spared...on the single condition that you identify the body...or the living person of the slave called Spartacus.'

The battle-ravaged faces are on full alert. Spartacus himself is about to disclose his identity when every one of his followers shouts out, 'I'm Spartacus!—I'm Spartacus!' The eagle eyes of Crassus are, however, able to locate Spartacus among the prisoners of war. He orders a combat-to-death between Spartacus and his friend Antoninus, with the rider that the survivor would be crucified.

Keen to save the other from the torture of crucifixion, each tries to kill the other. When Antoninus tells him, 'I love you, Spartacus, as I loved my own father,' Spartacus answers, 'I love you...like my son that I'll never see.' With that he thrusts his sword into Antoninus with the words, 'Go to sleep.'

Crassus's political rival Senator Gracchus does not allow Crassus to satisfy his lust upon Spartacus's wife. He buys her and her child, and lets her go free, helping her cross the Roman limits through a secret passage to reach Aquitania. As she travels, she sees bodies hanging on both sides of the road, some of them still with traces of life. She then comes to the crucifix on which Spartacus is nailed. She lifts her baby towards him and says, 'This is your son. He's free, Spartacus! Free!' The movie ends on this note of poetic justice.

The sublimity and grandeur of an epic historical movie does not depend only upon glittering costumes and massive, expensive settings. A substantial burden is carried by the dialogues that help reveal the invisible throbs that palpitate inside the epic. The screenplay of *Spartacus*, based on the novel by Howard Fast, had been written by Dalton Trumbo and owed a good part of its success to its high quality, intelligent dialogues: 'Politics is a practical profession,' says Senator Gracchus while talking about democracy.

Spartacus was a joint production of Universal Studios and Kirk Douglas's firm Bryna. Douglas wore two hats: hero on-screen and producer off it. The actual shooting began in January 1959. At first Universal Studios contracted the experienced and established Anthony Mann as director. Some of the biggest British stars like Lawrence Olivier, Peter Ustinov and Charles Laughton were chosen to play Roman noblemen. Mann was so heavily under their influence that it is believed Ustinov had gone to the extent of directing his own scenes. Douglas was upset at this that he immediately dismissed Mann and brought in 30-year-old Stanley Kubrick to replace him. *Gone with the Wind* had also had a change of director within a month of starting. Here it took just 15 days to take this tough decision. Kubrick was phoned up on a Friday and asked to take charge by next Monday. It was a risky step but Douglas had studied Kubrick during the making of *Paths of Glory* and was convinced he was the man.

Kubrick was a spirited, intelligent and courageous young director with a firm understanding of the technical aspects of film-making. But his arrival did not signal 'all well' either. He would often get into scraps with the cinematographer Russell Metty, and did not give Olivier the respect due to his seniority.

Kubrick did not much like Dalton Trumbo's screenplay either. Consequently, scenes would be re-written almost every night, and the actors would be required to rehearse their dialogues immediately afterwards. There would be many a nitpicking even after that. Out of this process, however, a good piece of work was taking shape; the script was steadily getting tighter and cleaner and the dialogues more impactful.

The shooting went on for 150 days. When the first run was shown on the screen, the director and the actor-producer were convinced that they had a disaster on their hands. The grand dreams they had dreamt, the plans they had executed, none of it were visible on the screen.

Kubrick and Douglas tightened their belts again and decided to leave for Spain with their unit. Thousands of soldiers had to be quickly mobilised and sent in advance. They had to capture scenes of their teeth chattering with cold, their bodies soaked to the skin in rain, their hard training and their combat with nature, on the rocky terrain.

The new round of shooting added richness and grandeur to the final product. The advance of the armed soldiers was captured in a single long-panning shot. The effect created by the back-tracking camera are images one can see only in the rarest of rare films. The camera tilts up to capture thousands of soldiers scampering down the mountainside like tiny ants; in the same shot the camera tilts down to show a cavalry charge rushing from the frame in front straight at you. Kubrick had woven many such magical effects into the film.

Stanley Kubrick is listed high among the best directors of the world. *Killer's Kiss*, *Lolita*, *Paths of Glory*, *Full Metal Jacket*, *The Shining*, and most importantly *2001: A Space Odyssey* are some of the great movies credited to him. *Spartacus*, of course, belongs to a different genre. It bagged four Oscars but it was neither for Kirk Douglas nor Lawrence Olivier or Stanley Kubrick.

Peter Ustinov won one for Best Supporting role. The rest were for Best Cinematography, Best Art Direction-Set Decoration and Best Costume Design.

After David Lean's *Lawrence of Arabia* it had begun to appear that the new generation audience would never get to see movies of such epic dimensions again. However, in the beginning of 1995 Mel Gibson's 70 million dollar movie *Braveheart* arrived on the screen. This 177 minute movie created history by capturing the imagination of millions of filmgoers the world over. Knocking the hats off the heads of the critics, it created a new reference point among war movies. The story, based on Blind Harry's epic poem *The Actes and Deidis of the Illustre and Vallyeant Campioun Schir William Wallace,* had been adapted for the screen by Randall Wallace. There are in fact many legends and eulogies around him in Scotland. Randall wove these stories into the rich fabric of his screenplay.

William Wallace was an ordinary Scot who had later rebelled and risen against the unjust, cruel and despotic rule of Edward I, King of England. The movie begins with a shot of white mist in the horizon. From behind the gossamer screen of the mist peeps the eye-catching natural vista of Scotland—its tall, crooked mountains, its blue-green meadows, its milky water bodies. A kind of magic starts happening. Like the *djinn* of Alladin's lamp picking up a thumb-sized man on his palm and depositing him on a far-away fairy land, within minutes the shot transports one to Scotland, amidst the resilient, aggressive, war-like denizens of the 13th century.

After dealing with Wallace's childhood, the scene shifts to London, the palace of the wicked, cruel English king, Edward Longshanks, who is seen in conversation with his advisors. He is looking for ways to subjugate Scotland and has a novel idea. His newly-wed daughter-in-law listens to this in amazement:

The trouble with Scotland... is that it's full of Scots! Perhaps the time has come to reinstitute an old custom. Grant them *prima noctes*. First night, when any common girl inhabiting their lands is married, our nobles shall have sexual rights to her on the night of her wedding. If we can't get them out, we breed them out. That should fetch just the kind of lords we want to Scotland, taxes or no taxes.

To prevent attracting this law upon himself, Wallace gets married on the sly to his beloved Murron MacClannough, who is beautiful, charming and an inspiring person. News of his secret marriage reaches the magistrate, who feels cheated out of his sexual rights on Murron. He, therefore, has the girl arrested, tied to a post and killed in public view. What begins as a private spark soon becomes a public conflagration. Wallace rebels against his wicked, death-dispensing enemy, with guerrilla tactics. He and his collaborators take advantage of the inimical nature of the land to keep the fire of revolt burning. With his robust, aggressive assaults Wallace administers one jolt after another to the English crown.

When it seems impossible to defeat Wallace by force, the scheming Edwards starts weaving silken threads round his neck to hang him by. First, he sends his beautiful daughter-in-law Isabella on the mission of arranging a compromise with the rebel leader. This daughter of the French king gets so influenced by Wallace's bravery that she falls in love with him. This ruse having failed, Edward then reaches out to the traditional nobles of Scotland. Noblemen everywhere, he knows, are in a class by themselves, and would do anything to safeguard their interests. One such lord, the 16th Robert Bruce happily uses his son as a pawn in an effort to save his possessions and sends him to join the rebel group. Through the clever use of his son's friendship, he lures Wallace to a deserted spot. Despite being warned not to go alone, Wallace places his trust in Robert Junior, who, innocent of all the plottings of his father, leads his friend into the snare. The lion is caught and caged and transported to England.

Being sold down the river by one's confidants seems to be a curse under which most revolutionaries labour. As Umaji Naik was betrayed by his own sister, as Rango Bapuji was done in by the foolish officials of the Bhor pilgrim town, so was Wallace led to his doom by some of his nearest ones. He is tortured in public before being executed. The uncontrollable lamentation of his followers, and the vision of his late wife Murron among the grieving crowds, paying him homage, are scenes that leave the audience choked with emotion towards the end.

The script of *Braveheart* had turned out to be compact and brilliant. The totally enamoured producer Alan Ladd, Jr. and the writer Randall Wallace could think of only one person to play the revolutionary, and that was the well-built Mel Gibson and so they approached him for the lead role.

In an interview, re-living his experience of first reading of the script, Mel Gibson said it was like an electric current passing through his head. It wasn't just the character, it was a tale of bravery that percolated to every cell in his being. Initially, it didn't stir the actor in him. It was the image of a

A still from *Braveheart* (1995), directed by Mel Gibson. COURTESY: WWW.DOCTORMACRO.COM

A still from *Spartacus* (1960), directed by Stanley Kubrick. COURTESY: WWW.DOCTORMACRO.COM

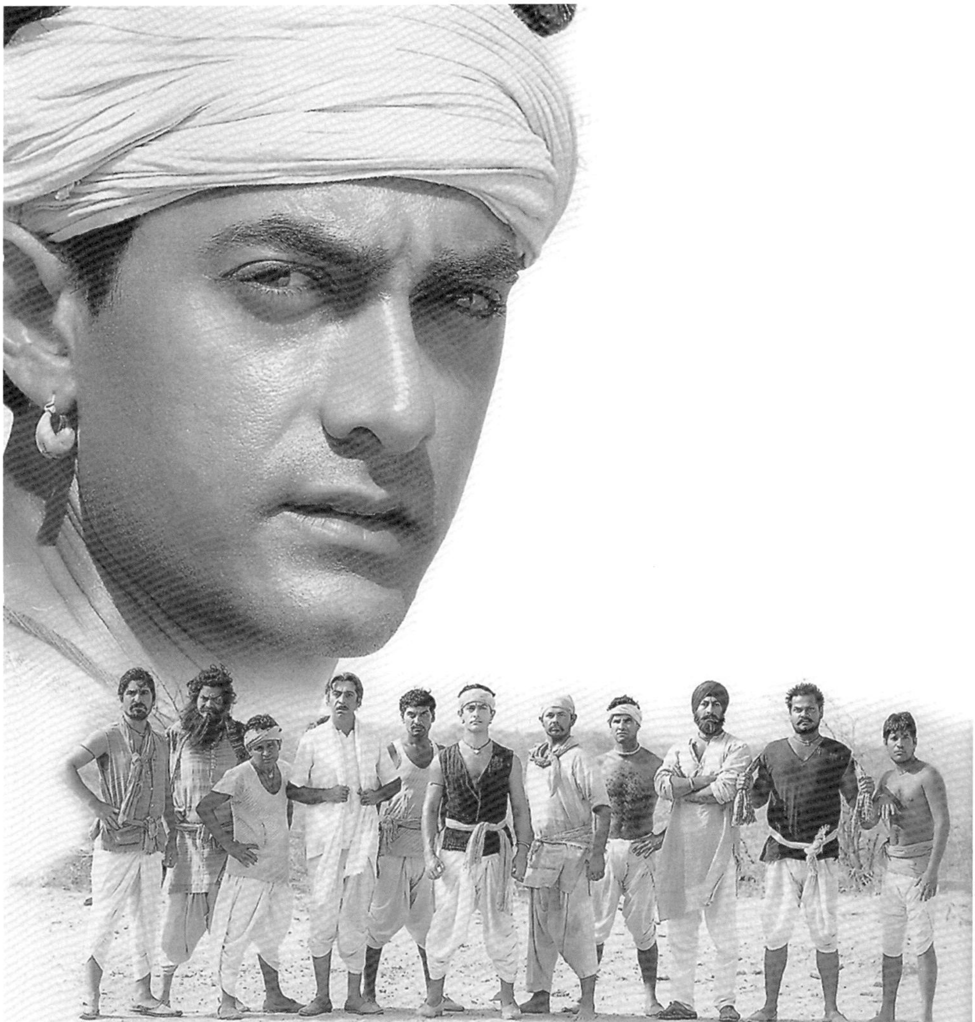

A poster of *Lagaan: Once Upon a Time in India* (2001), directed by Ashutosh Gowariker. COURTESY: AUTHOR

purposeless man out of a cave that stood before his mind's eye. The character was as bellicose as he was strong. As a director it was a greater challenge to bring to the screen all the events of his life narrated by the writer. How would he do it? Gibson, impressed by the script, declared to them that he would be delighted to direct the movie instead.

Gibson, the tall, well-built actor with sparkling blue eyes had made his debut in 1979 with *Mad Max*. He learnt acting at the National Institute of Dramatic Art, Sidney, Australia. *The Year of Living Dangerously* (1983), where he played a journalist who lived dangerously; *The River* (1984) where he was an exemplary farmer; Part I (1987), Part II (1989) and Part III (1992) of the serial movies *Lethal Weapon*; *Hamlet: The Prince of Denmark* (1990)—were some of the movies where he had shone as the hero before the arrival of *Braveheart*. *The Man without a Face* was his first directorial effort.

As an actor or as a director, he is known to completely immerse himself in his work. To play the character Sergeant Martin Riggs in *Lethal Weapon* Gibson is believed to have located an eccentric person who had fought in Vietnam and later joined the police force and become the nemesis of many a criminal. Gibson met this person, made a close study of him, his idiosyncrasies, his methodology, and poured this experience into the character which he played with great panache.

When the producer saw Gibson was hooked on to the idea of directing *Braveheart*, he attached a rider to it—he had to play the lead role of William Wallace as well. Gibson picked up the gauntlet and eventually proved to the world that he could bring the same dedication and passion to his work both before and behind the camera, and that too simultaneously.

With the original story and the screenplay already tuned to satisfaction, the shooting began within a few months. A movie with this big a budget generally requires a number of rehearsals. However, since they did not have enough time in hand, they had to manage without much preparation.

Gibson has always had a fondness for movies dealing with patriotism and other purposeful issues. He loved *The Big Country*, *Double Indemnity* and *Spartacus*, and from the very beginning he wanted to handle such larger-than-life themes. For an ambitious big-budget movie of such epic dimension, the first big obstacle is locating the right cast. A wrong judgement here and the chariot wheels could well get stuck in the middle of the battlefield. Chocolate

'They may take away our lives, but they'll never take our freedom!

BRAVEHEART

hero Gregory Peck never looked right for Captain Ahab in *Moby Dick*, and despite the presence of the celebrated director John Huston and a novel of the highest literary worth, the ship didn't succeed in reaching the shore of success.

Gibson picked Patrick McGoohan to play the scheming Edward I. McGoohan had a rather petite nose, so to give a lift to his Irish feaures he had to be fitted out with a Roman looking rubber nose to make him look like a proper king. The veteran actor proved from the first shot that his talents were no less majestic than the sets erected around him.

Murron, Wallace's beloved, appears in a few scenes in the early part of the movie. She then appears again as an ethereal vision in the crowd as Wallace is about to be decapitated. Despite being absent in almost seventy per cent of the movie it was important that her spirit hovered over it. This country belle needed to be transcendentally beautiful; despite her humble birth she had to create the illusion of divinity. Gibson chose the new comer Catherine McCormack for this role. She was just one-film old, yet her performance fully satisfied the director's expectations.

For Princess Isabella, he tested out many stars from England and Europe, but none met his expectations. Finally, he settled on French actress Sophie Marceau. Her statuesque figure, her royal arrogance and her proud body language that exuded rank and distinction in any company, made her stand out. She had begun her career as a child actress in France, so Gibson did not have to work very hard on her.

Most of the movie was shot in Scotland where rains were forever their companion, and the crew had to wait under their umbrellas to let the latest shower pass. But Scotland with its rocky, hilly terrain, made it difficult for shooting cavalry movements. The war scenes, therefore, had to be shot on the plains of Ireland.

To make his war scenes authentic and intense, Gibson fought with the passion of a soldier. Along with *Spartacus*, he saw the clips of war movies again and again. A storyboard was prepared where every frame was discussed in detail. A battleground chart was laid out on the table like a chessboard, and toy soldiers were placed to determine their movements.

For the battle scenes he needed disciplined extras. He got in touch with the army to procure a regiment or two. The Scottish Government disappointed him and turned down his request. The Irish government was willing to oblige and 1600 soldiers of the reserve forces marched out for the shooting. Gibson had the option to use advanced technology, but he preferred to field additional soldiers to create the real feeling. He finished off the battle scenes in eight weeks.

When the king's cavalry comes charging down upon the rebel soldiers, the latter pick up sharp wooden staves and pierce them into the horses' chests. To avoid causing injuries to the real horses, Gibson used technology interspersed with dummy animals. Mixing the real and fake ones cleverly, he got the shots he wanted.

The jungle skirmishes in *Gladiator,* one of the recent movies, and the battle scenes in *Seven Samurai* are outstanding and frightening as well, but the hand-to-hand combat scenes of *Braveheart* are unmatched. Similar scenes of close-quarter battles had been shot for *Spartacus* as well, but they were not granted permission for screening.

All said and done, *Spartacus* occupies the highest position of all. Even today when one watches its massive army, the heart skips a beat; the crowd of extras assembled for the battle scenes was truly vast. And one does not need reminding that there were neither computers nor mechanical horses back then. Real horses were being whipped to action.

When I talk of *Lagaan* in the same breath as *Spartacus* and *Braveheart*, I think of the thread of revolt and the struggle against injustice that bind them together. While the central event of the first two movies is based on history, in *Lagaan* it is pure fiction. But in its style, as with *Spartacus* and *Braveheart*, and in its grandeur, *Lagaan* has long established its position of eminence in the history of Hindi movies.

Unlike the earlier two movies, *Lagaan* does not offer us armed struggle against authority. Instead, a small village called Champaner in the Central Provinces stands up against the might of the British Empire, not with swords and cannon, but with bat and ball.

‘*Chulhe se roti nikale ke liye, chimte ko apna mooh jalaye padi*

(To remove the bread from the hearth, the tongs have to take the heat) *LAGAAN*

Caught in the throes of famine, the villagers find it impossible to pay their land tax (*lagaan*). An altercation takes place between British Captain Russell and a village lad, named Bhuvan (Aamir Khan). Captain Russell offers a deal that if the village can beat the British in a game of cricket, two years of land tax would be waived. Excited, the villagers take up the challenge. On the one side is the arrogance and colonial mindset of the whites, on the other is the resilience of the villagers. To add to that Captain Russell's pretty sister Elizabeth (Rachel Shelley) is so enamoured with Bhuvan that she secretly gives the villagers cricketing lessons. There is also the pretty village belle Gauri (Gracy Singh) who is not too happy to notice the sparks of love between the foreign lady and Bhuvan. Finally, after about 50 minutes of a thrilling cricketing contest when villagers beat the English at their own game, under the leadership of Bhuvan, it feels nothing less than winning a war.

One wonders where the story idea of this unusual conflict movie came from. A Hungarian director called Zoltan Febri had come out with a wonderful movie called *Two Half Times in Hell* in 1962. It is about these Hungarian prisoners of war who try to escape from a Nazi concentration camp and are caught. In order to teach them a lesson the German officers order the famous Hungarian footballer player Onodi, who is a prisoner there, to play a football match against the German soldiers. Onodi takes it as a challenge, and begins training the novice prisoners in earnest, making them sweat blood in the effort. As the match progresses, the Germans, who had been leading at half-time, suddenly begin to lose after the break. They can't take the insult, and mow the prisoners down with machine-gun fire.

The Hollywood director John Huston had taken this tragedy as the basis of his own lovely 1981 film *Escape to Victory*, which starred Sylvestor Stallone and the football legend Edison Arantes do Nascimento, better known as Pele. This film too had all the elements of determination, ambitions, sweat, blood and tears. In the end, taking advantage of the immense crowd that had assembled to watch the match, the prisoners do manage to escape.

There is also another popular tale that does the rounds in Kolhapur gatherings. It goes that during the time of Rajarshi Shahu Maharaj, some of his courtiers got into an argument with some British soldiers. The British soldiers challenged the hefty Kolhapuris for a cricket contest. Accordingly, the Kolhapuris had rustled up a cricket team and roundly defeated the British soldiers.

Which of these three stories inspired director Ashutosh Govarikar is difficult to say, but he did succeed in giving birth to a wonderful piece of cinematic art. With this one single film he had transported himself to the category of the best directors in Indian cinema. He had neither family connections, nor the support of government grants and yet he managed to take that massive leap. The grand success he achieved was totally self-earned.

Ordinary peasants, petty village officials, the rural ambience, the thrills and disappointments of the villagers—Ashutosh studied these well before he prepared a compact screenplay for *Lagaan*. Satyajit Bhatkal has written a book on *The Spirit of Lagaan*, so it does not need more elaboration. But there are some prominent features which can be gone over.

The pictures of famine-struck village Champaner hold audience attention from the first shot. The director and the producer visited a lot of spots in search for the ideal location, from Nashik to the ravines of Chambal to the hamlets of Rajasthan. Finally, Art Director Nitin Desai constructed the entire village, to look like that of the last century, near Bhuj in the Kutchh region. Nitin's workmanship is amazing. Bhanu Athaiyya's contemporary costume designs, and Anil Mehta's camera work are outstanding too. Period films often get crushed under the burden of unmanageable clothing, grand sets and stilted language (see Kamaal Amrohi's *Razia Sultan*); but the director of *Lagaan* has taken care to keep the pulsating sentience and the indomitable spirit of the villagers flowing in an unbroken stream. As for looking for a British cast, Bollywood has spent decades walking over to Tom Altar's doorstep to help them out. *Lagaan* did not take the easy route; going to London for auditioning, casting prospects, inviting them over for the movie, along with all the other pains taken, had finally borne fruit.

Lagaan is essentially the creation of the combination of great direction (Ashutosh) and great photography (Anil Mehta). The other important feature of Lagaan is A.R. Rehmaan's superb music. The lyric, the music and the rendition of '*Radha kaise na jaley*' have taken the number to such a height that one needs to travel ten to fifteen years back in film music to find a match.

There is an important piece of dialogue in *Braveheart*: '...history is written by those who have hanged heroes.' Universities, thinkers, PhD students, they are all happy to make merry under the shadow of the victor. They don't remember those who first lit the torch of revolution for the benefit of the people. A Mel Gibson, however, arrives to take charge of the medium of the cinema and presents the story of the revolutionary 'Braveheart' Wallace; or a Kirk Douglas-Stanley Kubrick team shows the fearless face of Spartacus, who first picked up a weapon for the freedom of slaves; or a young Ashutosh who, with his art, immortalises a fictitious persona, an ordinary Bhuvan who represents the deepest urges of the common people. These great cinematic talents create an archive that an army of 500 historians cannot, and pay their homage to the intrepid revolutionaries. This is my homage to the creators. ↑

INDEX